Petronius

Petronius

A Handbook

Edited by Jonathan Prag and Ian Repath

WILEY-BLACKWELL

A John Wiley & Sons, Ltd., Publication

This paperback edition first published 2013
© 2013 Blackwell Publishing Ltd

Edition history: Blackwell Publishing Ltd (hardback, 2009)

Blackwell Publishing was acquired by John Wiley & Sons in February 2007. Blackwell's publishing program has been merged with Wiley's global Scientific, Technical, and Medical business to form Wiley-Blackwell.

Registered Office
John Wiley & Sons Ltd, The Atrium, Southern Gate, Chichester, West Sussex, PO19 8SQ, UK

Editorial Offices
350 Main Street, Malden, MA 02148-5020, USA
9600 Garsington Road, Oxford, OX4 2DQ, UK
The Atrium, Southern Gate, Chichester, West Sussex, PO19 8SQ, UK

For details of our global editorial offices, for customer services, and for information about how to apply for permission to reuse the copyright material in this book please see our website at www.wiley.com/wiley-blackwell.

The right of Jonathan Prag and Ian Repath to be identified as the authors of the editorial material in this work has been asserted in accordance with the UK Copyright, Designs and Patents Act 1988.

Library of Congress Cataloging-in-Publication Data

Petronius : a handbook / edited by Jonathan Prag and Ian Repath.
  p.   cm.
 Includes bibliographical references and indexes.
 ISBN 978-1-4051-5687-5 (hardcover : alk. paper)
 ISBN 978-1-118-45137-3 (pbk.: alk. paper)
1. Petronius Arbiter–Criticism and interpretation.   2. Satire, Latin–History and criticism.
I. Prag, J. R. W.   II. Repath, Ian.
PA6561.P37 2009
873′.01–dc22

                                        2008028318

A catalogue record for this book is available from the British Library.

Cover image: Eleanor Antin, The Death of Petronius from *The Last Days of Pompeii*, 2001, chromogenic print, 469/16 × 941/2 × 13/4 inches (framed). Copyright © Eleanor Antin. Courtesy Ronald Feldman Fine Arts, New York
Cover design by Richard Boxall Design Associates

Set in 10.5/13pt Minion by SPi Publisher Services, Pondicherry, India

Printed in Malaysia by Ho Printing (M) Sdn Bhd

1   2013

For Ewen Bowie
magistro optimo et ingenti flumine litterarum inundato

Contents

Illustrations

Contributors

Jean Andreau is Directeur d'Études at the École des Hautes Études en Sciences Sociales in Paris. He specializes in the economic and social history of the Roman world. In 1999 he published *Banking and Business in the Roman World* (Cambridge). His most recent book is J. Andreau and V. Chankowski (eds), *Vocabulaire et expression de l'économie dans le monde antique* (Bordeaux 2007). He is currently working on a history of the Roman economy and collaborates, along with Jonathan Prag, in a group directed by Sylvie Pittia which is preparing a new edition and commentary of Cicero's third speech against Verres (the *De frumento*).

Shelley Hales is Senior Lecturer in Art and Visual Culture at the University of Bristol and specializes in the roles and meanings of Roman domestic art and architecture. She is the author of *Roman Houses and Social Identity* (Cambridge 2003). She is currently working on the reception of Pompeii in nineteenth-century culture.

Stephen Harrison is Fellow and Tutor in Classics at Corpus Christi College, Oxford, and Professor of Classical Languages and Literature in the University of Oxford. He has written widely on the Roman novels and was a co-founder of the journal *Ancient Narrative* (www.ancientnarrative.com). He is editor of *Oxford Readings in the Roman Novel* (Oxford 1999) and author of *Apuleius: A Latin Sophist* (Oxford 2000).

Valerie Hope is Senior lecturer in the Department of Classical Studies at the Open University. Her main research interest is Roman funerary monuments and funeral customs. Publications include *Death and Disease in the Ancient City* (London and New York 2000, co-edited with E. Marshall); *Constructing Identity: The Funerary Monuments of Aquileia, Mainz and Nimes* (Oxford 2001); and *Death in Ancient Rome: A Sourcebook* (London 2007).

J. R. Morgan is Professor of Greek at Swansea University. He has published widely on ancient fiction, particularly the Greek novel. His commentary on

Longus's *Daphnis and Chloe* was published in 2004 (Warminster). He is co-editor, with Meriel Jones, of *Philosophical Presences in the Ancient Novel* (*Ancient Narrative Supplementum* 10, Groningen 2007), and, with Ian Repath, of another forthcoming *Ancient Narrative Supplementum* on lies and metafiction. Other projects include an edition of Heliodorus for the Loeb Classical Library, and a monograph on Longus for the Duckworth Classical Literature and Society series. He is Leader of the KYKNOS Research Centre, which brings together colleagues working on the narrative literatures of the ancient world at Swansea and Lampeter (www.kyknos.org.uk).

Costas Panayotakis is Reader in Classics at the University of Glasgow. He researches on the Roman novel and Roman drama, and he is the review editor of the journal *Ancient Narrative*. His books include *Theatrum Arbitri: Theatrical Elements in the Satyrica of Petronius* (Leiden 1995) and annotated book-length translations into Modern Greek of one play of Plautus and two of Terence. His new book, *Decimus Laberius: The Fragments*, is forthcoming in the series *Cambridge Classical Texts and Commentaries*. He is now collating manuscripts to establish a new critical text of the *sententiae* attributed to the mimographer Publilius, and he has recently undertaken to write a new commentary on Petronius's "Dinner at Trimalchio's."

Joanna Paul is Lecturer in Classical Studies at the Open University. Her research specialism is modern receptions of the ancient world, especially in the cinematic medium. She has a particular interest in adaptations of ancient literature for the cinema, and is working on a book entitled *Film and the Classical Epic Tradition* for Oxford University Press.

Jonathan Prag is a university lecturer in Ancient History at the University of Oxford, and a tutorial fellow of Merton College. He has published briefly on Petronius (in *CQ* 2006), but his main areas of research are Hellenistic and Republican Sicily and the Roman Republic. He is the editor of *Sicilia nutrix plebis Romanae: Rhetoric, Law, and Taxation in Cicero's Verrines* (London 2007) and collaborates, along with Jean Andreau, in a group directed by Sylvie Pittia which is preparing a new edition and commentary of Cicero's second and third speeches against Verres. He is currently co-editing (with J. C. Quinn) a series of papers on *The Hellenistic West* (forthcoming, Cambridge) and working on a book on the non-Italian auxiliaries of the Roman Republican army.

Ian Repath is Lecturer in Classics at Swansea University. His principal research interests are Greek and Latin prose fiction, and literary aspects of Plato. He is author of "Plato in Petronius: Petronius *in platanona*," and co-editor, with John Morgan, of *Where the Truth Lies: Fiction* *and Metafiction in Ancient Narrative* (forthcoming). He is a founding member of KYKNOS, the Swansea and Lampeter Centre for Research in Ancient Narrative Literatures.

Amy Richlin is Professor of Classics at the University of California, Los Angeles. She works on the history of sexuality, Roman humor, women's history, and feminist theory. Her most recent books are *Rome and the Mysterious Orient* (Berkeley 2005) and *Marcus Aurelius in Love* (Chicago 2007).

Victoria Rimell is Associate Professor of Latin Literature in the Department of Greek and Latin Philology at La Sapienza, University of Rome. She has published books on Petronius (*Petronius and the Anatomy of Fiction*, Cambridge 2002) and on Ovid, and edited *Seeing Tongues, Hearing Scripts: Orality and Representation in the Ancient Novel* (*Ancient Narrative Supplementum* 7, Groningen 2007). *Martial's Rome: Empire and the Ideology of Epigram* is forthcoming with Cambridge University Press.

Niall W. Slater is Samuel Candler Dobbs Professor of Latin and Greek at Emory University. His research interests focus on the prose fiction and drama of the ancient world, as well as the conditions of their production and reception. His books include *Plautus in Performance: The Theatre of the Mind* (Princeton 1985; second, revised edition 2000), *Reading Petronius* (Baltimore 1990) and *Spectator Politics: Metatheatre and Performance in Aristophanes* (Philadelphia 2002). His current project is a study of Euripides' *Alcestis*.

Koen Verboven is Lecturer in Ancient History at Ghent University. He specializes in ancient social and economic history, Roman friendship, and voluntary associations (*collegia*). He is the author of *The Economy of Friends* (Latomus, Brussels 2002), and co-editor (with K. Vandorpe and V. Chankowski) of *Pistoi dia tèn technèn: Bankers, Loans and Archives in the Ancient World. Studies in Honour of Raymond Bogaert* (Leuven 2007).

Caroline Vout is a University Senior Lecturer in Classics at Cambridge and a Fellow of Christ's College. She is a cultural historian and art historian with a particular interest in the Roman imperial period and has published widely on topics related to Rome and its reception. Recent publications include *Power and Eroticism in Imperial Rome* (Cambridge 2007) and "Sizing up Rome or Theorising the Overview," in D. Larmour and D. Spencer (eds), *The Sites of Rome* (Oxford 2007). Her interest in the *Satyrica* stems from several years of teaching it at the University of Nottingham.

Preface and Acknowledgments

The idea for this book was born over a couple of pints of beer in a pub in Nottingham. While chatting about teaching and related matters we came to realize that one of us, Jonathan, was using the *Satyrica* as part of a course on ancient society and economy at the University of Leicester while the other, Ian, was teaching a literary course on the ancient novel at the University of Nottingham. It seemed a good thing that a text could be used in such different ways, but also a shame that such different approaches are often segregated. We decided, therefore, to propose a volume in which we would invite leading scholars to write chapters on a range of topics, a range both broad and mutually complementary, all focusing on the one text: Petronius's *Satyrica*. That our contributors were so eager to help seemed to suggest we had struck a chord, and we hope that this book will be valuable for all those with an interest in this novel and its influence.

We gratefully acknowledge the generosity of Eleanor Antin and of Ronald Feldman Fine Arts, New York, for their willingness to let us use the image reproduced on the cover; Merton College, Oxford, for financial assistance with other illustrations; and Paul Dilley for translating the chapter by Jean Andreau.

We are indebted to Al Bertrand and his colleagues at Wiley-Blackwell for being so receptive to the idea in the first place and so helpful throughout the editorial process. We are no less grateful to the contributors, who have been both prompt and patient – editing a volume by multiple academics can, in the unforgettable words of one of our contributors, be rather like herding cats – but happily not on this occasion!

Abbreviations

All references to chapters of the *Satyrica* are prefaced with a §. Although the division into chapters is almost certainly later than Petronius himself (and the numbering sequence in use today certainly is), they have been universally adopted, are now printed in all texts and most translations, and are the standard form of reference.

References to all other ancient authors and their works follow the standard abbreviations listed in *The Oxford Classical Dictionary* (third, revised edition 2003, edited by S. Hornblower and A. Spawforth, Oxford University Press), at pp. xxix–liv.

Other abbreviations used in this volume are:

CIL = *Corpus Inscriptionum Latinarum, consilio et auctoritate Academiae litterarum regiae Borussicae editum.* Berlin. 1863–. The standard collection of Latin inscriptions, arranged in multiple volumes, organized primarily on a geographical basis (for example, vol. 6 is the city of Rome, vol. 10 is central and southern Italy, Sicily, and Sardinia). Production of the series is ongoing.

LGPN = *Lexicon of Greek Personal Names*, edited by P. M. Fraser and E. Matthews, I (Oxford, 1987); II (M. J. Osborne and S. G. Byrne eds; Oxford, 1994); III.A (Oxford, 1997); III.B (Oxford, 2000); IV (Oxford, 2005). See the website: www.lgpn.ox.ac.uk

P.Oxy. = *The Oxyrhynchus Papyri*, edited with translations and notes by B. P. Grenfell and A. S. Hunt et al. London. 1898–.

Introduction

Jonathan Prag and Ian Repath

About this Book

Petronius's fragmentary novel, the *Satyrica*, is a text as amazing as it is puzzling. It combines startling originality, outrageous and raunchy humor, literary genius, and brilliant characterization. It provides an insight into the seedier side of life in the ancient world and an unusual perspective on first-century municipal Roman Italy and beyond. It has a unique place in the history of literature as the first substantial novelistic text and has been enormously influential on writers of fiction and on those trying to understand ancient Rome. Its attractiveness as a text to be read, studied, and researched, whatever one's interest, has long been clear, and, as is evident from the bibliography to this volume, there is no shortage of material written on it. What, then, does this book aim to achieve?

In this volume there are a dozen especially commissioned, original essays by leading scholars in the fields of the ancient novel and of the culture and history of the early Roman Empire. These essays have Petronius's *Satyrica* as their sole focus and students as their primary audience, although we are confident that anyone interested in this text will find much that is useful and illuminating. The essays each present a survey of one aspect of the *Satyrica* taking into account the vast amount of scholarship, both specialized and general, and, in a "Further Reading" section, point the reader towards other works on the particular topic. (Works are referred to by author and date, and full details can be found in the comprehensive bibliography towards the back of this book.) The aim is not a synthesis of material so that you do not have to read anything else; rather, the essays act as introductory pieces to provoke thought and guide you on your way. They enable you to gain a valuable insight by themselves, but they can also form the basis of in-depth research. However, they will be much more valuable if you read the text of the *Satyrica* first. This book cannot be, and is certainly not intended to be, a substitute for reading the text itself: it is a handbook to it, a help in interpreting it and making sense of it. In addition, we hope that this volume will prove invaluable for not only students, but also those who are lucky enough to teach this text, whether exclusively or as part of a broader course.

The rich variety of Petronius's *Satyrica* means that there are many angles from which it can be approached, and we have tried to reflect this range. You might be interested in Latin literature, for instance, or Roman art, or the Roman economy, or Classics in the cinema: whichever aspect of the ancient world you find most appealing there is something for you in the *Satyrica* and its influences, and there is something for you here. However, one of the main problems when approaching the *Satyrica* is the frequently sharp divide between literary and historical studies; this volume seeks to challenge and overcome that division. A full understanding of a text involves an appreciation of all its aspects, and, although the essays are free-standing and may be read independently and in any order, in the course of their different approaches they often provide complementary readings of the same passages; cross-references will usually alert you to this. We think that this multi-dimensional approach is essential to studying the ancient world, and that Petronius's *Satyrica* is one of the best texts that survive with which one can attempt an integrated interpretation of one snapshot of ancient life. It can be read as a literary text, as a social document, or as evidence for historical reality, but none of these readings can properly exist without the others. Our advice, then, whether you are an ancient historian whose focus is funerary monuments or a literature student who is keen to see what Petronius does with the literary heritage of the ancient Greeks, is the following: read the other approaches presented here, since they are not long and you should soon enough get an idea of what they are about and, more importantly, you may well find your understanding and appreciation deepened by alternative perspectives. Having said all that, and although the chapter titles should make it clear enough, a brief summary of how the volume fits together now follows.

In the next section of the Introduction we will briefly consider the questions of who Petronius might have been, and when we might date the text. This is followed by a short outline of the *Satyrica*, a glossary of the main characters' names, some initial suggestions for background reading, and a map of Italy. Then, in the first of the chapters, we start by looking at what kind of text the *Satyrica* is and the state in which it has come down to us, asking questions about its fragmentary nature, its genre, its narrator, how its narrative functions, the use of poetry as well as prose, and whether there have might been an overall narrative thread: in short, the fundamentals for being able to read the text (Slater, READING THE *SATYRICA*). We move on to look at how the *Satyrica* relates to other literature, since, for a Roman writer, and reader, how one reacts to both Greek (Morgan, PETRONIUS AND GREEK LITERATURE) and Roman (Panayotakis, PETRONIUS AND THE ROMAN LITERARY TRADITION) texts is a crucial part of the literary process and can tell us a great deal about what kind of text we are dealing with and what its author is up to. The *Satyrica* is a densely literary and allusive work, and an understanding of how it relates and reacts to other literature is essential to a full appreciation of the text. Next comes a chapter on the extraordinary language of the *Satyrica* and the interplay that takes place in the narrative between sound-effects and metaphors; in addition, the *Satyrica* not only alludes verbally to other texts, but it also demands in its use of repeated vocabulary that the reader have a keen eye and ear for detail (Rimell, LETTING THE PAGE RUN ON).

The extent to which "literature" is part of culture and society will already be apparent from these first few chapters; literary effects do not exist in isolation either from literary traditions, or from the wider world of language and the senses. The next two chapters consider aspects of the society within which the *Satyrica* belongs: the fascinating problems of gender and sexual practice in a society that is ultimately very different from our own, and the ways in which this is presented in the *Satyrica* (Richlin, SEX IN THE *SATYRICA*); and the no less intriguing problems raised by deciding which socio-cultural context we should put the *Satyrica* into in the first place – in this book, as in most studies of Petronius, into the world of Nero (Vout, THE *SATYRICA* AND NERONIAN CULTURE).

We continue the exploration of the social and historical context of the *Satyrica* with four chapters which increasingly focus upon the historical, and material, world of the *Satyrica*. The first of these (Andreau, FREEDMEN IN THE *SATYRICA*) begins with the important question of how we can use such a text to write "history" before going on to examine what we can learn about the social class of the "freedmen" in first-century AD Italy, whose central role in Roman life is reflected by their prominence in the *Satyrica*, and in particular in the *Cena Trimalchionis*, "Trimalchio's Dinner Party." This is followed by a study of the *Satryica* as a source for what might loosely be called economic history (Verboven, A FUNNY THING HAPPENED ON MY WAY TO THE MARKET), but which, as the chapter reveals, is a much bigger topic than the word "economic" suggests, and one for which, again, the *Satyrica* provides both important and unusual evidence to place alongside what we know from elsewhere. Two further chapters develop this particular approach, examining the ways in which comparison between the archaeology of the Roman world and the text of the *Satyrica* can illuminate our reading of the text, but also give us invaluable perspectives on the surviving evidence from other sources. In the first of these (Hope, AT HOME WITH THE DEAD) we consider the unique and unusual light which the *Satyrica* casts upon the subjects of death and burial, and on contemporary attitudes to them, comparing this with the rich material evidence that survives from the Roman world. In the second (Hales, FREEDMEN'S CRIBS), we confront the question of domestic space and the nature and use of the house and its decoration – something which, again, the *Satyrica* presents differently from any other source.

To bring the discussion up to the present day, we conclude with a pair of chapters on the more recent reception of what remains of the *Satyrica* in two distinct media – novelistic fiction and film. The first (Harrison, PETRONIUS'S SATYRICA AND THE NOVEL IN ENGLISH) examines the use and impact of our surviving text, and in particular of the *Cena Trimalchionis* – something which can be traced from literary works of the eighteenth century through to the most recent works of fiction. The second (Paul, FELLINI-SATYRICON) discusses the famous and challenging film by the Italian director Federico Fellini, inspired in diverse ways by both the content and the nature of Petronius's text. The volume concludes with a bibliography for all the contributions, an index of ancient passages cited in the text, and a general index.

Before taking a brief look at who Petronius might have been, two general points:

1   This is a handbook to Petronius's *Satyrica*, but you will see from the bibliography and further reading sections that the novel has frequently been referred to as the *Satyricon*. For an explanation of the difference and the argument that *Satyrica* was the original title, see Slater, READING THE SATYRICA (p. 20). Throughout this book we use the form *Satyrica*, since that is now the commonly agreed title: we hope that any confusion is minimal (and in any case, the difference is rather less confusing than between the two received titles of Apuleius's novel: *The Metamorphoses* and *The Golden Ass*!).

2   All Latin in this volume is translated, and translations are generally the contributor's own, unless stated otherwise. However, depending on the nature of the topic being covered, the Latin is often quoted or referred to,

since the *Satyrica* is a Latin text, and a text can never be fully divorced from its original language.

Who Was Petronius?

Among the questions that can be crucial for understanding and interpreting a text we might single out four particular ones in this instance:

1 Who was the author?
2 Where did they live?
3 What was their social status?
4 When did they write?

Such questions may seem obvious if we want to use the text as a source for historical information, but they are no less relevant when trying to locate a text in its literary context. In the case of Petronius the answer is unfortunately not a simple one. If we could answer the question of his identity with confidence then the rest would of course follow; but, for the very reason that we cannot be entirely sure of the identification of the author, it remains possible to dispute the other questions also, and in particular that of when he wrote. Much the fullest discussion of this problem is to be found in Rose (1971), with shorter summaries in, for example, Walsh (1970: 67–8, 244–7).

The basic elements of the problem are these:

1 The majority of our (mediaeval) manuscripts containing the text of the *Satyrica*, and later writers also, identify the author simply by the name (*nomen*) of "Petronius."

2 However, some manuscripts, and several later writers, refer to the author as *arbiter*, or even as "Petronius Arbiter."

3 The Roman historian Tacitus, in his *Annales* (16.18–19), provides a lengthy obituary notice of an individual of consular status called Petronius who was forced to commit suicide in AD 66 by the Emperor Nero (emperor from AD 54 to 68). It is worth reproducing this notice in full:

> Petronius deserves a brief obituary. He spent his days sleeping, his nights working and enjoying himself. Others achieve fame by energy, Petronius by laziness. Yet he was not, like others who waste their resources, regarded as dissipated or extravagant, but as a refined voluptuary. People liked the apparent

freshness of his unconventional and unselfconscious sayings and doings. Nevertheless, as governor of Bithynia and later as consul, he had displayed a capacity for business. Then, reverting to a vicious or ostensibly vicious way of life, he had been admitted into the small circle of Nero's intimates, as Arbiter of Taste (*elegantiae arbiter*): to the blasé Emperor nothing was smart and elegant unless Petronius had given it his approval. So Tigellinus, loathing him as a rival and a more expert hedonist, denounced him on the grounds of his friendship with Flavius Scaevinus. This appealed to the Emperor's outstanding passion – his cruelty. A slave was bribed to incriminate Petronius. No defence was heard. Indeed, most of his household were under arrest.

The Emperor happened to be in Campania. Petronius too had reached Cumae; and there he was arrested. Delay, with its hopes and fears, he refused to endure. He severed his own veins. Then, having them bound up again when the fancy took him, he talked with his friends – but not seriously, or so as to gain a name for fortitude. And he listened to them reciting, not discourses about the immortality of the soul or philosophy, but light lyrics and frivolous poems. Some slaves received presents – others beatings. He appeared at dinner, and dozed, so that his death, even if compulsory, might look natural. Even his will deviated from the routine death-bed flatteries of Nero, Tigellinus, and other leaders. Petronius wrote out a list of Nero's sensualities – giving names of each male and female bed-fellow and details of every lubricious novelty – and sent it under seal to Nero. Then Petronius broke his signet-ring, to prevent its subsequent employment to incriminate others. (Trans. M. Grant.)

Because Tacitus describes Petronius's position at Nero's court as *elegantiae arbiter*, "Arbiter of Taste," many scholars from the sixteenth century onwards have been tempted to identify the Petronius described here by Tacitus with the author of the *Satyrica*. This is the most likely source of the use of the term "Arbiter" in some later writers mentioned in Point 2 above. It will doubtless be apparent that the description of Petronius's character provided by Tacitus would seem to fit the author of the *Satyrica* extremely well – although the suggestion which is sometimes made, that the *Satyrica* is the same document as Petronius's list of Nero's debaucheries mentioned here by Tacitus, is surely going too far.

4   In the manuscripts of Tacitus, the consular Petronius appears either without a first name (*praenomen*), as at *Ann.* 16.17.1, or else with the initial C., short for Gaius, as at *Ann.* 16.18.1.

5   Both Plutarch and Pliny the Elder make brief references to an individual called T. (= Titus) Petronius, and the way in which they describe him

makes it very likely that he is the same man as that described by Tacitus, despite the different *praenomen* in the manuscript tradition:

> When the ex-consul T. Petronius was facing death, he broke, to spite Nero, a myrrhine dipper that had cost him 300,000 sesterces, thereby depriving the Emperor's dining-room table of this legacy. Nero, however, as was proper for an emperor, outdid everyone by paying 1,000,000 sesterces for a single bowl. That one who was acclaimed as a victorious general and as Father of his Country should have paid so much in order to drink is a detail that we must formally record. (Pliny, *Historia Naturalis* 37.20, trans. D. E. Eichholz.)

> But we come now to matters that are a serious problem, and do great damage to the foolish, when the flatterer's accusations are directed against emotions and weaknesses the contrary to those that a person really has. [...] Or again, on the other hand, they will reproach profligate and lavish spenders with meanness and sordidness, as Titus Petronius did with Nero. (Plutarch, *Moralia* 60D, trans. F. C. Babbitt.)

6   A number of families – as many as six – are known to us with the family name (*nomen*) "Petronius," of which several members reached the consulship in the period of the early Empire.

7   No other individual called Petronius is known to have had the surname (*cognomen*) Arbiter; indeed, study of Roman funerary inscriptions in particular makes it seem very unlikely that anybody used this as an official *cognomen* (almost no examples are known, and none among the elite).

8   At least three individuals called Petronius are known to have held consulships specifically during Nero's reign. One of these, suffect consul in AD 62, has frequently been identified as T. Petronius Niger in past scholarship (including the hardback edition of this book) and consequently has often been equated with the man mentioned by Pliny and Plutarch (point 5 above) and with the man described by Tacitus (points 3–4 above) assuming correction of the *praenomen* from Gaius to Titus. However, epigraphic evidence makes it certain that the suffect consul of AD 62 was called P. Petronius Niger, and so the equation with T. (or C.) Petronius, nicknamed 'Arbiter', now looks arbitrary and very hard to justify. Similar objections arise to identifying T./C. Petronius 'Arbiter' with either of the other known consuls of Nero's reign called Petronius (A. Petronius Lurco, suffect consul in AD 58; P. Petronius Turpilianus, consul in AD 61). However, there are gaps in the lists of known consuls for each of the years AD 54, 56, 60, and 61, into which it would be

theoretically possible to insert the consulship of T./C. Petronius 'Arbiter'.
See further Völker and Rohmann 2011.

With all of the above taken into consideration, most scholars are prepared
to accept the identification of the author Petronius ('Arbiter') with the
Petronius described in Tacitus (and Pliny and Plutarch), even if the further
identification of that Petronius with a specific consul in the reign of Nero
remains an open question. It should, nonetheless, be emphasized that the
identification is not certain, and that consequently a Neronian date is not
formally proven by this route, however likely it may be thought to be.

There is another way to try to resolve this problem, and that is to tackle
the last of our four original questions, instead of the first, namely, "When
was the *Satyrica* written?" The first reference to the work of Petronius
appears in an author called Terentianus Maurus writing around AD 200
(fragment XX in Müller's edition (2003: 181) of Petronius), so external
evidence does not narrow down the answer very much. There are two
remaining ways to confront this question: to examine the content of the
Satyrica and look for things which can only have been written before or
after a certain event or other text; and to consider the text more generally in
terms of the world it describes and what else we know of the Roman world
at the time of Nero and at other periods.

Scholars have found many things in the *Satyrica* which they have claimed
support a particular date, such as the names of famous individuals who can
reasonably be identified with known figures from the Neronian period (for
example, the gladiator Petraites at §52.3, or the lyre-player Menecrates at
§73.3 [cf. Suet. *Nero* 30.2]); or else the echoes of Lucan's *De bello civili /
Pharsalia* in the *Bellum Civile* of Eumolpus (§118–24; see Slater, READING
THE *SATYRICA*, p. 27, and Panayotakis, PETRONIUS AND THE ROMAN LITERARY
TRADITION). Most of these, however, provide no more than a *terminus post
quem*, a fixed point after which we can assume our own text to have been
written. Only if one also accepts the identification of Petronius with the
suicidal consul in Tacitus can these be used, for instance, to suggest a very
narrow time-span for the composition of certain parts of the *Satyrica*,
between Lucan's death in April AD 65 and Petronius's own death in AD 66.
Without this two-stage argument, this method cannot, technically, rule out
a later date for the *Satyrica*, and for this reason some scholars have suggested that we should consider, for example, a date in the Flavian period
(that is, AD 69–98, as Martin (1975); see, in general, the discussion in Vout,
THE *SATYRICA* AND NERONIAN CULTURE).

A number of the chapters which appear in this book, such as those by Vout (on Neronian culture) and Verboven (on economic history), make it very obvious that the *Satyrica* can be read perhaps most productively in the context of the 60s AD. By themselves, such readings do not prove that the *Satyrica* is a Neronian text, or that the author was T. Petronius, the *elegantiae arbiter* of Tacitus's *Annales*. Indeed, put as bluntly as that, the argument is simply circular. But what we might term "historical readings" are a two-way process, and unless clear contradictions emerge, the reinforcement is not merely encouraging, it is highly informative. Unless we choose to reject all such apparent correspondence as pure coincidence, which becomes ever more unlikely as the process itself continues – and the richness of what can be learned in both directions should become clear in the chapters that follow – then it becomes little short of perverse not to accept the general consensus and read the *Satyrica* as a Neronian text of the mid-60s AD. Although our contributors will on occasion remind the reader of the ultimate uncertainty in this question, and rightly so, in general all the chapters in this volume accept the basic hypothesis of a Neronian dating.

Two of our four questions remain – without a secure identification of the author the answers to these cannot be certain. But, accepting the general hypothesis that the author was T. Petronius, a consul in the reign of Nero, and the *elegantiae arbiter* of Tacitus, then he was a senator and a member of Rome's elite. This poses one very serious further question: as such, how much could he really have known about the sorts of people and the sides of life that the *Satyrica* describes? (The question is raised, for example, by Richlin, SEX IN THE SATYRICA, p. 91.) A superficial answer may be offered from the accounts in Tacitus (*Ann.* 13.25, 13.47), Suetonius (*Nero* 26.3–4), and Cassius Dio (61.8.1) of Nero's excursions into the city disguised as a private citizen or even a slave – if Nero could do this, then Petronius could doubtless have done the same. But it is probably unnecessarily modernizing to imagine that Petronius was writing a fully-researched "investigative" novel exposing the underclasses of his time. A second response, accepting the senatorial authorship, would be either to keep this authorship in mind throughout, with all its implications for skepticism or at least a very top-down perspective; or else to be prepared to rethink our assumptions about the true solidity and exclusivity of the "class-divide" in the ancient world.

However, Petronius was writing a work of entertaining literature, whose realism is not to be pushed too far, although presumably his aim was to create a world that was recognizable, or realistic, or at least plausible to his readership/audience. Many of the contributors make this kind of point: see for example, Panayotakis on dining/satire (p. 51), Richlin (p. 84) on "The *Satyrica* as Document," and in particular Andreau's chapter on freedmen. As mentioned above, and notwithstanding the problem of dating, there is no evidence as to who Petronius's contemporary readership might have been. However, such a sophisticated, ambitious, and richly allusive text would only be appreciated fully by those with the education to understand its far from straightforward Latin (see Rimell) or recognize the extensive and playful allusions to other literature (see Morgan and Panayotakis), and with the time to read it (or listen to it: see Slater, p. 16). Such people could realistically come only from the elite: Petronius was writing for those of his own social class, and it is important to bear this in mind when assessing to what extent we can take the *Satyrica* to be an accurate or useful historical source on the life and behavior of low-lifes, freedmen, and slaves.

Episodic Outline of the Extant *Satyrica*

The extant remains of the *Satyrica* are full of incident: as far as we can tell, the overall plot concerns Encolpius and his affairs (primarily with Giton), and this is then interspersed throughout with what seem to be smaller episodes. The following outline is designed to help you keep your bearings when considering different aspects of the text and to locate within the over-all narrative the passages and episodes discussed; it is not intended to be a comprehensive summary (cf. the outline of the "plot" of *Fellini-Satyricon* in Paul's contribution to this volume, p. 202, and Slater on the fragmentary nature of the *Satyrica*, p. 17).

1–5	Encolpius and Agamemnon at the school of rhetoric
6–11	Encolpius and Ascyltos fight over Giton
12–15	arguments over stolen clothing at a market
16–26	Quartilla and a bisexual orgy
26–78	the *Cena Trimalchionis*, or Dinner of Trimalchio (the whole episode is full of eating, drinking, and Trimalchio being boorish):
26–31	arrival and preliminaries
31–6	food, drink, and entertainment
37–8	Encolpius learns about those present
41–6	Trimalchio goes out and the guests, other freedmen, take the opportunity to talk

Glossary of Important Names

We list only those who play a significant part in the action, and not those who appear briefly or who are mentioned by other characters and do not appear; of course, it goes without saying that the contents of this list are affected by the fragmentary nature of the text. We do not list those historical characters, deities, or mythical persons referred to in the text since they can be found in standard reference works. The vast majority of the names are etymologically Greek; Latin names are denoted with *, and those of Semitic origin with #. It is worth noting that almost all the names employed are attested for historical persons – see *LGPN* – and also that all the freedmen names at Trimalchio's house are attested on inscriptions from *CIL* 10 (which covers southern Italy;

for both these references, see the list of abbreviations). However, many of the names are not especially common, and some are very rare: what is of primary importance in the majority of cases is the literary and/or etymological significance of the name, as indicated below. We are indebted to Costas Panayotakis for the rendering of many of the characters' names and for the descriptions of their roles and characters. Slightly fuller lists for comparison can be found in Sullivan (1986: 179–81) and Branham and Kinney (1996: 169–71). Particularly useful on names is Courtney (2001, especially 40–3).

Agamemnon ("Very Resolute"): hypocritical teacher of rhetoric; the name of the leader of the Achaean fleet against Troy (see, in particular, Homer's *Iliad*)

Ascyltos ("Untroubled" or "Indefatigable"): Encolpius's formidably well-endowed former lover and lover of Giton

Circe: Attractive but insecure nymphomaniac; the name of an immortal witch in Homer's *Odyssey*

Corax ("Raven"): servant of Eumolpus

Daedalus ("Artist"): Trimalchio's cunning cook; the name of the archetypal ingenious inventor, who built the labyrinth to house the Minotaur

Dama: freedman at Trimalchio's dinner; his name is frequently found belonging to a slave in literature

Echion: freedman at Trimalchio's dinner; his name is redolent of Greek words to do with snakes

Encolpius ("In The Bosom/Lap"): bisexual protagonist and principal narrator

Eumolpus ("Sweet Singer"): lecherous and terrible versifier

Fortunata* ("Mrs Blessed/Wealthy"): wife of Trimalchio

Ganymede: freedman at Trimalchio's dinner; in mythology Ganymede was taken up to Olympus by an eagle to be Zeus's (Jupiter's) cupbearer. From his name derive the Latin word *catamitus* and its English equivalent "catamite"

Giton ("Neighbor/Boy Next Door"): unfaithful male concubine of Encolpius

Habinnas# : freedman at Trimalchio's dinner and monumental mason

Hermeros: freedman at Trimalchio's dinner; his name means "a pillar with a bust of Eros"; he shares it with a gladiator mentioned at §52.3

Lichas ("Captain Blowjob"): superstitious ship-captain

Menelaus: another teacher of rhetoric, Agamemnon's assistant; in epic the name of King Agamemnon's brother, husband of Helen of Troy

Niceros: freedman at Trimalchio's dinner; his name combines elements of "victory" and "desire"

Oenothea ("Goddess of Wine"): old witch

Phileros ("Amorous"): freedman at Trimalchio's dinner

Philomela: unprincipled fortune-hunter; this was the name of a mythical woman transformed into a nightingale (see, for example, Ovid *Metamorphoses* 6.424–674)

Proselenus ("Older Than The Moon"): old witch who tries to cure Encolpius of his impotence

Quartilla* ("Quartan Fever Lady"): orgiastic priestess of the phallic god Priapus

Scintilla* ("Spark"): Habinnas's wife

Seleucus: freedman at Trimalchio's dinner; the name of the founder of the Seleucid dynasty, which inherited control of Alexander the Great's conquests in Asia

Trimalchio# ("Thrice Blessed/Lord"): excessively wealthy and eccentrically vulgar freedman

Tryphaena ("Luxurious Woman"): seductive lady

Introductory Reading

Each of the chapters has its own section of further reading, pointing you to scholarship relevant to its particular topic. What follows here is a list of readily available translations and texts and some (necessarily selective and subjective) suggestions of introductory works and resources for the study of Petronius.

Two recent and accessible translations into English are Sullivan (1986) and Walsh (1996); Sullivan's translation is due to be re-issued shortly with a new introduction and notes by Helen Morales. Other translations available include Arrowsmith (1959, often reprinted), Branham and Kinney (1996), Heseltine (1913, revised 1969, with facing Latin text in the Loeb Classical Library series), and Ruden (2000, with brief chapters on a number of topics). A number of translations (normally those out of copyright) are also available online, including Burnaby (1694), courtesy of Project Gutenberg (www.gutenberg.org).

The standard edition of the Latin text is Müller (2003, in the Teubner series). Other editions include Smith (1975, text and commentary of the *Cena* only), Sage (1969, including commentary), Habermehl (2006 and Forthcoming, §79 to end, with detailed commentary in German), and Schmeling (2011, comprehensive English-language commentary).

There are several general introductions to the ancient novel, including Hägg (1983), Holzberg (1995), and the collection of papers in Schmeling

(2003). On the Latin novel in particular, recent surveys include Walsh (1970), Harrison (1999) and Hofmann (1999). On Petronius specifically, Courtney (2001) provides a commentary-style companion, and there are a number of monograph-length studies of the *Satyrica*, including Sullivan (1968a), Slater (1990), Conte (1996a), and Rimell (2002).

General introductions to the Roman Empire can be found in Potter (2006) or, more briefly, in Wells (1992). On Nero, see the biography by Griffin (1984). For the historical context of the *Satyrica* / Trimalchio in particular, see D'Arms (1981) and Veyne (1961, in French).

There are several comprehensive bibliographies on past scholarship on Petronius: Schmeling and Stuckey (1977), Smith (1985), and Vannini (2007). The primary tool with which to find recent bibliography (and a full list of journal abbreviations) is the annual French publication *L'année philologique*.

Petronian studies are now well-served by online resources. The website www.ancientnarrative.com contains a journal which specializes in ancient narrative literature, with a particular focus on the ancient novel. Articles and books on this site require a subscription or access from a subscribed network; however, within this site, note in particular the online version of the *Petronian Society Newsletter*, all of whose contents are freely available: www.ancientnarrative.com/PSN/index.htm (accessed 3 May 2012).

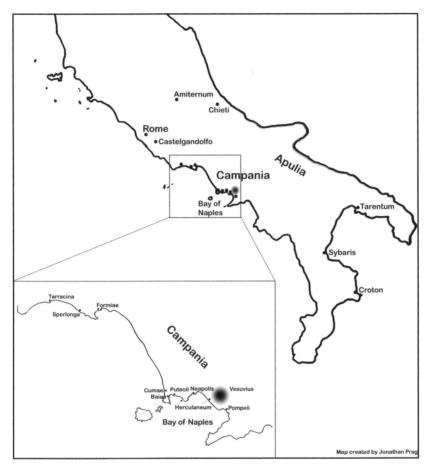

Map of Italy showing locations mentioned in the text, with an inset of the Campanian coastline.

1

Reading the *Satyrica*

Niall W. Slater

No Roman in Petronius's original audience read the *Satyrica* as you are now reading this book. Unless you have a Xerox or screen copy before your eyes, you are holding in your hands the form of book the Romans called a codex, a volume of pages folded or sewn together. This remarkable technological innovation of the late Hellenistic age only gradually replaced the papyrus scroll (Reynolds and Wilson 1991: 1–5, 34–6). Although the codex is attested before Petronius's time, we have no reason to believe it was yet used for such literary works.

Even more importantly, the *Satyrica* that comes down to us is a fragment of a much larger work. Notes in the much later copies that have survived suggest that what we can read today are parts of Books 14, 15, and 16 of the whole – originally, therefore, three separate scrolls out of a group of at least 16, and perhaps as many as even 20 or 24, if Petronius lived to finish whatever plan he had for the *Satyrica*.

Nor is it necessarily the case that a first-century Roman who wanted to know the *Satyrica* pulled a scroll from a shelf or a box in order to read it. Elite Romans often had slaves read to them, alone or in gatherings, as the polymathic elder Pliny did (Pliny the Younger, *Ep.* 3.5.7–17). Trimalchio does both: he listens to his clerk read news from his estates at dinner (§53), but when a troop of performers enters to recite in Greek, he takes up his own scroll to read in Latin (out loud, though perhaps only for his own benefit – and to prove that he *can* read? [§59]).

Such details are not merely of antiquarian interest: it is important to understand that the bound copy of the *Satyrica* that you pick up today to read is a profoundly different object, offering a different experience from that of the Roman two millennia ago. Awareness of the differences can do much to bridge the gap, even as some things remain tantalizingly beyond our grasp.

Reading Fragments and Fragmented Readings

The fragmentary nature of the *Satyrica* poses an ongoing challenge for readers. The text that we read today reflects an active struggle, particularly by scholars in the fifteenth to seventeenth centuries, to put together as complete and readable a narrative as possible, as they rediscovered two groups of manuscripts preserving different parts of the text (Reeve 1983). Sometimes those manuscripts indicated where there were gaps (of words, a few lines, or even pages) in the now lost exemplars from which they were copied, but interruptions in sense indicate other losses as well. Most modern translations indicate where material has likely been lost, but we can rarely be certain how much.

This process of construction is not just an additive one, since various manuscripts sometimes present even the text they do preserve in conflicting order. Readers must decide what the "right" order is by reading, and, where the text does not make sense, whether the problem stems from there being something missing or textual corruption. The reading mind fights against the fragmentary state of the text, with results that have varied widely over the centuries. Most of our reading here will proceed sequentially through the text as reconstructed. Realize that your own reading experience is part of the process of patching the tattered scrolls together.

When our text begins, someone is talking, denouncing the way public speaking is currently taught and practiced. Only when the person addressed interrupts do we discover that this speaker is also the overall first-person narrator of the *Satyrica* and a young man (*adulescens* §3) to boot. It will be 17 more chapters in the current text before we learn his name from someone else's passing remark: Encolpius.

The loss of so much text, particularly the opening, means that we cannot come to this story as the author originally planned. Did Encolpius introduce himself to the reader, narrate any background to his story, or just plunge in? The two obvious comparisons for such a long fictional story told in the first person are both later than Petronius: Achilles Tatius's Greek novel, *Leucippe and Cleitophon*, told to us by Cleitophon after a brief introductory frame story, and Apuleius's *Golden Ass* or *Metamorphoses*, with its puzzlingly playful prologue (Kahane and Laird 2001 offer multiple views of its games) followed by Lucius's narrative of his adventures. Neither of those prologues tells us right at the beginning where the story is going, though Cleitophon explicitly sets out to tell what love has made him suffer, while

Lucius, after a first-person prologue probably *not* in his own voice that nonetheless promises us readerly pleasure, simply begins his adventures on the road.

The loss of any initial frame forces us as readers to make (and continually revise) judgments about what we read as we go along. The temporal stand-point from which Encolpius narrates has been keenly debated. While drama enacts its events in a fictive present, right here and right now, narrative fictions (except for a few recent experiments) are always told after the fact: but how much after? Roger Beck (1973) and even more Gottskálk Jensson (2004) have insisted that Encolpius the narrator speaks from a much later point in time than Encolpius the character within the narrative; therefore the "older" Encolpius can and should have a very dif-ferent point of view. The textual basis for this theory amounts to three passages looking back in time and two looking forward, all within the narrative of Trimalchio's dinner. Arriving at Trimalchio's house, Encolpius says apologetically "if I remember correctly" (§30.3) just before he quotes the wording of a notice. After reporting a number of jokes, he says "600 such have escaped my memory" (§56.10). Later, though, some dishes come to the table "the memory of which offends me" (§65.10). Together, these three passages do indicate that Encolpius's telling of the story is logically later than the actual events themselves, but given how much they have to drink, he could easily have forgotten 600 jokes by the next morning. Two other passages refer, with extreme brevity (§47.8, "we did not yet realize," and §70.8, "what follows"), to things just about to happen. Thus, while a much older Encolpius *may* have begun the story, many readers will find that nothing *requires* such an assumption, let alone the view that his later self wanted us to see his youthful adventures through a lost and sharply different evaluative frame.

This matters, because the world of the *Satyrica* is full of surprises, of sudden and sometimes violent changes of action, scene, or mood, and many readers yearn for something to hold on to over the bumps. The literary texture can change, sometimes with warning, sometimes without. When Encolpius stops quoting himself at the beginning, we discover his interloc-utor is Agamemnon, a local teacher of rhetoric, who agrees with him about the decay of eloquence in their day. Agamemnon tries to express part of his agreement through reciting a poem of his own composition, after praising the style of Lucilius, the early Roman satirist. (Based on later experience of both characters, a reader may also decide Agamemnon has personal, even sexual reasons for wishing to ingratiate himself with Encolpius.)

This poem is the reader's first encounter with a fundamental feature of style in the *Satyrica*, the shift back and forth between prose and poetry, sometimes announced, as here ("I shall express myself in verse"), sometimes not. What most Roman readers could detect as well is an odd lurch within what looks like a single poem on the page, but which would not sound like one read aloud, an effect most translations fail to reproduce. The first eight lines of the poem at §5 are in an iambic meter, the remainder in hexameters. As a pioneer in Roman verse, Lucilius wrote poems he termed "satires" in both iambics and hexameters, though there is no evidence he combined these normally disparate meters within individual poems. While the two sections might individually resemble Lucilius, Agamemnon's homage therefore looks and sounds like bad gene-splicing: a hippogriff of a poem (see Courtney 2001: 59–61 for a different and more complicated view of the poem). Encolpius has no chance to respond to or comment on Agamemnon's argument or his poem, as the audience listening to the next speaker now exits, and he seizes the opportunity to slip away.

We, as readers, could easily race after Encolpius, but this little poem offers a good example of both the potential and limits of an approach to the novel based in the experience of readers, ancient and modern. While there are many variations within reader-response criticism, all approaches acknowledge that no text is either written or read in a vacuum. Readers bring their own experiences and expectations to the task of reading, and authors of any skill write with this in mind. Wolfgang Iser (1978) designates the experience the reader brings, both of life in general and literature in particular, as the reader's repertoire. For example, in order to read about declamation (*declamatores* §1.1; *declamare* §3.1) with enjoyment, it helps a reader to have some notion what declamation is. An exchange during the *Cena* illustrates just this point. Trimalchio demands that Agamemnon entertain him and the other guests with an outline of his declamation (*peristasim declamationis* §48.4) earlier in the day, and the guest obliges:

> When Agamemnon had said, "A poor man (*pauper*) and a rich man were enemies," Trimalchio said, "What's a poor man?" "Very witty," said Agamemnon and laid out some debate scenario (*controversiam*).

Trimalchio's heavy-handed joke is based on the pretence that he is so rich that he does not even know what the basic word *pauper* means. Since Agamemnon's theme is among the tritest *controversiae* (see Richlin, SEX IN THE *SATYRICA*, p. 94, on these rhetorical exercises), a Roman reader would recognize that Trimalchio, whose vocabulary and repertoire includes such Greek rhetorical jargon terms as *peristasis*, is being deliberately obtuse as well as self-aggrandizing.

What then is the joke, if any, in Agamemnon's "Lucilian" poem, and on whom? The modern reader needs help to figure out who Lucilius was and what he wrote. It seems very likely that Petronius expected his Roman reader to know both, and know better than Agamemnon. Part of the joke, then, is that Agamemnon knows Lucilius as a writer of famous quotations but does not grasp that, even though Lucilius used different meters for his poems, patching two different meters together into one poem makes the result completely un-Lucilian (cf. Panayotakis, PETRONIUS AND THE ROMAN LITERARY TRADITION, p. 60, on Trimalchio's "Publilian" poem). The unanswerable question here, though it will become much more interesting at other moments, is whether the narrating Encolpius realizes this. If he does, he is in on the joke. If not, we as readers can enjoy a laugh at his expense too.

Genre, Narrator, Narrative

Let us backtrack briefly. When we pick up a book today, a number of signals (author, title, cover art, jacket blurb, as well as the place in the bookstore or library where it is found) help us classify it: is it a novel, biography, history, or a cookbook? This notion of genre creates expectations for the reader that may be fulfilled or played with: a recipe in a cookbook is expected, but one in a novel is an interesting surprise. The ancient reader had some such signals (scrolls often had a tag called a *titulus* attached which might include the author's name as well as a title), but might need to read some of a work's contents as well to decide what to expect. The few ancient references to the *Satyrica* call it a *fabula*, a narrative, but that is not enough to tell us exactly how ancient readers classified its genre.

The surviving manuscripts and most older translations give the title of Petronius's work as *Satyricon,* but this is the Latinized form of a Greek genitive plural understood with *libri* ("The Books *of the Satyrica*"). The original title was therefore *Satyrica*. Roman readers knew both fictional works (such as Aristides' *Milesiaca* or *Milesian Stories*; see Morgan, PETRO-NIUS AND GREEK LITERATURE, p. 45) and historical works (such as Ctesias's *Persica* and *Indica*) with similar titles. Surviving Greek prose fictional narratives with such titles, including Xenophon's *Ephesiaca* (*Ephesian Tale*) and

Heliodorus's *Aethiopica* (*Aethiopian Tale*) are later than Petronius, so whether *Satyrica* would arouse reader expectations of a long fictional narrative is questionable (see Whitmarsh 2005, especially 602–3). The exact meaning of the title is still debated, but the root in *Satyrica* seems to allude both to the tradition of Roman satire (*satura*) and to the novel's satyr-like subject matter, though ironically, since the narrator Encolpius often fails as a satyr.

The first episodes (Encolpius's and Ascyltos's separate adventures in a brothel, their quarrel over the boy Giton back at their lodgings) soon establish a theme of erotic misadventures and sufferings. Combined with the title, this might make it tempting to read the *Satyrica* through the frame of romance or novel (Walsh 1970). Differences soon appear, however. The Greek novel typically shows us the sufferings of devoted couples, separated by dire circumstances (Konstan 1994). While these can include homosexual couples, fidelity to each other is still the hallmark of these stories, rousing readers' sympathies. In the surviving *Satyrica*, Encolpius and Giton are never long separated, and their sufferings, real enough at least to Encolpius, are portrayed comically rather than tragically. Parody of romance is therefore a possible frame for the *Satyrica*, but this will not account for other elements. (See Morgan, PETRONIUS AND GREEK LITERATURE, p. 40.)

The *Satyrica*'s mixture of both prose and poetry within its text (also known as *prosimetrum*) is one of its most striking features and often thought to be fundamental to how we should read this text. In this it differs sharply from the major Greek novels, which contain at most a few quotations from well-known poetry or inscriptions or oracles in poetic meters. Some papyrus fragments, notably of the *Iolaus* romance (Parsons 1971, Reardon 2008, Stephens and Winkler 1995), show that lost Greek fiction could use more poetry, but nothing closely resembles Petronius. The *Charition Mime* (*P. Oxy.* 413), though perhaps a century later than the *Satyrica*, shows that stage mime could mix prose and verse as well. The *Satyrica* contains both poetry that seems to be performed by characters in the narrative (Agamemnon's poem, Trimalchio's improvised versions at §55.3, and Eumolpus's two long poems, §89 and §119–24, of which more below) and poems that do not seem to be spoken within the real-time present of the narrative. The next poem that a reader encounters follows Encolpius and Ascyltos's decision to go out and try to sell what is probably a stolen cloak in a shady market (§12–15, see Verboven, READING PETRONIUS TO WRITE ECONOMIC HISTORY, p. 125). When their first customer, a man from the countryside (*rusticus*), proves to be carrying a tunic that Encolpius and

Ascyltos once possessed, with money hidden in its seams, they debate how to get the garment back. Ascyltos argues against trusting the local authorities to help them out; then comes – at least in the text as now printed – a six-line elegiac poem (§14.2) on the theme of corrupted justice. No manuscript puts it there, however. The group of manuscripts we call the *L* tradition (see Reeve 1983) places the poem earlier, after §13.4. Konrad Müller, editor of the standard modern text, follows the decision of an earlier German editor, Bücheler (1862), to move it to its present position (such details are found in the *apparatus criticus*, the standard listing of manuscript sources and editorial judgments; Müller 2003: 10). Bücheler thought that, since the poem continues Ascyltos's theme, it should follow and be a continuation of his direct speech. All current texts now read this way, and many, though tellingly not all, translators print the poem as a part of Ascyltos's speech – but how can we be sure? What apart from theme makes Ascyltos the probable author or improviser of these verses? He composes poetry nowhere else in our surviving text. Is he quoting another authority? If so, we might expect him to cite that authority, or at least his inspiration, just as Agamemnon appeals to the authority of Lucilius. The uncomfortable truth is we simply cannot tell whether Ascyltos speaks the poem, but we should not forget that for most readers even contemplating the possibility that he might do so is the consequence of one earlier reader's decision to put the text together in this order.

The third bit of verse we encounter certainly tilts in the other direction. A woman accuses Encolpius and Ascyltos of stealing the cloak, and they make a counterclaim for the tunic, with which they eventually succeed in making off. They stumble back to their rooms, laughing over their success "as we thought" (§15.8), says Encolpius, hinting at some failure or disaster we never learn of. Immediately after Encolpius tells us this come two brief lines of poetry:

> *nolo quod cupio statim tenere,*
> *nec victoria mi placet parata.* (§15.9)

> To grasp desire at once is not my wish;
> and there's no fun when once the fix is in.

This could be an utterance in character by Encolpius, and the first person verb might initially incline us in that direction, but it is certainly not part of the story being told. Instead it seems to be a reflection after the fact, but with no way of telling how much after the fact.

The character Encolpius, then, is not the same as the narrator Encolpius, though the latter possesses a key story-telling resource usually unavailable to the former in the form of verse reflection. Many see the verses as Encolpius's later reflections (Courtney 2001: 31–9), though this does not explain everything about them. Others note that the poems often moralize or reflect parodically on the context and so categorize the *prosimetrum* as the diagnostic feature proving the narrative to be Menippean satire (Relihan 1993), an unfortunately shadowy genre that does little to explain the *Satyrica*'s particular appeal. We will return to the key problem of how to read verse in the novel when we meet longer poems below.

Since its rediscovery, the *Cena* – the narrative of Encolpius's, Ascyltos's, and Giton's dinner at the home of the fabulously wealthy freedman Trimalchio – has been the most read and studied part of the *Satyrica*. The fact that it is also the best preserved part, with the least evidence for significant gaps or losses, also makes it the easier reading, but it is in many other ways too a different kind of reading experience from the surrounding, more fragmentary text.

One or two examples from the *Cena* will further illuminate the problem of how to understand the narrator Encolpius apart from the character. Encolpius and his friends largely act as observers here, allowing Trimalchio and his fellow freedmen center stage. Food, entertainment, and fellow guests alike astonish and appall our narrator. One dish features a wooden hen nesting in a basket of straw, out of which the slaves pull peahen's eggs for the guests. Trimalchio then says:

> "Friends, I ordered peahen's eggs set under an ordinary hen. And by Hercules, I'm afraid they're addled. Let's try, though, and see if they can still be sucked." We took our spoons, weighing half a pound at least, and broke through the eggshells made of rich pastry. I almost threw mine away because I thought the chick had already formed in mine. Then I heard a veteran guest say, "There ought to be something good in here," so I poked my finger through the shell and found the fattest little fig-eater, surrounded by peppered yolk. (§33.5–8)

From what perspective is this story told? It seems to be happening simultaneously with the narration: Encolpius sees the dish, identifies the peahen's eggs as they are served, tries breaking one open, and sees enough (with Trimalchio's prompting that they might be addled) to make him want to throw it away, until he hears a fellow diner speak. The problem, though, is that he has already registered that the eggshell is made out of pastry; even Encolpius has to know that real birds do not lay pastry eggs. Is this then a proof of an older narrator, telling a broadly comic story at his own expense?

("I was so stupid then I didn't know that peahen's eggs weren't made of pastry.") Perhaps more likely is the notion that Encolpius is deliberately playing along with his host. If Trimalchio says the eggs might have gone bad, he will play along with the game, until someone else takes the lead to show what proper guest behavior is in these circumstances.

Indeed, Encolpius shows an almost desperate desire to fit in. Later a roasted wild boar appears on a platter wearing a freedman's cap (*pilleatus* §40.3). Deeply puzzled, he finally asks his fellow guest for an explanation. The explanation is that the boar was served yesterday, but the overfed guests sent it away, so today it returns as a freedman. Encolpius then pointedly tells us his internal response to this information:

> I cursed my own stupidity and asked nothing more, for fear I'd seem like
> I never dined with decent people (*honestos*). (§41.5)

Such a response seems to raise the question: is the *Satyrica* a satire, and if so, of whom or what? Dinner with a boorish host is perhaps the clearest overlap with the themes of traditional Roman verse satire (see Vout, THE SATYRICA AND NERONIAN CULTURE, on resonances with Horace's satire on dinner with Nasidienus, but also other, more recent targets as well), while greed and legacy hunting, fundamental to the novel's final scenes at Croton, are almost as common satiric targets. Attempts have been made to read the *Satyrica*'s women as Juvenalian terrors, but as dangerous as Quartilla, Tryphaena, and even Circe prove, Fortunata, Scintilla, and above all the unnamed widow from Ephesus have struck other readers as much richer characters than satiric motives would dictate. Classifying the *Satyrica* as satire then does not fully account for either its narrator or its narrative.

Reading a Poet and his Poetry

The great bulk of verse in the *Satyrica* comes from the mouth of Eumolpus, whom Encolpius encounters in an art gallery, though verse is not his best talent. After Giton abandons him, Encolpius goes there to console himself by looking at the paintings of primarily homosexual lovers and their sufferings. He is soliloquizing in front of the art, "as if in a desert" (§83.4), when a white-haired old man comes up to him and introduces himself as a poet. He promptly offers a sample, a lament for the state of "eloquence" (*facundia*

§83.10) in a materialistic age. After a gap of indeterminate length, we find Eumolpus (presumably he has given Encolpius his name by now) telling the racy tale of seducing a young boy at Pergamum while serving on the Roman quaestor's staff. The story is often classed as a "Milesian Tale" (Lefèvre 1997: 8–15; for a different view of "Milesiaca" see Jennsen 2004), on which more below. In this context, Eumolpus is clearly trying to establish a sympathetic relation with Encolpius (whether he overheard his laments or only observed his interest in the homoerotic paintings) and perhaps even to pick him up.

This bawdy narrative encourages Encolpius to ask Eumolpus more about the paintings. He gets potted art history followed by 65 verses of a poem on the theme of the sack of Troy, the *Troiae Halosis* (§89), supposedly the subject of a painting that had captured Encolpius's attention.

The poem is presented as an ecphrasis, a vivid representation in words of visual subject matter, and often in the ancient novel of a work of art (see particularly Bartsch 1989, Fowler 1991). Such a description launches two surviving Greek novels, Achilles Tatius's *Leucippe and Cleitophon* as well as Longus's *Daphnis and Chloe*. While no ecphrasis is ever *just* a visual description, the problem in the *Satyrica* is that Eumolpus's poem narrates much too much to fit into any one painting; in fact, it sounds more like a soliloquy from a Senecan tragedy delivered in character. If it is supposed to be understood as descriptive of the art, it should then be an improvisation based on looking at the painting. Since it bears no clear relation to any imaginable painting (perhaps its events could fit into a series of paintings), the suspicion arises that Eumolpus has seized the opportunity to recite a previously composed poem. Even if the poem fits neither the painting nor the tranquility of the gallery, however, the reaction of the other viewers, who drive him away by throwing stones, seems excessive.

The Wrath of Priapus?

Giton rejoins Encolpius, and while Eumolpus's presence represents a threat to their relationship, the three decide to skip town by ship. Only after embarking do they discover they have boarded the ship of Lichas, with whom Encolpius and Giton have had earlier unhappy encounters in portions of the narrative now lost. Avid attempts have been made to reconstruct previous events, with results that seriously affect our reading of the surviving text. Particularly interesting is the role the god Priapus appears to play.

Eumolpus tries to disguise Encolpius and Giton as his slaves, but Lichas and
Tryphaena, the rich woman traveling with him, discover them nonetheless.
This discovery is foreshadowed by parallel dreams in which Priapus tells
Lichas that he has personally led Encolpius onto the ship, and Neptune tells
Tryphaena that she will find Giton (§104.1–3). Their sharing of these
dreams instigates the search of the ship that reveals Encolpius and Giton.

  More than a century ago Klebs (1889) linked these events both to
Encolpius's earlier adventures with Quartilla, the priestess of Priapus, and
his problems yet to come with impotence at Croton (which Encolpius
blames on the "terrible anger of Priapus" – *gravis ira Priapi* §139.2) to
suggest that a theme of the "wrath of Priapus" helped structure our narrative
(see Richlin, SEX IN THE SATYRICA, p. 92, on Priapus's presence). This would
be a parody of epic, in particular the wrath of Poseidon (Neptune for
Romans) against the hero Odysseus in Homer's *Odyssey* (cf. Morgan,
PETRONIUS AND GREEK LITERATURE, p. 34, and Richlin, SEX IN THE
SATYRICA, p. 95, on literary epic parody, and Vout, THE SATYRICA AND
NERONIAN CULTURE on Neronian resonances). The suggestion is initially
quite appealing, drawing together apparently disparate sections of the
surviving narrative, and it gives a point to the parallel appearance of Priapus
and Neptune here in dreams. Yet all adventure narratives after Homer
possess some Odyssean characteristics, and the frame of epic parody does
not account for everything that is interesting in the *Satyrica*. Encolpius
might well *perceive* himself as a victim of the "wrath of Priapus" (Conte
1996a: 94–103), yet it is but one theme among many here, despite
the wickedly funny parody of a famous recognition scene in the *Odyssey*:
the fugitives are detected first by their voices rather than their disguised
faces, but Lichas confirms his recognition of Encolpius by reaching into his
crotch (Encolpius's unusual name is derived from a Greek word that can
mean "crotch") and grabbing his genitals. Encolpius the narrator compares
this to Odysseus's nurse recognizing him years later by a hunting scar
(§105.9). (For more on the relationship between the *Satyrica* and Homer's
Odyssey see Morgan, PETRONIUS AND GREEK LITERATURE.)

  Conflict breaks out over how to treat the fugitives, and Giton even threatens self-castration before a truce is reached. Eumolpus contributes to calm-
ing things down by telling another racy and entertaining story, "The Widow
of Ephesus." The famously virtuous widow, trying to starve herself to death
over her husband's body, is seduced back to both life and love by a soldier
guarding crucified bodies nearby. When one body is stolen, the soldier plans
suicide for his dereliction of duty, but the widow persuades him to hang her

deceased husband's body on the cross as a substitute, and both live happily thereafter. In its immediate context, this internal narrative offers a study in varied audience response: Lichas thinks it outrageous, the rest of the men laugh, and Tryphaena is embarrassed (compare Richlin, SEX IN THE SATYRICA, p. 89), but on the whole it fulfills Eumolpus's intention of restoring good feeling after conflict. The thematic import is more controversial: it can be seen as a traditional misogynistic tale, proving no woman is really virtuous (Conte 1996a: 104–7), as a triumph of life in the midst of death (Arrowsmith 1966), or as a microcosm of the way the *Satyrica* devours other literature (Rimell 2002: 123–39).

The harmony is short-lived. A storm wrecks the ship and apparently drowns all, except our protagonists and Eumolpus's servant Corax. The others find the poet in the wreckage, at work on a poem, and drag him ashore. Discovering they are near Croton, they concoct a scheme to pretend that Eumolpus is a rich widower from Africa, traveling to forget the loss of his only son and heir, and they are his slaves. Since Croton is presented as a culture that lives by legacy hunting, it will provide them with a living from would-be heirs to Eumolpus as long as they can keep up the charade.

On the road to Croton, Eumolpus recites the poem he was composing, an epic fragment on Rome's civil war, the *Bellum Civile*. This poem too has generated much discussion of possible parody of or relation to other poetry in the Neronian age. Unlike others in the narrative, Eumolpus is certainly a competent versifier, though by no means a great poet. His theme is current: while the first few generations after the civil war avoided it as subject matter, loath to re-open the conflicts that preceded the Augustan settlement, the Neronian poet Lucan was at work on a civil war epic around the time that the *Satyrica* was being composed. Though originally writing in praise of the emperor, Lucan fell foul of Nero and was forced to commit suicide (as Petronius too would be). In contrast to Aeneas's divine mission to found Rome in Virgil's epic, Lucan's unfinished poem excised the gods as motive forces of history. Eumolpus puts the gods back in with a vengeance, and some have seen here a counterattack on Lucan.

Bound up in this is the question of where, if anywhere, we should see the possible views or sympathies of the author Petronius in or behind the views and sympathies of characters in his narrative. The *Satyrica* is a richly comic text, and readers often wish to feel that they are laughing not just *at* its subjects, but *with* its author. The most heated discussion focuses around a poem late in the Croton episode, after Encolpius, afflicted with impotence, tries to take vengeance on his own body and castrate himself to the tune of his own verse.

He fails, upbraids his own member in extravagant rhetoric (see Panayotakis, PETRONIUS AND THE ROMAN LITERARY TRADITION, p. 57, on this debate!), and ponders his plight in a pastiche of Virgilian verse. When he claims to feel embarrassed over his conversation with a body part, he decides he should not, since Odysseus addressed his own heart. These elegiacs follow:

> Why do you Catos frown at me
> > And condemn a work (*opus*) of fresh simplicity?
> A cheerful grace laughs in my pure speech,
> > And what people do, a frank tongue reports.
> Who doesn't know sleeping together, the joys of Venus?
> > Who says you can't heat your members in a warm bed?
> Epicurus, father of truth, commanded the learned to love
> > And said that life had this *telos*.
>
> > > > > > > > > > > > (§132.15)

To a modern reader, this sounds very much like a defence of a literary work (*opus*) against censorship, and some have heard Petronius speaking here in defence of the "realism" of his novel (notably Collignon 1892: 53, and Sullivan 1968a: 98–102). More recently such biographical criticism has become ideologically suspect: would we even think of the author breaking out of the dramatic illusion of the text to speak directly to us as readers if we did not imagine that author as the Petronius we meet in Tacitus (see INTRODUCTION)? Compare Vout's thought experiment on dating (THE SATYRICA AND NERONIAN CULTURE): would a Flavian author defend his "realism" through the persona of Encolpius? It seems fair to ask how many Catos (that is, stern Stoic moralists) would have made it this far through Petronius's text to be the readers the author really wants to argue with (Conte 1996a: 187–94). Encolpius, not for the first time, has taken on a role to argue with an imagined audience.

(Without) a Sense of an Ending

The *Satyrica* becomes more fragmented as we near the end of what survives. Encolpius's adventures with Circe, the witches' attempts to cure his impotence, and Philomela's plan to use her children to seduce Eumolpus follow in quick succession.

The legacy hunters, though, are becoming exhausted and suspicious, as someone advises Eumolpus in the last section (§141.1). Immediately thereafter follows a quotation apparently from Eumolpus's will:

> All recipients of legacies under my will, except my freedmen, shall inherit what I have left on this condition: that they cut up my body and eat it in public view ... (§141.2)

The state of the text here makes it impossible to know whether Eumolpus is in fact dead, and this is the public reading of his will, or whether he has ordered it read, in order to make the prospective heirs less eager for his immediate demise. What we do know is that someone, possibly Gorgias (namesake of the great Sicilian sophist), then argues in favor of carrying out the terms of the bequest, citing examples of cannibalism from Roman history.

The prospect or presence of death lends a spurious sense of closure to the narrative. The end of the confidence game in Croton seems imminent, but Encolpius, Giton, and even Eumolpus might have escaped to defraud and debauch yet others for several more books, if Petronius lived to finish whatever design he had for the *Satyrica*. Our preserved text ends, as it began, in the midst of a rhetorical performance by a speaker trying to gain an immediate advantage.

We can read the *Satyrica* for many purposes, and do. It tantalizes us with the hope of seeing the Roman world under Nero through the eyes of freedmen and would-be intellectuals, of experiencing life on its gritty streets and in its luxurious, or at least expensive, homes. It engages the Greek and Roman literary heritage in richly subversive ways that seem all the more appealing in light of the seriousness of much of the ancient literary canon. Its voyeuristic vignettes illuminate Roman sexual mores as well as the dangers and potential violence of its world as virtually no other text can.

The temptation to see the meaning of the *Satyrica*, therefore, as something to be excavated is very strong, and another, much discussed poem in the text seems to guide us in that direction:

> A troupe acts a mime on stage: that man's called "father",
> > This one "son", that one's named a rich man.
> Soon when the page shuts up the smiling characters,
> > The true face returns, while the pretended one perishes.
> > > (§80.9, based on Bücheler's text (1862))

Editors differ as to whether this is a free-standing poem or part of another, but let us simply focus on these lines now. They are a powerful evocation of the metaphor of life as a stage performance, a notion we first see emerge in Greek thought only a couple of centuries before Petronius (and as Hales, FREEDMEN's CRIBS, p. 174, shows, the Romans then domesticated this theatricality particularly in their private interior spaces). Indeed, when the surviving novel text breaks off, the mime that Encolpius, Eumolpus, and Giton have been performing in order to fleece the legacy hunters may be about to reach its final page. Yet Eumolpus the poet is no more a "true face" (*vera … facies*) than the shipwrecked rich man he plays in Croton – both are constructs of the words we have read.

There are many ways of reading the *Satyrica*, though none now available to us is precisely the way it was read in the first century AD. We cannot even be absolutely sure Petronius wrote for readers, rather than listeners, although the survival of his text shows his enduring appeal as writing. The *Satyrica* can be read for insight into the age that produced it, and that age can be read for more material to enrich our reading of Petronius. As you put this essay down and pick up the *Satyrica*, though, be prepared to play along with the mime as well as study the performance.

Further Reading

There is no complete modern commentary in English on the *Satyrica*, while translations abound (including one falsely attributed to Oscar Wilde!). The standard text is Müller (2003), although it still displays a keen enthusiasm for deletion and emendation learned from Fränkel. Smith (1975) is an excellent guide to the *Cena*, while Habermehl (2006 and forthcoming) offers detailed commentary and parallels for the text thereafter. Courtney (2001) is a companion in continuous narrative with much valuable material and many lapidary judgments. Most (1997) collects numerous approaches to the problems of reading fragmentary texts, while Casson (2001) adds much to Reynolds and Wilson (1991: 1–32) on Roman books and their readers.

Arrowsmith (1959, and often reprinted by various publishers) was the first modern unexpurgated translation and remains highly readable. The lively version of Branham and Kinney (1996) conveys the range of both Petronius's prose and poetry, while Walsh (1996) can guide readers through some of the difficulties of the Latin.

While literary studies have multiplied in recent years, the pioneering work of Sullivan (1968a) remains invaluable despite a now dated concern with how the novel might represent Petronius's own psycho-sexual character. So too the genre-based study by Walsh (1970), to which Selden (1994) offers a counterpoint. Zeitlin's classic article (1971) illuminates the picaresque quality of both novel and age. Slater (1990) offers a reader-response approach to the experience of the text. Connors (1998) is a sensitive and sympathetic reader of all the poetry in the novel. To find a way through the last three decades of a vast and growing critical literature we are fortunate to have the annotated bibliography of Vannini (2007), with Schmeling and Stuckey (1977) and Smith (1985) for earlier periods.

2

Petronius and Greek Literature

J. R. Morgan

The Greekness of the *Satyrica* is palpable at many levels. The action of the surviving portions of the text plays out apparently in the cities of Magna Graecia in southern Italy, and the cast list is populated by characters with Greek names. The thematic prominence of homosexuality is no doubt an aspect of the Roman representation of Greek ambience. It is equally clear that the novel would not be the way it is were it not for the Greek literature which underlies it. This chapter addresses the ways in which the novel actively enters into intertextual relationships with the Greek literary canon as part of its own creation of meaning (see Panayotakis, PETRONIUS AND THE ROMAN LITERARY TRADITION). This is less a matter of listing the literary influences to which Petronius might have been subject than of exploring what he did with his own and his reader's awareness of Greek literature. The discussion will concentrate on three main areas of Greek literature: firstly Homeric poetry (with a vaguer mythological penumbra), secondly Plato, and finally the vexed issue of the extent to which the *Satyrica* draws on Greek traditions of fictional narrative.

Homer

Petronius's novel could hardly advertise its relation to the *Odyssey* more clearly. The extant text ends with a fragmentary sequence in which Encolpius is disguised as a slave called Polyaenus, one of the Homeric epithets for Odysseus, and is the object of the amatory attentions of a beautiful seductress named Circe. The characters themselves are aware of, and draw attention to, the Homeric connotations of their own situation:

"So my maid hasn't told you that I'm called Circe? Not that I'm the child of the Sun – my mother never stopped at will the course of the revolving heavens. Yet if the fates unite us, I shall have something to thank heaven for. A god, in fact, is already working his mysterious purposes to some end. It is not by chance that Circe is in love with Polyaenus – a great flame is always kindled between these names." (§127.6–7; the translation of all Petronian extracts in this chapter is from Sullivan 1986)

But the Homeric hypotext (an earlier text which forms part of the background to later texts) in this episode is not confined to the perception of the characters. Encolpius's narrative responds with a verse description of their lovemaking (§126.9) that references the famous scene in *Iliad* 14 (especially lines 346–51) when Hera seduces Zeus to distract his attention from the battlefield around Troy. This is a symptom of what Conte (1996a) has described as the narrator's "mythomania": he is characterized by his tendency to assimilate his own mundane and sleazy experiences to grandiose literary analogues. Even as Encolpius is identified with Odysseus through his name and his liaison, multiple ironies are at work below the surface of the narrative. In the *Odyssey*, the hero's companions are metamorphosed into animals by Circe's witchcraft (10.203–43), while Odysseus, armed with a powerful counter-charm, is able to bed the enchantress (10.274–347). In the *Satyrica*, Encolpius is likewise immune to Circe's spell, but only in the sense that he is repeatedly impotent with her. Here it is not the companions but the hero himself who is metaphorically dehumanized, and as he casts himself in the role of Odysseus, he is simultaneously revealed as an ineffectual version of that hero. And yet at the same time, Encolpius's companions are living in luxury as the result of the scam that Eumolpus has concocted to exploit the legacy hunters of Croton. At a level far removed from the narrator's own perception of the situation they are being equated to the swine feeding at Circe's troughs, an element in the work's satirical critique of a life concerned only with the pursuit of material goods.

The Circe/Polyaenus episode, however, is not an isolated fleck of intertextual coloring. Rather it is paradigmatic of a sustained interaction with Homeric epic. Indications in the manuscript assign the extant parts of the *Satyrica* to Books 14, 15, and 16, and there are no obvious signs that the final resolution of the plot is imminent (see Slater, READING THE *SATYRICA*, p. 17, on the fragmentary nature of the remains of the *Satyrica*). Given that the overarching plot-structure concerns the adventures of a wandering protagonist, in the course of which he also encounters characters bearing such Homeric names as Agamemnon and Menelaus, it would be perverse not to entertain the possibility that the novel was conceived as a comic rewriting of the *Odyssey* on an epic scale; I am convinced that the original text comprised a Homeric 24 books. It goes without saying that most of the plot is lost beyond hope of reconstruction, but it would be surprising if there were not macro-structural correspondences to the Homeric epics as well as allusive details. One such feature has long been remarked (first by Klebs 1889; discussion in Courtney 2001: 152–7), and, despite the cautious skepticism of some scholars, there is no reason to discard it. After his debacle with Circe, Encolpius complains that he is hounded by the wrath of Priapus of Hellespont, a predicament that he compares to that of other victims of divine anger, including Odysseus (in Latin Ulysses) pursued by the wrath of Poseidon (in Roman terms, Neptune).

> Others have been hounded by gods
> And implacable fate, not I alone.
> Hercules hounded from Argos,
> And propping heaven on his shoulders.
> Impious Laomedon
> And those two angry immortals:
> He paid the price of his offences.
> Pelias felt the weight of Juno.
> Then there was Telephus –
> He took up arms in his ignorance.
> Even Ulysses went in fear of Neptune's power.
> Now I too take my stand among these –
> Over land and white Nereus' sea, I am hounded
> By the mighty rage of Priapus of Hellespont.

(§139.4)

In the *Odyssey*, Odysseus incurs the anger of Poseidon after blinding his son the Cyclops Polyphemus (9.105–566), and this underlies many of his sufferings in the first half of the poem; Poseidon's final act of spite is to petrify the ship of the Phaeacians that finally conveys Odysseus back to Ithaca (13.125–87). In the *Satyrica*, Priapus makes his presence felt at several junctures: Encolpius bursts into secret rites in the shrine of Priapus (§17.8); Priapus appears to Lichas in a dream and reveals Encolpius's presence on his ship (§104.1); Encolpius tries to conciliate the hostile divinity, pleading poverty as an excuse for an act of temple robbery which must have been narrated in one of the lost sections of the text (§133.2–3); shortly afterwards he renews the god's anger by unwittingly killing Priapus's favorite goose (§137.2). The ithyphallic deity appropriately exacts his vengeance through the infliction of impotence; his agency is thus to be perceived in contexts where he is not named, as when Encolpius blames an unspecified divine power for his failure to perform with Giton (§140.11). From the repeated references to the remarkable size of Encolpius's organ, we can even guess that the origins of Priapus's hostility lie in his jealousy of the hero's male endowment; this seems to be confirmed by the verses of Sidonius Apollinaris, in which, confusing the author Petronius with the narrator Encolpius, he describes Petronius as "equal to Priapus of the Hellespont" (Petronius frag. IV, Müller 2003: 177). (Compare Slater, READING THE SATYRICA, p. 25, and see Richlin, SEX IN THE SATYRICA, p. 83, 92, 95, on Priapus.)

In the *Odyssey* the anger of Poseidon ceases to be operative after Odysseus's return to Ithaca; the wrath of Priapus in the *Satyrica* seems to be sustained for longer, and periodically renewed by fresh offences. The basic point remains, however, that one fundamental structure of the text casts its hero as a comic Odysseus hounded by the wrath of a comic god. Within that frame we cannot know how closely Petronius did or did not follow the plot of the *Odyssey*, but it does not take a fevered imagination to suppose that some of the major episodes of the poem found an analogue of some sort in the novel. The novel of Heliodorus, written several centuries after Petronius, may serve as a parallel: the overall plot structure is an Odyssean *nostos* ("return home") for the heroine Charicleia, who was born an Ethiopian princess; her 10-year stay at Delphi, where she lives unrecognized and unaware of her own identity, echoes Odysseus's 10-year detention by Calypso; her encounter with an Egyptian necromancer (6.14–15) is linked by precise allusion to Odysseus's meeting with the dead (*Od.* 11.13–640); the protagonists' tribulations in the luxurious but brutal Persian palace (7.12–8.13) correspond to the Cyclops episode (*Od.* 9.105–566); and at the very end of the novel, like Odysseus, the heroine is united with her father and her true-beloved. There is no slavish one-for-one correspondence here, but the reader's recognition of the Homeric hypotext activates a whole series of meaningful resonances.

If Petronius were doing something similar, the obvious candidate for identification with Odyssean set-pieces is the *Cena Trimalchionis*. It is well known that a cluster of images towards the end of the episode connect Trimalchio's house with the Underworld; in particular Giton's feeding of scraps to the watchdog (§72.9) recalls Aeneas throwing sops to Cerberus in the sixth book of the *Aeneid* (6.417–23; Newton 1982, Courtney 1987, Bodel 1994). In retrospect, then, Encolpius's visit to Trimalchio's house

becomes a rewriting of Virgil's rewriting of Homer: a metaphorical
katabasis (κατάβασις – "descent"), beginning, like Virgil's, with an entry
through an imposing gateway decorated with significant images (§28.6–
29.8 – *Aen.* 6.14–41), and ending with an exit through a different door
(§72.10 – *Aen.* 6.893–8). As this intertextual dimension belatedly becomes
clear, the reader is compelled to reassess what has just been read.
Trimalchio's house is retrospectively revealed as the realm of the dead; its
inhabitants are insubstantial wraiths, spiritually, if not physically, lifeless.
Aeneas in Virgil's Underworld was granted a vision of what Rome would
become (*Aen.* 6.752–892); Encolpius in Petronius's metatextual version is
granted a vision of what Rome has become (except that he is incapable of
recognizing it for what it is: see further Hope, AT HOME WITH THE DEAD,
p. 142, on Trimalchio's house as Underworld). Simultaneously, the *Cena*
recalls the Cyclops episode of *Odyssey* 9. Like Polyphemus, Trimalchio is a
monster baited in his lair, whose guests are destroyed by eating. The difference is that Polyphemus's guests are killed and eaten, whereas
Trimalchio's eat and thus enter the state of figurative death implied by the
Underworld imagery (see Vout, THE SATYRICA AND NERONIAN CULTURE,
p. 110, on the imagery of the Cyclops in relation to emperors). In addition,
there are also hints that Trimalchio's house is like the labyrinth (§73.1;
note that one of Trimalchio's servants is called Daedalus, and see Hales,
FREEDMEN'S CRIBS, p. 173), casting its master in the role of Minotaur,
another flesh-devouring monster. These two intertextual patterns reinforce each other and add to the implicit ethical commentary of the episode
(see A. Cameron 1970). The conspicuous consumption, vulgarity and
materialism of Trimalchio's world are associated with death, in a manner
that effectively bypasses the narrator. In other words, an important layer
of ethical appraisal (belonging to the author not the narrator) is intertex-
tually activated.

Within the surviving parts of the novel, it is not possible to identify any
other episodes that are quite so clearly modeled on the *Odyssey*, although
comparisons, made by Eumolpus, of Lichas to the Cyclops and his ship to
Polyphemus's cave (§101.5–7) perhaps trigger a reading of this section as
another version of *Odyssey* 9. Certainly there is the same basic situation of
the hero trapped in an enclosed and hostile space, but the Lichas section
again relates to Homeric models in a complex way. The disguise adopted by
Encolpius and Giton (§103) recalls Athene's transformation of Odysseus
into an old man when he returns to Ithaca (*Od.* 13.392–438), and, sure
enough, the moment when Lichas recognizes the shaven Encolpius by the

abnormality of his genitalia is compared by the narrator to Eurycleia's recognition of Odysseus by his scar (19.335–507):

> Will anyone now be surprised that Ulysses' nurse after twenty years found a scar sufficient identification when this shrewd man so cleverly went straight to the one thing that identified the runaway, despite the total confusion of the lines we use for physical identification? (§105.10)

However, whereas Odysseus silences his nurse before she can give him away to his wife, Lichas's exclamation is the means by which Tryphaena too, unlike Penelope, can recognize the pair; her very name (connected with the Greek word τρυφή, *truphê* – "luxury" or "wantonness"), in fact, casts her as an anti-Penelope. The sequence on the ship becomes very fragmentary towards the end but is terminated by an epic storm and shipwreck, recalling Odysseus's ordeals after leaving Calypso (*Od.* 5.262–457), but overlaid with reference to the storm at *Aeneid* 1.81–156. The pattern is further complicated by the fact that not long before the encounter with Lichas, Giton hides from Ascyltos by hanging under a bed, a stratagem whose similarity to Odysseus escaping from the Cyclops' cave by hanging underneath one of Polyphemus's rams (*Od.* 9.415–63) is not lost on Encolpius the narrator:

> When the mattress was pulled back too, he saw our Ulysses, and even a hungry Cyclops would have had pity on him. (§98.5; cf. §97.4–5)

Trimalchio, Ascyltos, and Lichas are thus all at some stage and in some way assimilated to the Cyclops.

Although these items of epic coloring all contribute to the reader's sense that the novel as a whole is a parodic version of epic poetry, it is important to distinguish the levels at which the intertextual awareness resides. Sometimes, the characters are themselves aware of the analogy at the time of the action: Circe herself comments on her liaison with Polyaenus, and Eumolpus compares Lichas's ship to the Cyclops' cave. In these cases, the epic allusions are at the service of the characterization: these are people – particularly the poet Eumolpus – with literary pretensions. At other times, the reference seems to be the property of Encolpius the narrator, an element of what Conte has termed his "mythomania," his obsessive assimilation of his tawdry adventure to elevated literary genres. For instance, the explicit comparison of Lichas's recognition of Encolpius to its Odyssean analogue (quoted above) is placed in the mouth of the commenting narrator. Less overtly, the narrator forges mythic analogues for his younger self. For example, after Giton chooses to go with Ascyltos, Encolpius casts himself in the role of Achilles, rents a quiet place by the sea and sulks, like the warrior in his hut after Agamemnon's theft of Briseis (§81.1–3). After a bitter soliloquy he desperately sallies forth into the night, like Aeneas at the fall of Troy (§82.1). The third layer of epic reference, however, resides with the author, who has devised the story as a whole on an epic frame, with analogues which escape the notice of character and narrator alike. The satirical and moral implications of the mythic, and specifically Homeric, intertextuality that casts Trimalchio as both Cyclops and Minotaur, and his house as the Underworld, are never drawn by the narrator. At this level, it is a tool in the communication between author and reader.

Plato

The extended description of a dinner party at which a series of different speakers express their thoughts could hardly fail to evoke Plato's *Symposium*, in which seven guests of the dramatist Agathon speak on the nature of Love, culminating in Socrates' account of what he learned from the priestess Diotima. The *Symposium* became one of the favorite intertextual archetypes of the Imperial period, with resonances in literature of all types, from Athenaeus's *Deipnosophists* to the Greek romances. It is quite clear that Petronius had this text very much in his sights: at Trimalchio's dinner party too, seven of the guests address the whole company. Indeed, one of Plato's speakers, the comic playwright Aristophanes, speaks in a riotously humorous vein, telling the myth of primordial spherical beings with two sets of genitals in all possible combinations of gender, who were punished for their arrogance towards the gods by being split in two; human beings are literally seeking their other half, and Love occurs when they are at last united in a single being (*Symp.* 189c–193d). This conceit is toyed with in several of the Greek novels, and the homosexual Odyssey of Encolpius may well be read as a comically unsuccessful instantiation of the Aristophanic myth. Aristophanes' self-deprecating introduction (*Symp.* 189a–b) is verbally recalled as Niceros begins his tale of the werewolf (§61.3–4). The point about Trimalchio's party, however, is that its speakers are intellectually and culturally challenged. It is a Symposium of Idiots. In place of disquisitions on the nature of Eros, in some cases so profound and poetic that they became part of the literary patrimony of antiquity, Petronius's freedmen trade clichés – this is the limit of their philosophy:

> "Please, please," broke in Echion the rag-merchant, "be a bit more cheerful. "First it's one thing, then another," as the yokel said when he lost his spotted pig. What we haven't got today, we'll have tomorrow. That's the way life goes. Believe me, you couldn't name a better country, if it had the people. As things are, I admit, it's having a hard time, but it isn't the only place. We mustn't be soft. The sky don't get no nearer wherever you are. If you were somewhere else, you'd be talking about the pigs walking around ready-roasted back here." (§45.1–4)

A little later (§56.7) Encolpius sarcastically describes Trimalchio as "putting the philosophers out of work." This follows the host's attempt at a piece of moralizing verse in the manner of Publilius (see Panayotakis, PETRONIUS AND THE ROMAN LITERARY TRADITION, p. 60), and a series of would-be clever generalizations.

The importance of the *Symposium* as an intertext is signaled by a significant structural parallel. The arrival of the drunken and uninvited Habinnas (§65.3) closely echoes that of Alcibiades near the end of the *Symposium* (212c–213b). Within the similarity, the two are contrasted point by point. Alcibiades has been, one presumes, at an aristocratic party; he is accompanied by a beautiful flute-girl, apologizes for his inebriation, and asks whether he can join the gathering: Habinnas has been to a funeral, is supported by his hideous wife, Scintilla, calls for more drink, and sits down in the praetor's chair. Cameron (1969) argues that both arrivals set the action on a new direction, and pave the way for the culminating revelation about the main character: Socrates' chastity and endurance at Potidaea (*Symp.* 215a–222b), contrasted with Trimalchio's morbid obsession with death and his plans for his own tomb monument (§71–8).

Although Encolpius can sarcastically suggest that Trimalchio's nonsense was putting the philosophers out of business, this intertextual alignment with the *Symposium* resides again with the author: neither as character nor as narrator does Encolpius suggest any explicit comparison with the *Symposium*. The implications of the comparison therefore constitute a judgment on Trimalchio and his circle communicated by the author to the reader.

Alcibiades' speech with its account of his unmolested night, despite his worst efforts (*Symp*. 216d–219e), with Socrates, is explicitly recalled by Giton in the context of Encolpius's impotence:

> "So thank you for loving me in such an honourable Platonic way (*Socratica fide*). Alcibiades himself couldn't have been safer when he slept in his teacher's bed." (§128.7)

That this episode was demonstrably in Petronius's mind adds credence to the idea that Eumolpus's story "The Boy of Pergamum" (§85–7), in which a tutor seduces his pupil but ends up being embarrassed by his failure to meet the boy's demands, is to be read as a comic deconstruction of the Platonic passage (the case is argued at length by McGlathery 1998, and see Richlin, SEX IN THE SATYRICA, p. 88, 95).

The Greek Novel

The final area of Greek literature to be considered is the most obvious one: the Greek novel (to which must be added other forms of Greek fiction). The case for a connection rests on the two pillars of form and motif: briefly put, the fact that the *Satyrica* and the Greek novel are both lengthy fictional narratives in prose has suggested that there is a causal connection of some sort between them, and the frequency with which it is possible to find correspondences between episodes and details in Petronius and the Greek novels appears to confirm this. Since Heinze (1899), the idea that Petronius was parodying the ideal Greek love romance has found wide, if not universal, acceptance.

As far as the form is concerned, the first factor is that of scale: at 24 books, the *Satyrica* would have been rather longer than the most extensive of the surviving Greek novels, the *Ethiopian Story* by Heliodorus (10 books). But the *Wonders beyond Thule* of Antonius Diogenes (now lost but read by the Byzantine patriarch Photius in the ninth century; his summary of the text can be found, translated by Sandy, in Reardon 2008; see also Stephens and Winkler 1995) was also 24 books in length, and was also, so far as one can judge, playing games (albeit not quite the same ones) with the *Odyssey*. The *Babylonian Story* by Iamblichus is said by the *Suda* (a Byzantine encyclopaedia) to have run to 39 books; but Photius's summary of this text appears to end with Book 16; in any case it was clearly a very lengthy novel, and would serve as another parallel to a *Satyrica* of the size envisaged here. Secondly, most of the Greek novels are narrated in the third person by an external and more or less omniscient narrator, but there is one example, *Leucippe and Cleitophon* by Achilles Tatius, whose eponymous hero's narration of his own experiences forms the bulk of the novel. Cleitophon tells his story to an anonymous frame narrator, who describes their meeting at Sidon; the loss of the beginning and end of the *Satyrica* means that we cannot be sure whether Encolpius's narrative was framed in the same way and delivered to a narratee within the fiction. Third, the title of the *Satyrica* is often taken as parallel to the geographical titles attached to some of the Greek novels: the *Ephesiaca* of Xenophon of Ephesus, the *Babyloniaca* of Iamblichus, the *Phoenicica* of Lollianus, or the *Aethiopica* of Heliodorus. Finally, even the prosimetric mixture of prose and verse that we find in the *Satyrica* can be paralleled, for example by Chariton's incorporation of Homeric verses into his narrative.

To turn now to the matter of motif, although the five extant Greek novels are each highly individualized they do share a definite generic thematic. Canonically, the central characters are a beautiful young man and woman, who fall in love and undergo a series of adventures before achieving an ending of the "They lived happily ever afterwards" sort. In most cases, the adventures are strung on a thread of travel, as the protagonists are either separated and seek each other, or else undertake a journey of some other sort – to the heroine's homeland and family in Ethiopia in Heliodorus, or to escape the lust of the Persian king in Iamblichus. The mix of travel and adventure allows, naturally, for frequent intertextual play with the *Odyssey*. In the course of their adventures, the lovers generally become involved with pirates or outlaws, and undergo shipwreck (descriptions of storms are a staple). At every turn, their extreme beauty, particularly that of the heroine, provokes the unwelcome attention of rival lovers, but throughout their tribulations, the lovers remain true to each other, with just one or two infringements. The tone is predominantly romantic, but here again Achilles Tatius is exceptional. Cleitophon is far from the ideal hero for a novel. Early in the novel he infiltrates his beloved's bedroom, and is only prevented from fulfilling his desires by the arrival of her mother, who has dreamed that her daughter was being attacked by a man with a naked sword. Later, believing Leucippe dead by decapitation, he enters into a marriage with a wealthy and amorous widow (a widow of Ephesus, in fact), but does not consummate it. Only when he discovers that his sweetheart is alive after all, and that his wife's husband is not dead either, does he finally agree to service his wife, as an act of kindness, on the floor of a jailhouse, before making his escape in drag. Even the happy ending is somehow destabilized: the introductory frame narrative is never taken up again, and the situation with which Cleitophon ends his narrative is disquietingly not quite that in which he is found in the introductory frame; the reader recalls that there he was alone and apparently not too happy (see Repath 2005). As a narrator, Cleitophon is heavily characterized by his tendency to digress and preen himself on his erudition; the unreliability or at least partiality of this internal narrator bears comparison to that of Encolpius, and similar reading strategies can fruitfully be applied to both texts (see Morgan 2007).

It is not difficult to see how the *Satyrica* might be held to relate to these Greek novels, by either participating in or parodying their repertoire of themes and motifs. Encolpius and Giton take the place of the central pair of lovers; instead of an ideal heterosexual relationship, which leads inexorably to socially sanctioned marriage, we have a homosexual couple whose adventures take place in the lower reaches of the social pool (see Richlin, SEX IN THE SATYRICA, p. 84, 94). The principal rival figure is Ascyltos, but Eumolpus, Lichas, Tryphaena, and even Circe also pose potential threats to the stability of the protagonists' love, attracted by their physical beauty. Amatory commonplaces cluster around Encolpius and Giton. They are, for example, caught in a storm, whose rhetorical elaboration is reminiscent of those found in Achilles Tatius (3.1–5), Heliodorus (5.27), and the fragmentary "Herpyllis-romance" (translated by Reardon in Reardon 2008; see Stephens and Winkler 1995). At the point of shipwreck, Encolpius clasps Giton and looks forward to union in death, as romantic heroes are prone to do:

> "We deserved this of heaven – death alone would unite us. But our cruel luck does not allow it. Look, the waves are already overturning the ship. Look, the angry sea is trying to break our affectionate embraces. If you ever really loved Encolpius, kiss him while you can and snatch this last pleasure from the jaws of death." (§114.8–9; cf. Achilles Tatius 3.5.4)

Their wanderings are analogous to those of many Greek romantic heroes, and the wrath of Priapus against the hyper-endowed Encolpius, which drives their travels, is analogous to, for instance, the anger of Eros against Xenophon's haughty hero, Habrocomes. Encolpius's frequent invocations of Fortuna are similar to all those occasions in the Greek novels where the protagonists protest against the cruelty of Tyche. Where romantic heroes and heroines give vent to their feelings in genuinely tragic laments, Encolpius's pretensions to tragic or heroic status are systematically deflated as part of his "mythomanic" characterization. There are ways in which Eumolpus, too, might be connected to several figures in the Greek novels. His encounter with Encolpius in the art gallery recalls the frame of Achilles Tatius's novel, in which Cleitophon is inspired to tell his story by a painting of Zeus and Europa; Longus's *Daphnis and Chloe* also parades itself as the extended ecphrasis of a painting (a vivid representation in words of visual subject matter). Elements in the characterization of Eumolpus connect him with figures such as Longus's *praeceptor amoris* ("teacher of love"), Philetas, or the substitute father-figure Calasiris in Heliodorus. From evidence of this sort, Holzberg (1995: 68), typically of many scholars, concludes, "It is easily seen that these episodes ridicule the heroic pathos of scenes from the typical idealistic novel by taking it to extremes or confronting it with the hard facts of real, everyday life and thereby revealing its hollowness."

However, I believe this conclusion is incorrect. In the first place, comparatively recently published papyrus fragments have demonstrated that Greek fiction was generically less restricted than had hitherto been realized. The existence in Greek of analogous fictional narratives of comic low-life weakens the explanation of the *Satyrica* as a parody of idealistic love-romance. *The Phoenician Story* by a certain Lollianus, for example (translated by Sandy in Reardon 2008; see Stephens and Winkler 1995), features first a scene in which an innocent, not to say intellectually challenged, young man is paid for his virginity by a predatory female, and then one in a bandit lair where a boy is sacrificed and his heart cooked and eaten, with dire digestive results. Other Greek fragments show the same combination of comic, or at least non-idealistic, subject matter with prosimetric form, as in Petronius. The so-called "Iolaus-novel" was even first published as a "Greek Satyricon" (Parsons 1971; see Stephens and Winkler 1995), and was rapidly interpreted as a better generic stablemate for Petronius than Menippean satire, whatever that might be (Astbury 1977). This fragment seems to revolve around a plot for a lover (Iolaus) to get close to his girlfriend by posing as a eunuch; to enable him to act the part with verisimilitude a friend has apparently undergone initiation as a *gallus* or eunuch priest of Cybele and in the fragment addresses Iolaus and a *cinaedus* ("man who likes to be sexually penetrated") in Sotadean verse (see Panayotakis, PETRONIUS AND THE ROMAN LITERARY TRADITION, p. 57), a meter apposite to the cult of Cybele; the verse contains a Greek obscenity quite uncharacteristic of the manner and tone of the extant Greek novels.

Another prosimetric fragment, in which the name Tinouphis occurs, switches into meter as part of the narrative; the context here is rather harder to reconstruct, but seems to involve an intrigue in which Tinouphis escapes execution for adultery with a queen by hiding in a specially built tomb in which one brick has been deliberately left loose so that food can be passed in (Haslam 1981; see Stephens and Winkler 1995). The point with this evidence is not just that texts in some respects resembling the *Satyrica* existed in Greek, but that the Greek novel as a genre would have presented a rather more diffuse target for parody than Heinze's theory might suggest.

A more concrete difficulty is presented by the issue of dating. If we accept the Neronian date for Petronius (see INTRODUCTION), we must posit the existence of fully developed Greek novels, of a sort resembling the extant ones, at that date. Of the five surviving novels, four are certainly later than that. The one which has attracted most attention in this regard is Chariton's, a reference to which has been seen in Persius's first satire (1.134), where "Callirhoe" is suggested as appropriate post-lunch entertainment for the sort of person Persius does not wish for as reader of his poems. But it is by no means certain that this is a reference to Chariton's novel, named after its heroine, and in fact the logic of the context tells against this interpretation (Courtney 2001: 16–17); Persius may intend "Callirhoe" as a typical name for a prostitute. The earliest novel of which we know is generally reckoned to be the so-called *Ninus Romance*, the reverse of a copy of which was used for writing accounts in AD 99. To use this as an argument for the Heinze hypothesis, we would have to assume there was a population of similar texts not just in existence some 40 years earlier, but also in circulation in Rome in sufficient numbers for the genre to be recognized as such, with the motif-repertoire of the later novels already in place, and to have attracted the sort of critical attention which would make parodying them of any interest; there is, after all, little mileage in writing an enormously long parody of a type of literature which few have read and about which nobody cares. We have no direct evidence for the existence of these texts at that time anywhere.

There is also the question of how to construe Petronius's humor. Is the idea of a couple of promiscuous homosexual rogues making their disreputable circuit of the Mediterranean only amusing as a send-up of sentimental stories of idealized heterosexual lovers seeking reunion and return home? Does the humor of the *Satyrica* depend on the reader recognizing these features specifically as parody of the Greek romance? The answer to these questions must be, I think, in the negative. Encolpius and

Giton are funny because they contravene and subvert the conventional cultural and social norms and values of the Greco-Roman world (see Richlin, SEX IN THE *SATYRICA*). To a Roman reader they and their antics would have seemed intrinsically amusing, without the need to invoke any external literary reference. If, at a later period and in a different genre, the Greek novelists (with the exception of Achilles Tatius) produced texts which support and endorse much the same norms and values as those which Petronius's characters transgress, this signifies no more than that they and Petronius occupy positions along what is basically a single cultural spectrum, within whose widely shared assumptions they all construct their meanings, whether they be normative or critically subversive. When we look at the specific similarities which are taken as a sign of Petronius's parody, they turn out to be commonplaces of many literary forms, or straightforward reflections of reality: Petronius did not need to have read Greek novels in order to write about sex and travels, storms and shipwrecks, rivals, and lamentations about the malignity of Fortune.

Furthermore, in so far as we can form a picture of the overall shape of the *Satyrica,* it seems to have been significantly different in its structure from that of most of the Greek novels. Although characters such as Lichas and Tryphaena are clearly making their second appearance in the story, an episode such as the *Cena Trimalchionis* appears to be a sustained and self-contained piece of satire during which the protagonists' story was effectively put on hold. Although some of the novels – Xenophon's, for example – are very episodic, with secondary characters dropping out when they have served their function, the hero and heroine remain at the center of the text at every turn, and the most important of the secondary characters, the bandit Hippothous, is also a fixture. There is nothing remotely like Trimalchio's dinner party in the Greek novels that we know of. On the contrary, the plot of the other of the earliest cohort of Greek novels, Chariton's *Callirhoe,* is a true organic unity.

There was, in fact, another type of fictional narrative in Greek, which was almost certainly an ingredient in Petronius's literary mix. This was the Milesian Tale, created around 100 BC by Aristides, and translated into Latin by Sisenna. Ovid (*Tristia* 2.443–4) identifies this Sisenna with the Roman historian, praetor in 78 BC, but even if the identification is not correct, Ovid's reference is proof that these tales were in circulation in Latin in the first century BC. The title of Aristides' work, *Milesiaca,* is surely the true analogue for Petronius's title. Fragments of Aristides and Sisenna are few and far between: literature of this kind was not held in much respect. But all the evidence agrees that the average Milesian Tale was an erotic and dirty piece of work. A well known anecdote tells that a copy of the Greek version was found in the baggage of a Roman centurion after the battle of Carrhae (Plut. *Crassus* 32), providing material for Parthian propaganda about Roman decadence. Some of the comments made about the work suggest that Aristides presented himself as hearing the tales, within a narrative frame, perhaps rather like Chaucer's *Canterbury Tales*. At several points, most notably in his opening sentence, Apuleius affiliates his novel to the genre of Milesian Tales (*Metamorphoses*, 1.1, 2.21, 4.32); this seems to refer not just to the subject matter of his novel, but its structure of multiple inset tales within an overarching narrative (see Harrison 1998). There is no explicit reference to Milesian Tales in the surviving passages of the *Satyrica*, and we cannot even speculate intelligently about what Petronius might have said in his prologue. But there is a strong case for identifying some of his inset tales, such as Eumolpus's narratives about the widow of Ephesus and the boy of Pergamum as typically Milesian; this is paradoxically confirmed by the appearance of an Ephesian widow in Achilles Tatius, a mischievous generic intrusion of a personage from the Milesian Tales into an already subversive romance. The linking narrative about the wanderings of Encolpius provides a structure, much like that of Lucius's adventures in the *Metamorphoses*, into which stories told by a number of secondary narrators can be stitched. As we have seen, this is quite different from the structure of the Greek novels. The generic affiliation of the *Satyrica* to Milesian Tales goes a long way to accounting for both the subject matter and the tone of those episodes which are often taken for parodies of the idealistic novel.

Conclusion

The conclusions of this discussion are not startling. Petronius's humor bounces off the reader's intimate knowledge of canonical Greek literary texts, particularly Homer and Plato. His exploitation of this literature is in itself sophisticated and goes beyond mere "parody," sometimes serving to characterize the narrator Encolpius or characters within the action as bookish or "mythomanic," but on other occasions supplying the reader with analogies to the situations of the novel which invite him to think about the characters and actions in ways that bypass the narrator himself. Within the parts of the *Satyrica* that survive, it is harder to find sustained engagement with the Greek tragic and comic stage, but it is perfectly possible that there were episodes which exploited dramatic intertexts in similar ways. The Greek romance was not canonical literature in the same way, and so it should not perhaps be too much of a surprise that Petronius's supposed relationship to the Greek novel turns out to be a red herring.

Further Reading

Homeric elements in the *Satyrica* are discussed by most of the standard works on the author. Sullivan (1968a: 92–8) and Walsh (1970: 28–30) provide good starting points. The theory that the *Satyrica* is a sustained rewriting of the *Odyssey*, with the wrath of Priapus substituted for the anger of Poseidon, goes back to Klebs (1889), and has often been restated since. Much scholarly attention has been devoted to detecting detailed allusions, but rather less to analyzing their function and implications. The idea that the narrator Encolpius is characterized by his tendency to "epicize" his own decidedly non-heroic adventures is developed at book length by Conte (1996a). A. Cameron (1970) offers some important thoughts on how to read some of Petronius's larger mythical allusions.

The relation of the *Cena Trimalchionis* to Plato's *Symposium* is outlined in Cameron (1969). Recent work has suggested that Plato is a presence elsewhere in the novel. McGlathery (1998) advances a case for reading Eumolpus's story of the Pergamene boy as an inversion of Alcibiades' account of his chaste night with Socrates. Repath (2010) detects extensive and significant Platonic allusion, especially to the *Phaedrus*, in the Circe episode.

The idea that Petronius was writing a parody of the Greek romance genre was first raised by Heinze (1899). It is accepted by Walsh (1970: 7–9 and 78–80) and Holzberg (1995). Translations of the Greek novels are available in Reardon (2008), where most of the fragmentary material is included. Texts of the fragments, including the scabbier ones which provide parallels to Petronius, are in Stephens and Winkler (1995); discussion and further bibliography in Morgan (1998).

3

Petronius and the Roman Literary Tradition

Costas Panayotakis

For the elite Romans who grew up reading the canonical works of Virgil, Horace, and Ovid, and who were trained to speak in the rhetorical fashion exemplified in the moral tragedies of Seneca and the grand epic of Lucan, the *Satyrica* of Petronius was probably an amusing literary surprise situated in the periphery of what constituted "acceptable" creative writing. In what follows I offer general remarks on Petronius's complex literary texture – a popular scholarly topic since the end of the nineteenth century. I suggest that Petronius selects conservatively and exploits unconventionally the works of famous authors, from which he draws material to boost the melodramatic dimension of Encolpius's life, and that the indications deliberately planted in the text to signal the occurrence of learned jokes may be misleading.

The hedonistic and dangerous escapades of the (occasionally impotent) bisexual anti-hero Encolpius, his unfaithful male concubine Giton, and his formidably well-endowed former lover Ascyltos are probably situated in the Bay of Naples and are a far cry from the stories set in the palaces of tragic kings and queens and the world of epic heroes and heroines, whose sufferings occur in the temporally and spatially remote sphere of Greek mythology and early Roman history. The theatrically and satirically embellished adventures of the main characters of the *Satyrica* give Petronius the opportunity to satirize social, religious, educational, rhetorical, and poetic concerns of his time, and to invoke a host of widely differing Roman literary genres (epic, satire, elegy, historiography, oratory), often to subvert them for the amusement of his learned audience. In this he is aided by the form of the narrative (for further discussion of the first-person narration see Slater, READING THE *SATYRICA*), which combines prose and verse and enables Encolpius to vary his style from the low to the sublime and from mundane melodrama to lyrical poetry (the works of Courtney 1962 and

2001, Conte 1996a, and Connors 1998 are the most sophisticated and successful scholarly attempts in demonstrating these stylistic shifts).

Petronius has set a difficult challenge for his audience. We might expect that the principles of Stoic philosophy, which was popular in Petronius's era and constituted one of the reasons why Seneca, Petronius's predecessor in Nero's court, wrote some of his tragedies and most of his extant letters, could provide a key to reading the text. However, there is no clear indication in the surviving extracts to suggest that Encolpius's life is governed by "real wisdom," "reason," and "obedience to nature," and the meaning of the text remains elusive and hard to pin down (Slater 1990 makes the best case in support of this interpretation; for his views on multiple and "open" readings in Petronius see also his contribution to this volume, p. 20). In addition to this difficulty, modern readers may approach Petronius's text in a light-hearted fashion, as if it were an easily read pornographic book to be studied at night and under the blankets (on Petronius as porn see Richlin, SEX IN THE SATYRICA, p. 96). But the readers who, before embarking on their voyage with Encolpius, have not prepared themselves adequately by reading the best of Latin literature composed in the first century BC and the first half of the first century AD, will be unaware that a literary joke is played at various times in the life of the unfortunate protagonist.

The bookish character of the text is suggested in an amusingly inappropriate fashion by two characters, neither of whom is renowned for his erudition or poetic skills. To parade his half-baked scholarship Trimalchio informs his guests that "even when we're dining we must advance our learning" (§39.4), while the incorrigible poetaster Eumolpus recommends a thorough brain-washing in the sea of literature to anyone who attempts to compose a lofty literary piece: "The human mind cannot conceive or bring to birth its offspring unless it is first submerged in literature's vast flood," he says to his young friends at §118.3, and at §118.6 he adds that those who aspire to be epic poets "must be steeped in literature" (the translation of all Petronian extracts in this chapter is from Walsh 1996). The message is "Reader, pay attention" (as Apuleius, the other surviving Roman novelist, would say): if Encolpius's fondness for learned allusions escapes your notice and if you find yourself outwitted by Trimalchio's cunning tomfoolery, the joke is on you. In the context of the dish with the zodiac signs on it, Trimalchio explicitly advises his guests to be alert: "none of my arrangements is without a purpose," he declares proudly (§39.14). This is also the case with Petronius. Trimalchio's and Eumolpus's boastful remarks should act as warnings for the readers of the *Satyrica*.

In the following three sections I will look at a selection of scenes in the *Satyrica* which echo, explicitly or subtly, passages in the works of Horace, Virgil, and Ovid. My aims are to give an overview of the different forms of Petronian intertextuality, to demonstrate how it functions within the context of Encolpius's first-person narrative, and to consider how it affects the portrayal of the narrator Encolpius and of the remaining characters, and the interpretation of the plot.

Petronius and Horace

Often the instances of Petronius's appropriation of earlier literature are easy to detect because of the prominence of the literary model in the reading repertory of Petronius's audience. Which educated Roman was not expected to be familiar with the works of Horace, whose famous aesthetic principle of poetic composition – "I hate the common mob, and keep it at arm's length" (Hor. *Carm.* 3.1.1) – is voiced pompously by the incompetent poet Eumolpus, seconds before his recitation of 295 hexameters on the hackneyed theme of the civil war between Caesar and Pompey (§118.4)? The irony is palpable. Eumolpus even goes on to assert that the pithy sayings in his poem, whose metrical and stylistic idiosyncrasies are meant to recall the "flawed" epic poems of Neronian authors such as Seneca's nephew Lucan, form an integral part of the overall composition. This is intentional on his part, because he says he wishes to follow the practice of "Homer, the lyric poets, Roman Virgil, and Horace with his studied but happy gift of expression" (§118.5). Petronius, therefore, tells his readers that knowing Horace's works is important in order to understand Eumolpus's character both as an unsuccessful poet and as an excellent teller of rude tales.

Recognizing the value of Horace's contribution to the *Satyrica* also involves reading Horace's description of the eventful dinner party of the boorish host Nasidienus (see *Satires* 2.8 and Vout, THE SATYRICA AND NERONIAN CULTURE, p. 103) alongside Petronius's extended episode of Trimalchio's ostentatious banquet, and comparing Eumolpus's cunning scheme in the episode at Croton (§117.1–10) to Horace's presentation of unscrupulous flatterers who seek to inherit the fortune of elderly people (*Sat.* 2.5). The similarities are striking: for example, in both dinner parties there is an accident (the awning collapses in Nasidienus's dining room, while a boy-acrobat falls on top of Trimalchio), which causes exaggerated reactions and trite moralizing comments on the unpredictability of life and the power of Fortune over human affairs (Hor. *Sat.* 2.8.54–63 and §54.1–55.3); both Nasidienus and Trimalchio tend to dominate the conversation over dinner to such an extent that the guests are relieved when their hosts leave the table (Hor. *Sat.* 2.8.77–8 and §41.9); on both occasions the only means of escape for the narrator and his friends is to flee before the dinner is over (Hor. *Sat.* 2.8.90–5 and §72.5–7, 78.7–8). But there are also differences between these texts, which are as revealing as the similarities: for instance, Nasidienus is not a freedman, whereas Trimalchio is, and the motifs of death, superstition, and morbidity are not as clearly pronounced in Horace's poem as they are in Petronius's narrative (§26.9, §30.5, §32.3, §74.1–2, §76.10, §77.7–78.5). This selection of parallels and dissimilarities demonstrates not only Petronius's homage to Horace and the satirical tradition as a whole (this was to be expected in a text whose title, rightly or wrongly, invites satirical associations: see Slater, READING THE *SATYRICA*, p. 20), but also his attempt to break free from this tradition by giving it a new and refreshing dimension. This he achieves by combining traditional literary commonplaces on vulgar multi-millionaires with historical information on wealthy social climbers, whose eccentric habits were deemed distasteful by Nero's "Arbiter of Elegance." In other words, Petronius elaborates on his Horatian models and modernizes them by enriching them with allusions to the eccentric behavior of historical persons of the post-Augustan era. For instance, Seneca mentions several people (most of them freedmen) of the Neronian period, whose pretentious attitude and unconventional habits strikingly resemble some aspects of Trimalchio's life: Seneca (*Ep.* 12.8) describes the mock-funeral of the rich Pacuvius (cf. Trimalchio's "staged" death at §77.7–78.5) and he gives a detailed account (*Ep.* 27.5) of the tastelessly wealthy millionaire Calvisius Sabinus, who confuses Greek and Trojan heroes and forgets the familiar names of Achilles, Ulysses, and Priam (cf. Trimalchio's hopeless aspirations to erudition at §52.1–2 and §59.4–5).

On the other hand, modern readers of the *Satyrica* should not be deceived by the atmosphere of verisimilitude with which Petronius builds up the literary artifice of the episode at Trimalchio's house (on the caution required in the study of the social aspects of Trimalchio's episode see the salutary remarks of Hope, AT HOME WITH THE DEAD). For instance, John Bodel (1994 and 1999a) has convincingly shown that painted scenes, such as the murals Encolpius sees outside Trimalchio's dining room, have no parallel in extant Roman domestic decoration, but can be found in the tombs of non-Roman ex-slaves during the first century AD (for further discussion of this see Hope, AT HOME WITH THE DEAD, p. 142, Hales, FREEDMEN'S CRIBS, p. 179). The significance of this observation cannot be underestimated, because Encolpius's experience at Trimalchio's house is thus transformed from a potential document of Roman social life and manners into a comic descent to a literary realm of the dead (see also Morgan, PETRONIUS AND GREEK LITERATURE, p. 35). The literary tradition of the *katabasis* (κατάβασις – "descent") to Hades goes back to Homer (*Odyssey* 11), and includes the celebrated Virgilian account of how Aeneas, accompanied by the Sibyl, traveled into the Underworld to visit his father (*Aeneid* 6. 268–899); Anchises meets Aeneas in Elysium and shows him the souls of famous Romans whose military or civil achievements will make Rome glorious (6.756–846). In three famous lines (6.851–3) Anchises announces the duty of the Roman to the world and soon after informs his son of the future wars he will need to wage (6.890–2). Encolpius, the caricature of the epic hero Aeneas, enters Trimalchio's home, the home of the dead, and cannot escape easily from it (for Encolpius's two attempts to get out of Trimalchio's "labyrinth" see §72.5–7 and §78.7–8). Petronius's Underworld has no prophecies to offer, but is crowded with people and objects reminiscent of traditional Greek and Roman literary genres; in effect, it is inhabited by literary allusions in the shape of easily recognizable human types of Petronius's contemporary society. In this way Petronius creates a tension (which he does not resolve) between the satire of a specific social phenomenon of his era (the anxiety of the Roman aristocracy and the threat posed to it by the escalation in power of culturally inept but wealthy ex-slaves) and the literary representation of stock themes (in this case, the depiction of the boorish host in Horace, *Satires* 2.8).

Petronius and Virgil

It is not surprising that the lion's share of literary evocations in Petronius belongs to Virgil. This is so because of Virgil's high reputation in the Roman literary canon and because of the generic affinities between epic and the novel: both of these literary categories include lengthy narratives which deal with the adventures of wandering heroes who are vulnerable because of their emotions (which they try, often in vain, to control); furthermore, the presence of a divine force (a wrathful deity or an abstract concept such as Fortune) caters to the readers' entertainment by creating obstacles for the main character, whose inner strength is constantly tested (for further discussion of the wrathful god Priapus in Petronius see Morgan, PETRONIUS AND GREEK LITERATURE, p. 34, Slater, READING THE *SATYRICA*, p. 25, and Richlin, SEX IN THE *SATYRICA*, p. 92, 95). The *Aeneid* occupied such a central position in the socio-cultural dynamics of the Augustan regime, and so many authors draw from it and echo it in their compositions (often to parody it, but even more often to compete with it), that Virgil's epic forms an obvious target for Petronius, the "literary opportunist" (to quote the celebrated phrase coined by Sullivan 1968a: 255). If there were no trace of a Greek novelistic tradition, of comic travelers' tales such as those composed by Lucian, and of Greco-Roman satirical and novelistic texts combining prose and verse (Parsons 1971; Astbury 1977), I would be inclined to conclude that the *Satyrica* is Petronius's impertinent version of the *Aeneid*: an anti-heroic tale of epic proportions told by an unreliable narrator (not to be identified with the author) in the wrong narrative medium (prose interspersed with verse).

Extracts from Virgil's poem are cited no fewer than five times in the extant *Satyrica*. Even Trimalchio, in whose portrayal the thesis of Petronius's debt to literary verse satire finds its strongest exponent, quotes the ending of a Virgilian hexameter: "Is this the Ulysses you know so well?" (§39.3; *Aeneid* 2.44). The warning of the priest Laocoon to the optimistic Trojans not to believe so readily that the Greeks, having failed to capture Troy, had really departed and left the wooden horse behind them as a gift is borrowed here by the conceited Trimalchio: he wishes both to equate himself with the crafty Odysseus (but Trimalchio is cunning only in culinary, not in military affairs) and to show off that he knows his Virgil. However, Trimalchio's blunders about the Virgilian Sibyl at §48.8 and his account at §59.4–5 of the sequence of events which led to the Trojan war prove that, in his attempt to impress his guests, he memorized no more than these Virgilian words, just as some people nowadays cite isolated phrases from Shakespeare without having read his plays in full. The same outlook on literature is exhibited by a slave of one of Trimalchio's guests, who recites only the first line of the fifth book of the *Aeneid* (a line he has learnt from street-entertainers, §68.6), and combines it most offensively with verses from low comedies of Campanian origin (§68.4–5). Equally jarring is the literary effect produced in the tale of the widow of Ephesus, in which the narrator Eumolpus assigns to the two-faced, wine-prone servant of the widow the role of Dido's sister, Anna (§111.12 and §112.2). The remarkably cynical achievement of Petronius in this tale is not only that he uses two lines from the most tender episode of the *Aeneid* (a slight variation of *Aen.* 4.34 and two-thirds of 4.38) to demolish the most fundamental and traditional feminine Roman virtue – a woman's devotion to only one man, but also that he upsets literary hierarchy by bringing high epic into the seedy world of Milesian tales (on which see Morgan, PETRONIUS AND GREEK LITERATURE, p. 45). The exploitation of more Virgilian hexameters at §132.11 will be discussed below.

But Aeneas's adventures are not present in Encolpius's life only through direct quotations. In one of the episodes (§82.1–2) Encolpius has been betrayed by Giton, who abandons him for the erotic services of Ascyltos. The vocabulary with which Encolpius the narrator describes his emotions while looking for his lover and his rival effectively transforms the pathetic fury of a cuckold into the sorrow of the Homeric Achilles, when his slave-girl Briseis is taken from him to be given to Agamemnon (*Iliad* 1.345–56), or the frenzy of the Virgilian Aeneas, frantically searching for his wife Creusa on the night of the burning of Troy (*Aen.* 2.314, 2.671–2). Thus the down-to-earth situation of a pederastic trio has suddenly acquired epic grandeur and importance (on the imaginative fashion in which Encolpius presents this episode see Richlin, SEX IN THE *SATYRICA*, p. 85): Encolpius the narrator has reconstructed an incident of his past as stylized melodrama, casting himself in the role of the wronged masculine hero. It is at this point that the deflation of the high tone is achieved: Petronius "the hidden author" (as Conte 1996a cleverly names him) introduces into the plot a passing soldier who notices that Encolpius is wearing non-military white shoes (the incongruity might be conveyed today by the image of a soldier in pink socks), robs him of his weapons, and destroys the literary fantasy. Encolpius's talent for role-playing suits perfectly the theatricality of society in the empire (an issue on which see Hales, FREEDMEN'S CRIBS, p. 174) and squares well with the varied tone of the different episodes in the text. Only Giton may be said to be more obsessed with, and skilled in, living life through literature; he is the ultimate "drama queen," who reacts to the demands of people around him by pretending to be Livy's Lucretia (§9.5; Livy 1.58), Virgil's Nisus (§80.4; *Aen.* 9.426–7) and the Sibyl (§72.9; *Aen.* 6.417–24). His and Encolpius's exaggerated histrionics have been interpreted as the desperate attempts of these characters to define themselves as individuals and to fill the content of their inner selves (Slater 1990); the learned and refined Petronius has been seen as an author who sadly longs for the glorious literary past of Rome, which was, by his time, lost forever (Conte 1996a).

Petronius and Ovid

In addition to Horace and Virgil, Petronius expects his readers to know well at least one more Augustan poet. More than a century ago, Albert Collignon (1892: 258–67) showed how Encolpius's vocabulary and imagery in the events in Oenothea's hut echo Ovid's description of the humble abode of the elderly couple Philemon and Baucis (*Met.* 8.637), an episode modeled on Callimachus's difficult Greek poem *Hekale* (Courtney 1991). Those familiar with the Callimachean fragments and the Ovidian extract will instantly realize that, if we are to visualize Oenothea as a second Hekale or Baucis, we elevate the impotent Encolpius to the level of a masquerading deity or a hero such as Theseus. Furthermore, Ovid's memorable hag Dipsas (*Amores* 1.8.2–4) is often said to have been the literary antecedent of the bibulous Oenothea in Petronius. Like Dipsas, Oenothea ("Wine-Goddess") has a Greek name, but by giving her a name which makes her the female equivalent of Dionysus, god of wine, Petronius invites us to picture his hag as more than a "thirsty woman" (*dipsas*); moreover, he complicates her character by adding to it aspects of comic witchcraft and corrupt religious practices. Collignon has also shown that, in the scene of Encolpius's erotic encounter with Circe (more on her below), Petronius's allusions to the elegiac vocabulary of Ovid's erotic poems: (*Amores, Ars Amatoria, Remedia Amoris*) accentuate the sensual tone of the affair, so that, when things go wrong in Encolpius's performance, the desired anti-climactic effect (itself possibly echoing yet another Ovidian poem: see below) may be felt all the more. A good knowledge of Ovid, therefore, is crucial for the appreciation of the erotically charged atmosphere in the episode at Croton (§126.1–139.5), and it is possible that Petronius drew heavily from Ovid in this section precisely because both he and Ovid treat sexual relations and love in a humorous, even ironic, fashion.

So far I have looked at a small group of scenes from the *Satyrica* which signal that Petronius exploits literary material from *individual* major Augustan poets. I have yet to consider how he combines allusions from different sources in the same episode. For this purpose I wish to look at two incidents from the text: Encolpius's attempt to cut off his penis and the scene on board Lichas's ship.

Encolpius's Penis and Dido

Petronius's most entertaining and perhaps boldest experiment with literary tradition is to be found in the episode at Croton, where Encolpius is instructed by Eumolpus to assume the identity of a slave and, for some reason, takes the name Polyaenus – the Latinized form of the Greek adjective πολύαινος (*poluaenos*, "much praised"), which is one of Odysseus's epithets (for example, Hom. *Od.* 12.184). This disguise arouses the sexual interest of an aristocratic Crotonian woman who calls herself Circe, longs only for slaves and low-class men (§126.7), is aware of the literary existence of the Homeric witch Circe (she jokes about this at §127.6–7), and invites the "slave Polyaenus" to satisfy her lust in a grove of plane-trees (whose description, §126.12–18, evokes "erotic" landscapes in Homer, Plato, and Theocritus and shows similarities to the Greek novelistic tradition; on the exploitation of Greek authors in Petronius see Morgan, PETRONIUS AND GREEK LITERATURE). However, "Polyaenus" fails to rise to the occasion both at this point and later (probably in the missing part of the text before §132.2), after "Circe" had decided to give him a chance to redeem himself.

The anger of "Circe" and the humiliation of "Polyaenus" are expressed in terms which evoke the shame of the sexually enervated speaker and the irritation of his displeased girlfriend in an Ovidian love-poem (*Amores* 3.7): the fury of the protagonist towards his irresponsible penis inspires him to compose a poem of nine lines (§132.8) describing his attempt at penectomy. Here is the beginning of the poem:

> Though thrice my hand took up the fearsome, two-edged steel,
> Thrice did my body sudden enervation feel.

The shift of the narrative vehicle from prose to verse and the repetition of the adverb "thrice" (in the Latin text at the beginning of each of the first two lines) should function as signposts alerting us to the fact that Petronius wants us to think that Encolpius was not the first literary character who attempted three times (all of them unsuccessfully) to grasp something. Much more famously, the epic hero Aeneas tried, also three times, to embrace the ghosts of his beloved wife Creusa in the midst of burning Troy and of his dear father Anchises in the Underworld; on all three occasions, however, both Creusa's apparition and Anchises' ghost escaped his hands (Virgil. *Aen.* 2.791–3 and 6.700–1). Petronius takes it for granted that our familiarity with these two well-known episodes in Virgil's epic (the sack of Troy and Aeneas's visit to the Underworld) will ensure that we grasp the comic juxtaposition not only between the impotent, cowardly, and "bisexual" Encolpius and the sexually potent, brave, and "heterosexual" Aeneas, but also between the shadowy figures of Creusa and Anchises and Encolpius's shrinking and personified penis. Encolpius wishes to give epic grandeur to his low predicament, but he fails to exhibit the courage required to bring the mission (that is, penectomy) to an end. However, there is a further incongruity in the employment of Virgilian subject matter in Encolpius's sleazy narrative, and this lies in the meter of the poem: not heroic dactylic hexameters, but rarely attested sotadeans. This is a meter associated in Petronius with "effeminate" men, such as the one who sang a song (in sotadeans) before he began to abuse Encolpius sexually with his mouth and his body during Quartilla's orgy (§23.2–5; it may not be coincidental that sotadeans appear also in the fragmentary Greek text conventionally known as the "Iolaus-novel" (Parsons 1971), and that they are used there in relation to castration). So, although sotadeans are apt for an episode of sexual enervation, the trained ear of the Roman listener or reader would have spotted immediately the inappropriateness of having heroic words and ideas conveyed in an unmanly rhythm.

The playful evocation of Aeneas, Creusa, and Anchises paves the way for further tributes to Virgil and has implications for Encolpius's portrayal as an erudite narrator infatuated with literary myth (see Conte 1996a on Encolpius's "mythomania"): his shaping of the incidents of his low past in a supremely sophisticated fashion bears the marks of high literature and of lessons taught at the schools of rhetoric during the first century AD. Immediately after the sotadean verses the narrator continues the story in prose and cites in direct speech the words he uttered to rebuke his penis, which he addressed asking it to explain its behavior. But genitals do not normally speak; does the Greek rhetorical term ἀπόδειξις (*apodeixis* – "proof"), which Encolpius uses at §132.10, suggest that we are to visualize Encolpius and his penis as two opponents in a rhetorical school engaged in a debate? In any case, what we get are the following three hexameters (§132.11):

> She looked away, and kept her eyes fixed on the ground.
> Her face was no more softened by these opening words
> Than *pliant willow*, **or poppy with its drooping head**.

It has often been observed that the underlined text in the above extract comes from the *Aeneid* and describes how Dido responded to Aeneas's pleas in the Underworld (6.469–50; the correlation between Dido and Encolpius's penis works easily, because both the proper name "Dido" and the Latin noun for "penis" are feminine); that the italicized words occur in two Virgilian bucolic poems (*Eclogues* 3.83 and 5.16); and that the half-line in bold print, which comes also from the *Aeneid* (9.436), depicts the untimely death of the Trojan Euryalus, Nisus's comrade. The humorous juxtaposition between the heroic feat of Euryalus and the pathetic situation of Encolpius not only forms the result of Petronius's clever exploitation of Virgilian material, but also creates a comic dissonance between epic and the novel as literary categories: Encolpius's narrative is a low, debased epic story, whose mock-heroic nature may be seen in the way in which Virgilian poetry has been reduced to a collection of formulaic phrases skillfully assembled to form an elegant passage of hexameters on sexual enervation. Any feeling of compassion or pity which readers may feel towards "Polyaenus" vanishes at the sound of this literary appropriation, but the crudity of the event is not transmitted to the Virgilian models: when I read the fourth book of the *Aeneid*, I do not think about Encolpius's penis; but when I think about Petronius's association of Encolpius's penis with Dido, the learned humor dilutes the coarseness of the scene.

Petronius and Greek Novels, Roman Rhetoric, and Low Drama

Another interesting case study for the complementary combination of sources in Petronius is the trial of Encolpius and Giton on board the ship of their arch-enemy Lichas, who happens to be traveling with Giton's former mistress, the luxurious Tryphaena. The episode abounds in well-known motifs found in the extant Greek novels (sea journey, reversal of fortune, reunion with old enemies: see Galli 1996; compare Morgan, PETRONIUS AND GREEK LITERATURE, p. 40) and low drama (theatrical disguises; Panayotakis 1995), whose repertory is fruitfully exploited to produce a scenario, suggested by Eumolpus, which aims at deceiving Lichas and Tryphaena: Eumolpus's hireling shaves the heads and eyebrows of Encolpius and Giton (§103.1), while Eumolpus himself marks a neat inscription on their foreheads so that they may appear as branded slaves (§103.2). But the two rogues are seized and Lichas orders them to be flogged; the screams of the squeamish Giton (§105.5) and the familiarity of Lichas with Encolpius's genitals (§105.9) reveal the identity of the hero and his lover, for both of whom a court is set up.

Trial-scenes such as the courtroom scene on board Lichas's ship are a stock feature of Greco-Roman fiction (cf. the scenes at: Chariton 5.4–8, Longus 2.15–17, Achilles Tatius 7.7–12, Apuleius 3.1–9, and Heliodorus 8.9). However, Petronius's inspiration is the contemporary obsession with rhetoric: he structures the speeches of Lichas (the plaintiff) and Eumolpus (the counsel for the defense) in such a way that they resemble not a set of speeches delivered by fully fledged orators at court but the opposing sides in a formal debate between students of rhetoric. Eumolpus's arguments present inconsistencies which enhance his already established characterization as an incompetent poet, while Lichas sees through the trick of the painted letters, and defines it as "tricks of the low stage" (*mimicis artibus*, §106.1) – a type of theatrical entertainment which dominated the theatre in Neronian times and clearly influenced the character portrayal and subject matter of almost every episode in the action of Encolpius's narrative (Panayotakis 1995). The orderly trial scene ends up in mere slapstick and blows. This abrupt and inconclusive ending is typical of the way in which Petronius constructs his text to elicit humor: several literary sources are exploited for the composition of a single, multi-layered episode, whose plot dissolves into chaos and disarray. The same pattern may be observed in the structure of the episode at Trimalchio's house, where sustained allusions to Horace (see above) and Theophrastus (see Walsh 1970: 134–6, for parallels between Trimalchio and several of Theophrastus's *Characters*) give way to the low mime: the inability of Encolpius and his friends to cope with the overwhelmingly pretentious conduct of the uncouth host forces them to flee at the end of the episode, as if they were characters in a pointless farce (§78.8). This may also have been the way in which the episode at Croton ended, with the scheming comrades escaping the clutches of the deceived Crotonians who showered gifts at them with a view to receiving Eumolpus's non-existent fortune.

So, in the scene on board Lichas's ship the author enlists the services of Roman oratory (rhetorical debates proliferating in the first century AD and best exemplified nowadays through the rhetorical exercises collected by Seneca the Elder) and low drama. However, the synthesis of it all is far from orderly or harmonious. It may even be argued that this chaotic, literary polyphony is not a result of Encolpius's incompetence as narrator but a deliberate authorial strategy on Petronius's part. It may reflect not only the anarchic world populated by Petronius's imaginary characters but also the actual frenzy of ambitious authors in composing tragedies, comedies, elegies, and epics destined for recitation in the theatres and private halls of the wealthy in the second half of the first century AD. It is possible, then, that our novelist resembles the angry speaker who, at the beginning of Juvenal's first satire, complains that he is always a listener to other people's mediocre compositions and reacts by writing a series of vitriolic satires penned with declamatory and epic features. Petronius responded to the cultural polyphony of his time, and perhaps to the prolific corpus of Seneca's works or to Lucan's post-Virgilian epic, by writing *one* text which could not be given a specific generic label and encompassed a variety of widely differing literary genres.

Petronius and Publilius (No, I meant Seneca)

In the previous section I suggested that clusters of literary allusions in the *Satyrica* may be so complex that their structure eventually crumbles and they become a disorderly crowd of references, just like characters in a piece of low drama. I will now suggest that allusions can mislead readers, even when (or precisely because) the name of the literary source is mentioned. My case-study for this will be Petronius's 16 iambic verses on the condemnation of luxury. The important word in my previous sentence is the name "Petronius," for there is great dispute about the model and authorship of this elaborate composition, which Trimalchio recites in §55.5–6.

> Then Trimalchio said: "Tell us, master, how do you think Cicero differs from Publilius? I myself think that Cicero was the more eloquent, but that Publilius had more probity, for what could be better than these lines of his?
>
>> 'Neath Luxury's grin the walls of War soon fold.
>> Peacocks from Babylon clothed in feathered gold
>> To please your palate in their cages feed;
>> Numidian fowl and capons serve your need."

And so on. Publilius was a famous first-century BC Syrian writer and performer of low mimes, which contained moral apothegms. It is important to note that, although Trimalchio invites his guests to express an opinion on the comparison between Cicero and Publilius, he does not really allow them to do this. It is therefore tempting to dismiss Trimalchio's question to

Agamemnon as yet another pseudo-intellectual whim of the semi-educated host, who is constantly looking for an opportunity to draw attention to his ability to compose verses at the drop of a hat. On the other hand, scholars who discuss the relationship of Petronius's poem to the fragments of Publilius or to other poets in terms of language and style have argued that the poem is a genuine Publilian product, or that it was composed in the style of the plays of the other well-known mimographer of the republican era Decimus Laberius, or as a parody of the poetry of Maecenas, Augustus's "Minister for Culture." But Courtney (1991 and 2001) believes (mainly on stylistic grounds) that this composition is a parody of the poetry of Seneca, who was very fond of Publilius's moral maxims. The metrical features of these iambic lines corroborate Courtney's view and a careful analysis of their rhythmical patterns reveals that Petronius gives this pseudo-Publilian composition Seneca's prosodic peculiarities (Gratwick 1993: 40–59). But why would Petronius confuse his audience by making Trimalchio attribute to the mimographer Publilius verses which display the style of Senecan versification? If Petronius's aim was to parody Seneca, why does not Trimalchio mention Seneca's name explicitly in relation to these iambic lines? Petronius's practice, at least as far as the extant text is concerned, is to avoid explicit reference to other contemporary or near-contemporary literary authors. Even in the case of Eumolpus's poem on the *Civil War* (§119–24), which readily brings to mind Lucan's *Pharsalia*, Petronius does not mention Lucan by name, although he could easily have done so when Eumolpus gives an account of his own poetic principles before he starts reciting the poem (§118.1–6). Therefore, when Trimalchio misattributes to Publilius a poem whose content and metrical patterns echo Seneca's lofty tragedies, Petronius both pokes fun at the pretentious and hypocritical Trimalchio (he gets the author's name wrong and he delivers a tirade against luxury, although he himself is the personification of luxury) and attacks, under a different guise, Seneca, who was extremely fond of Publilius's moral maxims.

Petronius and Petronius

It has only recently been recognized that yet another important intertext for Petronius is the *Satyrica* itself. The idea of self-referentiality and of Petronius recycling Petronian material yields impressive results, if used cautiously, and Rimell (2002) makes several observations, most of them illuminating and persuasive, about Petronius at work creating a nexus of events that echo each other (see also Rimell, LETTING THE PAGE RUN ON). Her "ideal Petronian reader" is more attentive than the "alert reader" of Apuleius's *Metamorphoses*; he or she is a "scholarly reader," who pays attention to the minutest detail in a scene and is ready to identify and connect motifs even in episodes that are far away from each other. For instance, Rimell invites us to connect Encolpius who poses as a scarred slave in order to impress Circe with "the orator in *Sat*. 1 who displays and exaggerates his wounds in order to win over his audience" (2002: 147). In the same vein we could associate the reference to pirates mentioned by Encolpius in his declamation at §1.3 with the episode on board Lichas's ship, which may now be visualized as the lengthy dramatization of the scenario of a *controversia*, a formal debate at a school of rhetoric such as Agamemnon's. It is possible then to interpret Encolpius's hypocritical declamation in §1.1–2.9 as a programmatic statement about the elaborate style which he adopts to narrate his past, and about the literary format which he gives to some of the episodes of his story.

Conclusion

In this chapter I have presented an overview of the complex ways in which Petronius recycles Horace, Virgil, Ovid, Publilius, Seneca, and the *Satyrica* itself. Shortage of space does not allow me to go on with a discussion of Petronius's exploitation of writers and cultural trends of the post-Augustan era. This would have included an account of how the *Satyrica* pokes fun at philosophical ideas such as those articulated by Seneca in his letters and treatises; how it satirizes post-Augustan innovations in epic poetry such as those found in Lucan's lengthy *Pharsalia*; how it fits within the fashionable and powerful epideictic culture of rhetorical schools, whose mentality is revealed in the Elder Seneca's collection of rhetorical exercises; and finally, how it takes advantage of the unsophisticated crudity and the spectacular violence that dominated the theatres and the amphitheatres of the first century AD. For these issues I refer the reader to Sullivan (1968b), (1985a), and (1985b), Soverini (1985), and Panayotakis (1995).

But shortage of space is not the only reason why I have confined myself to an overview of the presence of the above authors in Petronius's work. Intertextuality in the *Satyrica* deliberately focuses on the "classics" of the major Augustan poets, with whom the readers are expected to be familiar.

However, Petronius's reasons for his intertextual choices are not dictated solely by the educational standards of his (actual or intended) readers, or by the kinds of texts which were the prescribed reading in the Roman educational curriculum. Petronius looks back at the Augustan era and self-consciously composes an anarchic work whose position is low and marginal in the literary canon, but whose sophistication aspires to be as high and as complex as the refined style of works belonging to the "respectable" genres (for example, epic and oratory) of previous generations. The best way for him to achieve this paradoxical aim is to embellish the narrative of Encolpius's scurrilous adventures with allusions to "high" literature composed by the most celebrated representatives of the Augustan literary "establishment." For this reason Petronian intertextuality may be viewed as "inclusive" or even "self-inclusive": when it comes to echoing authors (even himself), Petronius does not favor an "either–or" approach, and his mode of allusions requires erudition but does not seek to impress with obscure references of the sort which we would now associate with Hellenistic and neoteric poetry. The literary debt may be signaled with exact citations or brief verbal parallels or thematic connections. It is only rarely that literary evocations mock the work evoked; they usually function as effective narrative devices for the portrayal of the main and the minor characters and narrators in the text. More importantly, they bestow on Petronius's work the prestige of the distinguished authors echoed in Encolpius's narrative.

Further Reading

The ideal starting point for "beginners" in Petronius's treatment of Latin literature is Collignon (1892: 109–312); however, since this volume is no longer easily accessible, the most reliable introductory books to this topic are Sullivan (1968a: 115–231), Walsh (1970: 35–52, 67–140), Conte (1996a), and Courtney (2001: 54–222). "Advanced" readers would profit greatly from Slater (1990) and from some chapters in Connors (1998) and Rimell (2002). Hinds (1998) is an indispensable companion to literary allusion in general, and many of his ideas on intertextuality in Roman poetry can usefully be applied to Petronius's prose. Other valuable works on allusion and intertextuality are Russell (1979), Finkelpearl (1998: 1–35), and Conte (1996b).

In addition to the above general volumes, readers should consult the following works, which discuss how *individual* Roman literary genres are reflected in Encolpius's narrative. On satire: Révay (1922), Shero (1923),

Courtney (1962), Sandy (1969), and Rimell (2005). On Sisenna's "Milesian Tales": Harrison (1998) and Jensson (2004). On elegy: Schmeling (1971), Currie (1989), and Hallett (2003). On rhetoric: Kennedy (1978), Soverini (1985), Van Mal-Maeder (2003), and Panayotakis (2006). On comic theatre: Sandy (1974), Rosati (1983/1999), and Panayotakis (1995). On the Neronian literary context of Petronius and his relationship with Seneca and Lucan see Sullivan (1968b), (1985a), and (1985b). Good general accounts on Latin meter are in Halporn, Ostwald, and Rosenmeyer (1963), and Raven (1967), but the best analysis of the prosody of republican drama is in Gratwick (1993: 40–63, and 1999: 209–37).

Slater, Morgan, and Richlin, in this volume, offer information which complements my necessarily brief account of Petronius's Roman literary texture; my chapter should be read together with theirs.

4

Letting the Page Run On

Poetics, Rhetoric, and Noise in the *Satyrica*

Victoria Rimell

The *Satyrica* is a difficult text to read, and to listen to. As one history of
Latin literature puts it, "No classical narrative that we know of even remotely
approaches the literary complexity of Petronius" (Conte 1994: 460). The
first person narrator Encolpius often seems disoriented, his commentary
and notorious lapses tricky to judge. As we (struggle to) follow his adventures, made all the madder by a broken and cut-off manuscript, we
encounter a dazzling symphony (or some would say cacophony) of literary
references, voices, and sounds. Much has been written on the *Satyrica*'s
"rhetoricity," and the idea that rhetoric and rhetorical education play a huge
role in the development of novelistic discourse is on show everywhere in
this text. At the same time, Petronius mixes epic, elegiac, theatrical, and
satirical modes, verse and prose, the lofty and mundane, the fantastic and
the vulgar. Characters knock out their own poems, or quote bits of the classics, between low-life chat, courtroom style speeches, or random philoso-
phizing; we find folklore, fable, and mime alongside tragedy and epic,
dignified senarii alongside Priapic hendecasyllables and naughty sotadeans
(see Panayotakis, PETRONIUS AND THE ROMAN LITERARY TRADITION,
p. 57), odd Latin words not seen elsewhere mingling with cliches, archa-
isms, and bits of Greek. In the *Cena* the polyphony or clash of discourses
that characterizes Petronian *prosimetrum* (a mixture of prose and poetry) is
especially fascinating – not only because the speeches of the freedmen provide us with the best specimen we have of a text which appears to imitate
real spoken Latin, so all-important as the link between literary Latin and
the Romance languages of northern Europe (see, for example, Stefenelli
1962), but also because body language, gesture, music, and incoherent sounds
shape every page of Trimalchio's feast. Moreover, as we shall be seeing,
the kinds of literary and linguistic experiments on display here reverberate
through the remaining manuscript. The final result – which some scholars

(for example, Sullivan 1968a: 34–8) have claimed ran to 400,000 words in its original form, making this the *War and Peace* of the ancient world – is stunningly original, despite and because of a hyperactive jigsawing of almost every literary genre you could think of (see also Panayotakis and Morgan in this volume). This chapter gives an overview of Petronius's use of language and sound, and takes the *Cena Trimalchionis* as its starting point. I shall be looking in particular at how the extreme rhetoricization of speech and the overtly crafted narrative of the *Satyrica* combine with a carnivalesque poetics, which sees literary language blurring into violent action and incoherent noise.

Talking, Eating, and Characterization

Petronius revels in juxtaposing styles and tempos and seeing them interact in the shape of his larger-than-life characters, who also seem to speak differently according to the environment in which they find themselves. Encolpius in particular adopts various kinds of speech as costumes to suit each chapter of his adventure. In his speeches at §1–2, or §115, for example, he talks formally and uses refined rhetorical strategies (rhetorical discourse will be a recurrent feature of the rest of the extant *Satyrica*: Encolpius regularly refers to speeches as *orationes* or *declamationes*, and every episode contains the kinds of mannered outbursts both satirized and satirically exemplified by the speeches at §1–5). Elsewhere he uses much more melo-dramatic, overtly poetic language: in the shipwreck at §114 he is a soldier of love straight out of Ovid's *Amores*, sobbing in elegiac cliches about *iuncta mors* ("dying together") and frilling his prose with tragi-epic markers like *ecce* ("behold!"), repeated for effect (§114.9); at §129–30 his letter to Circe is written in a mock-naïve, confessional mode reminiscent of Ovid's *Heroides* (note the simple, short sentences). When he tells the story of Quartilla's orgy, however, his language is rambunctious and idiomatic (he uses lots of pronouns and Grecisms, and deviates from grammatical norms). In the *Cena*, his narrative is "looser," quite different from the elevated style of Roman oratory, historiography, or philosophy, yet it often contrasts noticeably with the Latin used by Trimalchio and his freedman guests. There is also a surprising amount of variation in the speech of each of the "low-class" speakers (see Boyce 1991, summarizing important works such as Dell'Era 1970 and Petersmann 1977, and refuting again the hypothesis that the *Cena* is written in a uniform vulgar style, in, for example, Marmorale 1948, Swanson 1963): when we look at the language of each in turn it is clear both that Petronius wants us to remember the characters as individuals, and that lively contrasts of tone, pace, register, and mood are carefully measured to entertain, providing a dramatic "soundtrack" to the dinner in parallel with the often mentioned musical accompaniment.

When the "tyrant" host (as they call him) leaves the room to relieve himself at §41, the first named freedman to speak is Dama. His contribution is the shortest, and translates into language the new "relaxed" atmosphere in Trimalchio's absence (the *Satyrica*'s verbal mania makes a political point, we might be tempted to say, about literary freedom amid imperial constraints – we are reminded that the Petronius of Nero's court, if he is in fact the author, is reported at Tacitus *Annales* 16.19 to have listened to lewd songs even as he committed suicide on the emperor's orders: for more on Neronian dating, see INTRODUCTION, p. 5, and Vout, THE SATYRICA AND NERONIAN CULTURE). This is possibly the only place in Latin literature, and certainly the most obvious, where a writer attempts to convey the slurring, crude speech of a drunk:

> *"dies" inquit, "nihil est. dum versas te, nox fit. itaque nihil est melius, quam de cubiculo recta in triclinium ire. et mundum frigus habuimus. vis me balneus calfecit. tamen calda potio vestiarius est. staminatas duxi, et plane matus sum. vinus mihi in cerebrum abiit."* (§41.10–12)

> "Day is nothing" he said. "You turn around, it's night. There's nothing like getting out of bed and going straight to dinner. Freezing cold it was. Could 'ardly warm m'self up in a bath. But a hot drink's as goodasacoat. I've downed a fair few, and frankly I'm wasted. That wine's gone straight to me 'ed."

Dama is capable only of blunt, childish sentences: note the extreme asyndeton (omission of conjunctions), and the staccato effect created by ending every sentence with a verb. Syncopated forms like *matus* and *calfecit* give the impression of a drunk's thick, lazy tongue, and Dama's slave origins are revealed in his "incorrect" conversion of neuter into masculine nouns (*balneus* §41.11, *vinus* §41.12).

Next to take up what Encolpius sardonically calls Dama's *fabula* ("tale" §42.1) is the depressive Seleucus, fresh from a funeral, with his lavish, almost hallucinogenic metaphors and imagery: unlike Dama, he does not bathe much because the "water bites, and a man's heart melts down a bit every day"; he announces that human beings are "bladders of wind," women are "vultures," and "old love pinches like a crab." Upbeat optimist Phileros shouts over him, introducing another contrasting vibe. Just like the dead man he criticizes for being rough and a "chatterbox," Phileros just cannot stop, speeding on maniacally, piling up connectives, or trilling out strings of words and tongue-twisting alliterations until we get the effect of a wall of chattering noise (be sure to read the Latin aloud, as it is impossible to convey the full effect in translation): *durae buccae fuit, linguosus, discordia, non homo. frater eius fuit, amicus amico, manu plena, uncta mensa. et inter initia malaam parram pilavit* [...] ("He had a rough gob on him, he was a talker, more of a noise than a man. His brother was a great guy, a loyal mate, open handed, always had good food on the table. To begin with, he plucked a bird of ill-omen [...]" §43.2). With poverty-stricken Ganymede, who reacts by plotting the real issues of the day, we swing back again to sober, serious topics. Then comes social climber Echion, whose vulgarisms expose his low origins despite his best efforts: note, for example, his use of masculines for neuters (*caelus* §45.3, *amphitheater* §45.6), his declension of Greek neuter nouns in *–ma* as first-declension feminines (*stigmam* §45.9), various types of irregularly declined nouns, his use of deponent verbs as though they were active, of accusative nouns with intransitive verbs, and of indicatives for subjunctives in indirect speech (for more on this see Boyce 1991). Echion's speech is also interesting for its abundance of hyperurbanisms, overcorrections that convey his bid to appear "posher" than he really is, especially when talking to the Prof., Agamemnon: for example, he puts masculine nouns in the neuter (*nervia* §45.11, *libra* §46.7, and *thesaurum* §46.8), makes active verbs deponents (*delectaretur* §45.7), indicative verbs subjunctive (*etiamsi ... sit* §46.5), and the object of a transitive verb a genitive (*artificii docere* §46.7).

The freedmen's storytelling kicks off once more at §57, when Hermeros hits back at Ascyltos's patronizing laughter with a tirade of abuse containing some of the best insults in the *Cena*: Ascyltos gets called "some vagabond fly-by-night not worth his own piss" (§57.3), a "just weaned baby that can't even go 'ga ga,'" a "claypot," and "a strip of leather soaked in water" (§57.8–9: whether these are "hypervulgarisms," a kind of mock-slang, or whether they really capture the typical jibes thrown about by mid-first-century drunks, is something we shall never know for sure). He concludes his proud outburst with a line that makes us picture Ascyltos's shocked, pale, and slightly intimidated face perfectly: *quid nunc stupes tanquam hircus in ervilia?* ("What you lookin' at me like that for, all wide-eyed like a goat in a field of vetch?!"). At §61 Niceros is called upon to speak up: unlike Echion and

Hermeros, he has an inferiority complex, yet is a comparative expert at storytelling (notice his vivid similes and long rhythmical sentences). Habinnas arrives at §65, becoming the self-satirizing clown, and life and soul of the party. And of course there is Trimalchio himself, who often tries (and fails) to talk in an elevated diction and sound superior to his freedmen guests. He spews verses, shows off what he thinks is his cultural acumen, uses long technical or rhetorical terms such as *anathymiasis* ("vapour") at §47.6, or *peristasis* ("theme") at §48.4, and frequently "overcorrects" his Latin before lapsing into idiom and gutterspeak (see Campanile 1957: 63–4; Boyce 1991: 94–102). His vocabulary and syntax are constantly working to perfect Petronius's portrait of the brash megalomaniac whose wild "errors" and drunken meanderings at the same time capture the ambitious modality of this novel as a whole (bearing in mind, as always, that most of the original manuscript has not survived).

In many ways the *Cena* presents itself as an extended oratorical performance of the likes illustrated in §1, a(nother) surreal enactment of Encolpius's florid metaphors. Students these days, he claims in his speech outside the school, are taught ridiculous set-pieces in which "every word and act is sprinkled with poppy-seed and sesame" (*omnia dicta factaque quasi papavere et sesamo sparsa*). A very similar image is used by Horace, at *Ars Poetica* 374–8: he compares a mediocre poem to a posh dinner party spoiled by over-thick sauces, a tuneless orchestra, or a dessert of poppy-seeds served with Sardinian, or bitter-tasting, honey. Yet in §31 Encolpius's verbal canapes are brought in on a plate as one of Trimalchio's *hors d'oeuvres* (*glires melle ac papavere sparsos* – "dormice rolled in honey and poppy-seed"). Similarly, while Encolpius in §1–2 compares the rhetorical school to a kitchen which brainwashes and traps students by overloading them with sickly "tastes" and "smells," so the *Cena* sees the guests stuffed with rich food to the point of nausea and finally trapped in a suffocating labyrinth (§73.1) from which they fear they will never escape. The point is always that consuming food and drink, and listening to or telling stories, are not just parallel activities, but processes that overlap, each one rendering the other more graphic: at §33, for example, the verb *consumere* is exploited for its multiple meanings (among which are "to exhaust," "to devour"): *interim dum ille omnium textorum dicta inter lusum consumit, gustantibus adhuc nobis repositorium allatum est cum corbe* [...] ("Trimalchio used up all his best lines as he played, and we were still busy with the starters when a tray was brought in with a basket on it [...]"). Compare the "acidic" songs of the waiters at §31 (*acido cantico*), which preview the appetite-spiking first course; Encolpius's use of *cibus* ("food") to refer to Trimalchio's singing at §36.1; or the phrases at §23.4 (*consumptis versibus*, "now that he was done with poetry") during Quartilla's feast, and at §109.8 (*consumpta frigidissima urbanitate*, "having exhausted his icy wit") during the feast on board Lichas's ship.

Encolpius's narrative is loaded with metaphors, and becomes most fantastic at climactic points (for example, at the end of the *Cena*, when the stowaways are discovered on board Lichas's ship, and when "Odysseus" suffers from impotence at §129–38). Metaphors connect scenes and tie together contrasting narrative styles; their abundance also makes it hard to tell whether Encolpius is being literal or not (and therefore whether we, too, are beginning to overtheatricalize). At §114.14, for instance, the "fishermen," who are about to pounce on their "prey" but then decide to come to the aid of the survivors of the shipwreck, are surely not really fishermen, given that we were introduced to the metaphor of professors of rhetoric as fisherman at §3, and that Croton is full of legacy hunters whom Eumolpus will later "bait" with his own flesh at §141. Yet this is never made explicit, and equally it is unclear whether Encolpius naïvely accepts the men's tale that they are fishermen, or whether he is making a poetic reference to the band of legacy hunters. All this in a context in which "shipwreck" can be used to describe any number of misfortunes (it is "everywhere" §115.16), and mock civil war onboard ship rehearses the "real" warring of elements in the storm that follows. We might also look at the scene at §132.2–8, which knits together real and metaphorical lashings within the same few lines (*matrona contumeliis verberata* [...] *verberibus sputisque extra ianuam eiectus sum*, "the lady, lashed by my taunts [...] I was beaten and spat upon and thrown out through the door"), and then plays on the proximity of *verbera* ("blows") to *verba* ("words") in a poem that stresses how words can be more violent than a knife (*ad verba, magis quae poterant nocere, fugi*, "I fled for refuge in words which could hurt more" §132.8 v. 9). This kind of verbal play is a microscopic example of how Encolpius's narrative repeats words and images to give a sense of continual reproduction and recontextualization of the same (critics, like Connors 1998, have also read the *Satyrica*'s strategies of refashioning, of itself and of other literary texts, as particularly Neronian). My point is that this entertaining and often satiric dynamic of interconnection always competes in the text with a sense of fragmentation (exacerbated no doubt by our mangled manuscript), and with the juxtaposition of sharply contrasting styles and registers that we see exemplified in the *Cena*.

Pump Up the Volume: Music and Metaphor

Yet the live buzz, the "orality" of Trimalchio's dinner party, is about more than just creative rhetoric and banter. Throughout the *Cena*, the narrator Encolpius comments on the rising and falling volume of the almost constant musical accompaniment: poetic recitations and gossip, full of sing-song proverbs and idioms (see Di Capua 1948), merge with imagined percussion, with singing slaves, with harps and trumpets, focusing our attention on sound in general. It is worth remembering that ancient literary criticism discussed the idea that prose fiction, like Encolpius's image of (bad) rhetoric at §1–2, was meant to be heard and be pleasurable to listen to. The oldest surviving critical remark about the *Satyrica* is made by Macrobius in his commentary on Cicero's *Somnium Scipionis*, amid a discussion about whether entertaining fiction can or should provide morally valuable truths. Macrobius (*In Somn.* 1.2.8) classes the *Satyrica* along with Menander's comedies and Apuleius's *Metamorphoses* as "engaging only in delighting the ears" (*quod solas aurium delicias profitetur*). Indeed, one of the first things we might notice about this novel, especially throughout the aesthetically exuberant *Cena*, where the voices of the freedmen boom over, and compete with, Trimalchio's orchestra, is how loud it claims to be. There is an abundance of shouting, shrieking, and exclamation (the verbs *clamare* and *exclamare* litter our text: see Biville 2003). Characters shout, cry, bawl, groan, erupt in uncontrollable giggles and rounds of jubilant applause; over and over, the narrative itself climbs to great heights of tragic passion before suddenly deflating, extremes of emotion giving way to relaxed moods and quieter narrative passages.

Again, the cue (or the bait) for turning up the volume seems to be taken from the speeches outside the school of rhetoric, and Agamemnon's Persius-like poem at §5. Declaimers look like they are possessed by the Furies when they "cry out" (*clamant*) an "empty noise" of *sententiae* ("opinions," *sententiarum vanissimo strepitu*), says Encolpius at §1.2. The noun *strepitus* ("din"), or the verb *strepere*, will be used many more times in the *Satyrica*: it describes, for example, the booming orchestra at §33.4, the climactic blast of Trimalchio's funeral march at §78.6, and the corrupt cry for gain (the seed of civil war), followed by the clash of arms thundering through the sky in wartime at *Bellum Civile* (§119–24) lines 40 and 134. According to Agamemnon, in his poem, the experienced scholar should leave the forum and let his page run loose (*det pagina cursum*), pouring out (*defundes*) poetry on feasts and wars *truci canore* ("in a fierce chant"). The major poetic episodes of the *Satyrica*, of course, are mini-epics revolving around and intertwining the themes of feasts and wars (equally, Trimalchio trumpets his dinner party as an epic event): in the *Troiae Halosis*, the Trojans feast and drink while the Greek soldiers lie waiting to pounce inside the Trojan horse, a loaded symbol also mirrored in Trimalchio's "pregnant" dishes in the *Cena*, slit open to reveal their unexpected contents; and in the *Bellum Civile*, Eumolpus connects civil war with gluttony, drunkenness, and a greed for luxury and wealth (see §119 vv. 1–44).

The idea of exuberant, noisy outpouring in the poem at §5 is carried through the rest of the fragmentary remains of the novel. Once again, we can look at how the first scenes that we have become the launch pad for Petronius's intermeshing of poetics and content. For instance, the angry, drunken, overexcited outbursts of the freedmen in the *Cena* are framed both by Trimalchio's philosophy of "letting loose" at §47–9, where he announces his forthcoming trip to the toilet and stresses that there is "no greater torture than holding oneself in" (compare again Agamemnon's *det pagina cursum*, "let the page run loose" §5 v. 16), and by Encolpius's wider narrative, which uses very similar terms to express the release of emotion, curiosity, laughter, and applause. At §58, for example, Hermeros is so enraged at Giton, who has just "burst out with an unseemly laugh which he had been holding back for a while" (*risum iam diu compressum etiam indecenter effudit*) that he can scarcely hold himself in (*vix me teneo*); he has just used the metaphor of worms breeding in rotten flesh (*in molle carne vermes nascuntur* §57.3) to describe his anger at Ascyltos, who at the beginning of §57 "let himself go completely" and "laughed until he cried." Niceros is ready to "burst apart" with joy at being asked to talk by a good-humored Trimalchio at §61 (*gaudimonio dissilio* §61.3, cf. Trimalchio himself at §75.9: *felicitate dissilio*, "I am bursting with happiness"). At §49.7, similarly, Encolpius cannot resist making a comment on the cook who "forgot" to gut the pig (*non potui me tenere*, "I could hardly contain myself"), involuntarily (?) predicting the bursting out of the pig's "insides" at §49.10. As I have discussed elsewhere, the verb *effundere*, employed paradigmatically by Agamemnon to refer to the writing or recitation of passionate poetry, is used over and over in the novel in various forms to refer to the whole gamut of intersecting bodily and literary effusions (see Rimell 2002: especially 203–5): at the X-rated dress rehearsal for Trimalchio's dinner party at Quartilla's house in §16–26, for example, Quartilla claps her hands and suddenly bursts out laughing so loudly that the men are frightened (*complosis deinde manibus in tantum repente risum effusa est, ut timeremus* §18.7); at §91.8, a weeping, groaning Encolpius pours out his heart to Giton (*haec cum inter gemitus lacrimasque fudissem* [...]); Greek soldiers pour out of the Trojan horse in the *Troiae Halosis* (§89 v. 57); the goddess Fortune pours out her speech to Pluto in the *Bellum Civile* (§121 v. 102, *levi defudit pectore voces*), just as Eumolpus himself pours forth the *Bellum Civile* (*cum* [...] *effudisset*, §124.2); and impotent Encolpius pours out a three-line poem in anger at §132.11 (*haec ut iratus effudi*). In all, the verb *fundere* and its cognates occur at least 61 times in our text. The repeated image links episodes, connects poetry with prose, and structures a text whose bitty pages seem paradoxically, as in Agamemnon's ideal, to run and run. In other words, close observation of Petronius's language (his vocabulary and use of metaphor) gives us another perspective on the theatricality of his characters, who seem now to be constantly rehearsing the production of (bad?) oratory and explosive imperial poetry, even as they laugh, cry, pray, or swear.

But is this raucous river of a text music to our ears? We have already touched on bits of conversation in the *Cena* which seem to indulge in what Encolpius describes as "superficial and inane sound effects" in contemporary oratory (*levibus enim atque inanibus sonis ludibria quaedam excitando effecistis*, §2.2). We are reminded, too, of what Tacitus later denounces as a terrible vogue among public speakers: the reproduction of the rhythms of stage-dancing in rhetorical prose: "Many of them," he sniggers at *Dialogus* 26.3, "actually boast that their speeches can be sung and danced to [*cantari saltarique*], as though that were something laudable, distinguished, and clever." As well as including multiple allusions to theatre and mime (on which see Panayotakis 1995), Encolpius's narrative is often unusually rhythmical even in the context of first-century oratory and prose writing, which placed great emphasis on quasi-musical effects (Di Capua's 1948 study of just 40 chapters of the *Satyrica* finds 435 *clausulae*, instances where sentences end in a recognizably metrical beat). Throughout, verse passages are woven into and rehearse or replay the prose narrative, and Encolpius's commentary is often made to "sing" in the form of Eumolpus's poetic set-pieces. To give just two salient examples: at §26.7, Encolpius announces the forthcoming *cena* but adds that "pierced by so many wounds [*confossis vulneribus*], we felt more like running away than resting," recalling orators' melodramatic moaning about war wounds deplored by the same Encolpius in §1.1; the phrase is then used of Furor ("Madness") in the *Bellum Civile* (*oraque mille / **vulneribus confossa** cruenta casside velat*, "she shields her face, scarred by a thousand wounds, with a blood-stained helm" §124 vv. 260–61). A similar pattern occurs at §79.10–11: when Encolpius discovers in the middle of the night that Ascyltos has stolen his Giton and reports, "I hesitated whether to run my sword through them both and make sleep and death one" (*dubitavi, an utrumque traicerem gladio somnumque mortu iungerem*), he previews Eumolpus's retelling of the fall of Troy at §89, where the drunken Trojans are slain in their sleep (*hic graves alius mero / obtruncat et continuat in mortem ultimam / somnos* [...], "One slaughters Trojans heavy with drink and makes sleep merge into the end that is death [...]" §89 vv. 62–4). Petronius's fervent aesthetic, celebrated in the *Cena Trimalchionis* as a loosening up of bodies, language, and even time, allows poetry to flow into prose and vice versa.

In the *Cena*, of course, Trimalchio regularly bursts into poetic song, and the freedmen talk against a background of music, dancing, and other acts. Moreover, the very mention of Trimalchio's orchestra, his *symphonia*, prompts Encolpius to play around even more than usual, and in what often looks like a self-consciously camp, amateurish way, with the idea of musical prose. At §33, for example, Trimalchio has just been conducted in to the sound of music (§32.1), and the guests are being treated to the latest of the hors d'oeuvres – a hen made out of wood that is "spreading out" her wings to cover the live eggs she is "incubating." Here, Encolpius's written account simulates the rising hiss and clash of the (bad) orchestra: we can almost hear what we imagine are shrill wind instruments and brash percussion in his next line, before we are instructed to turn our attention to the sight, or the "staged scene" (*scaena*) of the peahen eggs:

> Acce*ss*ere continuo duo *s*ervi et *s*ymphonia *s*trepente *s*crutari paleam coeperunt erutaque *s*ubinde pavonina ova divi*s*ere convivi*s*. (§33.4)

> The orchestra got louder, and two slaves came up at once and hunted in the straw, and peahen's eggs were pulled out and handed to the guests.

Encolpius adds his own similar sound effects to the scene at §36.6, where Carpus the carver is summoned to slice up the latest delicacy in time to the music, prompting us to think about just what kind of soundtrack would suit such a performance. The line *processit statim scissor et ad symphoniam gesticulatus ita laceravit obsonium* ("The slicer approached at once, and gesticulating in time to the music hacked the meat to pieces") again uses chopped-off "s" sounds, and onomatopoeic words, such as *scissor* and *lacerare* to imitate the aural assault, which Encolpius compares to "a gladiator in a chariot fighting to the accompaniment of a water-organ." As if in competition with Trimalchio's crass puns, Encolpius is perhaps also playing on the sound of the word *obsonium* ("food") and its "echoing" of *sonus*, "sound," or *obsono*, meaning "to interrupt by noise" (especially as the same verb, *lacerare*, is later used of Trimalchio's "massacre" of the harpist Menecrates' songs at §73.3: *coepit Menecratis cantica lacerare*). Certainly, this kind of attempt at a pun would be entirely in tune with the overload of allegory, similes, double meanings, and overlapping activities that characterize the *Cena* and this passage in particular.

Just before this scene at §36, moreover, after Trimalchio has ground out a tune from the tongue-twistingly titled musical comedy "*Laserpiciarius*" ("*Assafoetida*" = a foul-smelling resin used as a spice in cooking) and has introduced the next act, Encolpius's report of dancers running up in time with the music itself starts to skip to some kind of beat:

> [...] *ad symphoniam quattuor tripudiantes procurrerunt superioremque partem repositorii abstulerunt.* (§36.1)

> [...] four dancers ran up in time with the music, and whipped off the top of the dish.

The third-person plural verbs in the perfect tense, *procurrerunt* and *abstulerunt*, at the end of each quasi-poetic phrase, create balance and rhythm (*repositorii abstulerunt* is also a *clausula*), and the onomatopeic present participle *tripudiantes*, "dancers" (literally "people stamping out a dance"), which fits the beginning of a hexameter, seems to bring the scene alive. Later on in the *Cena*, when Echion winds up the first round of speeches at §46, Encolpius comments *eiusmodi fabulae vibrabant* ("stories of this nature flickered back and forth" §47.1): his metaphor evokes not just the buzz of conversation and blur of animated gesticulation in Trimalchio's dining room, but also the bluntness and speed of Echion's speech (it could also be a sarcastic reference to Echion's "scintillating" way with words). *Vibrare* is used intransitively of waving hands and limbs, of trilling bird-song, vibrating sounds, sudden movements, and fast, powerful speech (for example, Cic. *Brut.* 326, *Orat.* 70.234, Quint. *Inst.* 10.1.60, or 11.3.120), while Ovid and Lucretius use it transitively to refer to a serpent's darting tongue. Once again, Encolpius's imaginative narrative highlights the sounds of this text, and gets us hearing, as well as visualizing, each scene: listen again to Echion's snaky gossip (on Titus's games, §45.7–8: *videbis populi rixam inter zelotypos et amasiunculos. Glyco autem, sestiarius homo, dispensatorem ad bestias dedit*, "You'll see the crowd quarrel, jealous husbands and cocky little lovers. A guy like Glyco, not worth a cent, goes throwing his boy to the beasts"), and spiteful jibes (§45.8: *magis illa matella digna fuit quam taurus iacteret*, "that filthy piss-pot whore of his deserved to be tossed by the bull"; §45.11: *dedit gladiatores sestiarios iam decrepitos, quos si sufflasses, cecidissent*, "he produced some decrepit gladiators worth fuck-all, who would have fallen flat if you'd breathed on them"). The verb *vibrare* also links the freedmen's speeches with Eumolpus's literary theory at §118.2, where he dismisses writers who think a poem is easier to compose than "a declamation adorned with quivering epigrams" (*controversiam sententiolis vibrantibus pictam* §118.2). Echion's *declamatio*, of course, uses epigrammatic soundbites by the bucketload.

It is interesting that while in the Greek romances, and Apuleius's *Metamorphoses*, voices are almost always pleasurable and enchanting, singing and reciting voices in the *Satyrica* almost invariably grate on the ears (more on this *vis-à-vis* representations of writing in Rimell 2007): slaves sing in an "acid" tone at §31.6, a passage I mentioned above; Trimalchio's performance *taeterrima voce* ("in an awful voice") of a tune from a musical comedy at §35.7 leaves guests "really depressed" (*tristiores*); the same superlative, *taeterrimus*, is later used at §64.9 of the vicious dog Scylax, who fills the dining room "with a most hideous (*taeterrimo*) barking" – a repetition suggestive of the typical Petronian move of linking "high" with "low," human with animal, and poetry with incoherent noise; at §70.7 we see it referring to Daedalus, the mythical artistic genius metamorphosed here into a cunning slave, who while serving snails on a silver gridiron sings in an "extremely ugly, quavering voice" (*tremula taeterrima voce cantavit*: note the trilling alliteration of "t" sounds, and the *clausula* in the last two words) – giving us another perspective, perhaps, on how the freedmen's speeches "vibrate." Similarly, at §41.6, a slave impersonating Bacchus renders his verses *acutissima voce* ("in an amazingly shrill voice"); at §64.5, freedman Plocamus whistles some "offensive stuff" (*nescio quid taetrum*) that Encolpius doesn't quite catch, claiming afterwards that it was Greek; and at §68, a boy trying to imitate a nightingale is told to shut up (*muta!*), only for Habinnas's slave to start declaiming *Aeneid* 5, the "sharpest" sound Encolpius has ever heard:

> *Nam praeter errantis barbariae aut adiectum aut deminutum clamores miscebat Atellanicos versus, ut tunc primum me etiam Vergilius offenderit.*
> (§68.5)

"For besides making barbarous mistakes in raising or lowering his voice, he mixed up Attelane verses with it [a type of Italic farce], so that even Virgil jarred on me for the first time in my life."

It almost goes without saying that this kind of muddling is in evidence on a larger scale throughout our text: Encolpius's narrative before the storm that wrecks Lichas's ship at §114.1, for example, (*dum haec taliaque iactamus, inhorruit mare* [...], "While we talked over this and other matters, the sea rose [...]") seems to allude to the beginning of the *Aeneid*, where the "storm-tossed" Aeneas (*iactatus*, Virgil *Aen.* 1.3) faces a rising tempest as he "flings out" his words (*talia iactanti*, *Aen.* 1.102), while in the Milesian tale (see Morgan, PETRONIUS AND GREEK LITERATURE, p. 45) "The Widow of Ephesus" told onboard ship at §111–13, the soldier quotes bits of *Aeneid* 4 in order to seduce the woman. Eumolpus's recitation of his compressed version of *Aeneid* 2 in iambic trimeters at §89 (on which see also Slater, READING THE SATYRICA, p. 25) is just as badly received as the slave's declamation of *Aeneid* 5 in the *Cena*: crowds throw stones at him to make him stop (§90.1). (See Panayotakis PETRONIUS AND THE ROMAN LITERARY TRADITION for more on the use of the *Aeneid* by Petronius.)

Language Breakdowns and Civil War

As the *Cena* drags on, and the guests are all very drunk and sick at the very thought of more food and wine, ordered, controlled language is increasingly replaced by incoherent sounds and histrionic gestures. As the narrative builds to the crescendo of Trimalchio's funeral, Fortunata is anxious to get up and dance (*saltare* §70.10), and sparky Scintilla "clapped her hands more often than she spoke." As Trimalchio reads his lengthy will from beginning to end, the slaves "moan and groan," a lugubrious choir (*ingemescente familia* §71.4). At §72, after giving lengthy instructions for his theatrical funeral, Trimalchio bursts into floods of tears, followed by Fortunata, and then Habinnas, until "all the slaves [...] filled the dining room with lamentation" (§72.1). Encolpius, Ascyltos, and Giton then try to make their escape, but the guard dog welcomes them with "such a noise" (*tanto tumultu* §72.7) that Ascyltos falls into a fish pond (or epic "whirlpool," *gurges*), and they find themselves thrown back into the "labyrinth." At §73, as I mentioned above, Trimalchio retreats to his bath, and is encouraged by the bad echoes in a confined space to "open his mouth to the ceiling and lacerate Menecrates' songs," just as Carpus sliced up meat to the orchestra's beat at §36 (cf. §40.5 *qui atilia laceravit*, "who hacked apart the fowls"); at least, adds Encolpius, he was told they were Menecrates' songs by "those who could understand what he said." The verb *lacerare* is much used throughout our text of the *Satyrica*, linking the cutting up of meat, the ripping apart of animals, and the "murdering" of tunes in the *Cena*, with the anguish and breast-tearing of Tryphaena at §100.4 (*lacerata mulier indignatione*) or of the widow of Ephesus at §111.9 (*laceravit pectus*), the "tearing up" of bodies by vulture-like legacy hunters at Croton (*nihil aliud est nisi cadavera, quae lacerantur, aut corvi qui lacerant*, "you'll find nothing but corpses being torn apart and crows doing the tearing" §116.9), and the ravaged houses of the people, the torn clothes of Concord and Discord, and the entire world "rent in pieces" during civil war in Eumolpus's *Bellum Civile* poem (§119–24: *lacerata tecta*, v. 287; *lacera palla*, v. 254; *laceratam vestem*, v. 276; *laceratus orbis*, v. 121). In many different ways, Trimalchio's *symphonia discors* ("discordant symphony") chimes with Eumolpus's epic imagination, which reads Bacchic poetics and the metaphorics of ingestion, outpouring, and gluttony into the cosmic *discordia* ("discord") of civil war.

As Trimalchio wails at §73, other guests join hands and run round the bath, making a tremendous noise with their shrieking and laughter: *ingenti clamore gingilipho exsonabant* (§73.4). It is uncertain what *gingilipho* means here, as it is the only place this word appears in extant Latin literature, but it is normally conveyed as "giggling." What looks like a Petronian (again, onomatopeic) neologism further emphasizes the odd, innovative sounds being created here, rooting the carnival poetics of the *Cena* in the freed-men's drunken laughter. The men are then led into another dining room, and just as Trimalchio is announcing a revival of celebrations, a cock crows, or as Encolpius puts it, "sings": *haec dicente eo gallus gallinaceus cantavit* (§74.1). Notice again the play on sounds: *gallus gallinaceus*, "poultry-cock," perhaps alludes to the unmusical, repetitive calling of the bird. Trimalchio is confused by this "voice," reminding us of other references to the mingling of human and animal sounds, as well as to the bestializing of human voices in the *Cena*. Remember the boy who tried to sing like a nightingale and was so terrible he was told to be quiet at §68, or Trimalchio's retort at §59.3, where he calls Hermeros, who has just accused Ascyltos of "bleating" like a sheep, a "cockerel who likes to go cockadoodledo" (*et tu cum esses capo, coco coco*). Notice also that the repeated bisyllables of *coco coco*, an animal noise, are typical of the speech in the *Cena* more generally, and give the effect of fast-paced "blabbing" (for example, *super pisces duos mullos,* "over Pisces, two mullets" §35.4; *immo magis malus fatus,* "no, rather it was his bad luck" §42.5; *manus manum lavat,* "hand washes hand" = "one good turn deserves another" §46.1; *quicquid discis tibi discis,* "whatever you learn, you learn for your own good" §46.8; *velit nolit nomen meum legat,* "he will read my name, whether he wants to or not" §71.12).

At §74.5, Trimalchio then orders the cock to be killed, and it is *laceratus* (that word again) by Daedalus, the "most learned cook" (*illo doctissimo coco*). Another case, we might say, of someone who calls himself (after) an artist "murdering" songs, or songster birds. But this is also a great example of how Encolpius's narrative gets into the spirit of the *Cena* by imitating Trimalchio's love of puns and language play: the ablative of *cocus, coco,* is also the first part of the onomatopoeic phrase *coco coco* ("cockadoodledo") used by Trimalchio at §59.3, suitably "cut off" not just by Daedalus, but also by *doctissimus* Encolpius. In other words, we might hear *coco* as a sound-effect or stage-direction in brackets ("it was cut-up by that talented chef – cockadoo ... !"). The cockerel slaughtered mid-crow at dawn symbolizes Encolpius's imaginative rendering of Trimalchio's emperor-like reordering of time, as well as the metamorphosis of dining room into underworld, where no birds sing (cf. §120 v. 73: see Bodel 1994). Moreover, the concentration of meanings in *coco* serves to demonstrate the paradox that even "proper Latin" can be heard as meaningless babble or inhuman noise in the environment of the *Cena,* where elegant and vulgar speech is both marked and slurred drunkenly into one concoction.

There follows a loud slanging match between Fortunata and Trimalchio, which involves much shrieking, groaning, and crying, as well as a nasty eruption from Trimalchio which Habinnas calls a *fulmen,* a "flash of lightning" (§75.1). A weeping Scintilla joins Habinnas in asking him to calm down, but this triggers a flood of tears from Trimalchio (*non tenuit ultro lacrimas*) and another tortuous speech. As the "whole thing was becoming sickening" (§78.5), the inebriated host finally summons a new set of musicians, and the trumpeters start up with a "loud din" (*consonuere cornicines funebri strepitu*), one of them blowing hard enough to rouse the whole neighborhood. Firemen arrive, adding to the chaos and noise, and Encolpius and friends seize their chance to flee. The *Cena* ends in a musical crescendo and a barrage of brash, epic noise mixed with incoherent and unusual sounds that will later be recontextualized in Eumolpus's description of civil war, which is seen to be rooted in Trimalchian greed and excess (see §119–20 vv. 1–99). We might recall, too, Phileros's hypocritical blasting of Chrysanthus in §43.2 as "more of a *discordia* ['noise'] than a man": in Eumolpus's poem (§119–24), the noisy bitching of the freedmen is metamorphosed and comes to life in the form of the goddess Discordia, who calls all Romans to arms in vv. 282–94. In a world about to be "torn apart," mountains are excavated until they groan (*gemunt*, v. 92); and as war breaks out, the sky rings with thunder and the clash of arms (v. 134), strange voices sound (*insolitae voces sonuere*, v. 180), rumor beats its wings (v. 210), towns are full of weeping (vv. 225–31), and the gods unleash their thunderbolts of anger (v. 282). Similar peaks of intensity, when Encolpius emphasizes non-verbal noise, occur throughout our text of the *Satyrica*: the shameless *cinaedus* ("man who likes to be sexually penetrated") claps his hands violently and groans as he pours out his wanton poetry at §23.3; against the imagined roar of the storm, Eumolpus groans in the hull as he composes what we assume is the *Bellum Civile* (*audimus* […] *beluae gemitum* §115.1–2), a scene now mirrored by the groaning widow of Ephesus from her underground chamber at §111, and by Encolpius at §113, whose heart is "drowning" with tears as he groans and sighs, just before his *actual* near-drowning in the shipwreck (cf. §81.2, §134.5).

Conclusion

In his longest poem, Eumolpus sees the madness that leads to civil war as a "disease" that is "sewn in the marrow" and "spreads through the limbs" (§119 vv. 54–5), and it is tempting to borrow this image to describe the interaction between "episodes," and between poetry and prose, in the fragmented *Satyrica* as a whole. Petronius's metaphors are infectious, it seems: his suggestive repetitions create a brightly patterned narrative which constantly stimulates the imagination and gives all readers a touch of "rhetorical school madness." Just as civil war sees taboos broken and boundaries erased but at the same time produces torn bodies and worlds, so the *Satyrica* cuts up poetry and narratives while also emphasizing the flow and flux of ideas. We have also seen how Petronius is interested in making language stretch to communicate intense physical and emotional states, in exploring to what extent written representation can convey non-verbal, or incoherent orality – in the form of music, noise, drunken slurring, hissing, laughter, groaning, or other kinds of lamentations, both human and animal. Trimalchio's *Cena*, in which language (as in the fiction factory of the rhetorical school, depicted in §1–5) can seem to merge with a material world of bodies, food, tastes, and smells, becomes not just a pantomime stage for comically vulgar, "low" discourse, but a catalyst for rhetorical and poetic experimentation throughout the surviving novel. The result is sensory overload: we might read the *Satyrica* as the unapologetic literary equivalent of Nero's *Domus Aurea* ("Golden House"). Yet this is also a challenging text, as we have seen: just as the *Cena* tells the story of how even the most delicious cuisine and cleverest entertainments can become a torture, so Petronius's readers are forced to confront the paradox of a novel that makes us laugh by grating on our ears, in ways that continually test our literary knowledge and wit.

Further Reading

On the speeches of Encolpius and Agamemnon outside the school of rhetoric, and the role of rhetoric in the *Satyrica*, see further Cizek (1975a and b), Wooten (1976), Kennedy (1978), Courtney (2001), and Rimell (2002: 18–31). On Petronius's creative lexicon, see Oniga (2000). Much has been written on the language of the freedmen in the *Cena Trimalchionis*, but Boyce (1991) is still the most accessible account in English, and helpfully summarizes much of the earlier literature. Important articles on the topic, especially on how discourse relates to characterization and context, include Campanile (1957), Petersmann (1999), and Callebat (1998). On levels of volume, grating noise, and the abundance of exclamations and interjections in the text see Biville (2003), and Rimell (2007). On prose rhythm see the very interesting piece by Di Capua (1948). On animal sounds at §57–9 see Biville (1996), and on Trimalchio's puns see, for example, Newton (1991). Samatav (1975) collects instances of alliteration in the *Satyrica*. Rimell (2002) discusses Petronius's use of metaphor in greater detail, especially as it is used to connect episodes in ways reminiscent of Ovid's *Metamorphoses* in particular. Connors (1998) is also an unmissable study of how we might read verse passages interacting with the prose narrative.

5

Sex in the *Satyrica*

Outlaws in Literatureland

Amy Richlin

To a reader of the *Satyrica*, it can seem that one of the purposes of this novel is to run through all possible permutations of sexual behavior, a feature which certainly both appealed to and influenced pornographers in early modern Europe. Readers should bear in mind that we have only fragments, and that most manuscripts preserve just the material other than Trimalchio's dinner party, material particularly high in sexual content: is this a representative sample, or a collection of "good parts"? Moreover, this is a tricky text – not just a novel but a fiction about fiction – and plays with not just class and gender norms, but genre norms as well. Encolpius describes himself and his friends as "living outside the law" (§125.4): this applies to a lot of the sex and gender in the novel.

Sex Norms

Assuming the *Satyrica* was written in the first century AD (see INTRODUCTION, p. 5), we can compare a range of contemporary depictions of sexuality both in texts and in material culture (see Clarke 1998; Kampen 1996; Richlin 1992a, 1992b, 1993). Literary texts from Catullus (around 50 BC) to Martial (around AD 100), almost all written by elite males, manifest desire both for women and for teenage boys. Boys, like women, are said to be conscious of themselves as sex objects. There are no extant texts by boys from this period; the two extant women writers, both named Sulpicia, talk of adult male sex partners – there is no Roman Sappho. For a post-adolescent male to desire an adult male is considered abnormal, and texts present such men mainly to deride them; epithets include *cinaedus* ("man who likes to be sexually penetrated") and *mollis* ("soft"). Whereas the "normal" adult male is portrayed as the penetrator of women and boys, adult males who desire adult males are often said to want to be penetrated. If such hostile texts point to a real cinaedic subculture, it left no texts of its own to say who these men really were and what they really wanted. Erotic norms in texts are confirmed in art from cheap to pricey, and graffiti preserved at Pompeii and elsewhere confirm the non-normative as well.

These desires co-exist with traditional sanctions against citizen women having sex with men other than their husbands – made a crime by the Emperor Augustus – and against men having sex with freeborn boys. Moreover, and crucially, Rome was a slave society. The bodies of freeborn Romans were defined by law, custom, and morality as not to be penetrated, except for wives by husbands; conversely, the bodies of slaves were defined as penetrable. To be penetrated, in Roman culture, is thus to be aligned with the female and the servile. Adult males who allowed their bodies to be penetrated lost their honor and some civil rights, as did free prostitutes, although prostitution was legal. A citizen so dishonored was called *infamis*, a category both legal and moral. The humor in the complicated sexual behavior of the characters in the *Satyrica* depends on these norms, in which sex, gender, and class cannot be separated. The English word "lady" once signified a woman who was both upper-class and chaste; "freeborn" in Latin had a similarly double force.

The penetrability of the slave's body, male and female, made sex an expected part of servitude and left the freed slave with a life-long stigma. Slaves could not legally marry; a slave spouse was called a *contubernalis*, "tent-mate," originally army slang for "buddy," and also a word used in the *Satyrica* of Encolpius, Ascyltos, and Giton. Nor were slaves the legal parents of their children – slaves had no legal parents, nor, indeed, birthdays. Many were enslaved through warfare and conquest; such slaves in this period came from outside Italy, and their servitude entailed being forced to learn a sex/gender system that differed in key ways from those of some eastern Mediterranean cultures.

Perhaps unsurprisingly, images of the phallus (erect penis) were common Roman talismans – worn as amulets by freeborn children, hung beneath the chariot of the triumphing general, adorning walls, shop signs, and pavements in Pompeii (see Johns 1982: 61–75). In accordance with these practices, Roman worshippers adopted the god Priapus from the Greek East, and Roman writers and artists followed suit; he appears in literary texts by Catullus, Horace, Ovid, and Martial, and in the anonymous *Songs of Priapus*, probably from the first century AD (see Hales, FREEDMEN'S CRIBS,

p. 162, on the image that greeted visitors to the House of the Vettii). Priapus is the guardian of gardens, and his main feature is his enormous erection, with which he threatens to rape thieves.

The *Satyrica* as Document

Where other kinds of texts offer snapshots, novels appear to offer video to the historian of Roman sexuality. Historians nowadays are leery of taking any text to tell the truth, and the section below on "Literary sex" will explain what that means for the *Satyrica*. Meanwhile, giving in to temptation, let's take a look at sex roles in the novel and see how they complicate the norms depicted above, which, after all, are themselves derived from texts.

Encolpius + Ascyltos + Giton + Eumolpus + others

The predominant emotional relationship in what is left of the *Satyrica* is a love triangle between Encolpius, Ascyltos, and Giton; or maybe a love quad-rangle, adding in Eumolpus. It is clear from passing allusions to other relationships that Encolpius has been involved with women in parts of the novel now lost (Tryphaena, §113.7–8; maybe Hedyle, §113.3; Doris, §126.18), and each of the main characters has sex (or tries to) with other males and females in the extant text. Group sex scenes include the orgy with Quartilla (§16–26.6) and the scene with the children of Philomela (§140.1–11). Encolpius is said to look like a prostitute (§7.2), specifically an effeminate one (§126.2); Ascyltos is treated as one, first by a *paterfamilias* (male head of a household) who wants to penetrate him (§7.4–8.4), then by an *eques* (the rank below senator) who, judging from his characterization as *infamis* and his attraction to Ascyltos's huge genitals, wants to be penetrated by him (§92.7–10).

But Encolpius's love for Giton stands above all. The drama of their romance is played out in three major scenes, all set in sleazy rented rooms: in the first, Encolpius and Ascyltos fight over Giton but stay together (§9–11); in the second, they fight again, and this time Giton chooses to leave with Ascyltos (§79–81); in the third, Encolpius brings Giton back to a room where he fends off both Eumolpus and Ascyltos (§91–9). These scenes have some special features. Encolpius, Giton, and Ascyltos, here and elsewhere, refer to each other, or are referred to by others, as each other's *fratres* ("brothers"). This term in the *Satyrica* sometimes means "boyfriend," but is sometimes paired with terms like "companion" or "fellow soldier." *Frater* appears elsewhere in a sexual sense mostly in Martial. What is interesting about this term is that it implies equality and interchangeability among an indefinite number, unlike the man/boy norm described above, which defines hierarchical pairs with no role-switching allowed.

Moreover, both the first and second scenes involve insult matches – evidently a real feature in Roman popular culture, attested as far back as Plautus – and these insults suggest unexpectedly fluid roles for the *fratres.* Told by Giton that Ascyltos has tried to rape him, Encolpius says to Ascyltos, "What do you say, you whore of womanish passivity? Even your breath isn't clean!" Ascyltos replies, "Why don't you shut up [...] seeing as how you didn't even wrestle with a clean woman when you could do the job? Seeing as how I was your *frater* the same way in the garden that the boy is now in this motel?" (§9.6–10). Encolpius is accusing Ascyltos of having been penetrated anally and of having performed fellatio (Roman texts evince a feeling that oral sex dirties the mouth); this is a normal sort of Roman insult, impugning Ascyltos's virility. But Ascyltos says Encolpius has had sex with women tainted by performing oral sex (also an insult, though not as strong a one) – and that he himself was once to Encolpius what Giton now is. Everything in the novel suggests that Encolpius and Giton conform to the normative man/boy pair, thus that Encolpius penetrates Giton, though we never see this; it is extremely rare in Latin literature for a person to say, "I was penetrated by you," but that is what Ascyltos seems to mean. Or maybe Ascyltos means that he penetrated Encolpius in the garden, and that's what Giton is doing also. This would certainly be an insult, and there are jokes about such role reversals in Martial, but then why does Encolpius reply so mildly? The mysteriousness of this passage is compounded by the fact that the episode of the garden is lost.

Later, abandoned by Giton and Ascyltos, Encolpius rants about the two of them (§81.3–6):

"And who put this loneliness on me? A guy (*adulescens*) who's filthy with every form of lust, who's worthy of exile by his own confession; free by means of sex crime (*stupro*), freeborn by means of sex crime; whose youth was sold by a roll of the dice; people rented him as a girl even when they knew he was a man (*virum*). And what about the other one? On the day he was supposed to put on the man's toga, he put on a woman's dress; he was talked out of becoming a man by his own mother; he did woman's work in the slave

prison; and after he went broke and lit out for a new territory of lust, he
abandoned the name of his old friendship and, for shame, sold everything for
the touch of a single night, like some groupie (*mulier secutuleia*). And now
they lie, the lovers, entwined all night, and maybe when they're worn out by
their mutual lusts they laugh at my loneliness."

It is hard to say which is Giton and which is Ascyltos: both are accused of
having played the woman's part in sex (that is, of having been penetrated),
indeed to have acted the part of women; both are said to have been prostitutes. Encolpius insults both in conformity with norms for Roman insults –
Cicero says similar things about Antony in the *Second Philippic* (Richlin
1992a: 14). The phrase "mutual lusts" is unusual, and thought-provoking
here; so is the juxtaposition of this scene with the stanzas about role-playing
in friendship and on the stage that precede it (§80.9).

In other parts of the extant text, Encolpius and Giton behave more like a
normal man/boy pair. In the third rented-room scene, Eumolpus ogles
Giton while Encolpius defends Giton against him (§92, §94) and against
recovery by Ascyltos (§97); Encolpius is jealous of Eumolpus, here and later
(§100). Giton says he is to Encolpius what Alcibiades was to Socrates
(§128.7); the gullible Encolpius gets Giton to swear that Ascyltos never
forced him to have sex (§133.1–2).

The historian is still left with a threesome whose sexual relationship is
much more complicated than anything else in Latin literature. And this is
still further complicated by the difficulty of determining even the social
status of the main characters (on which see also Andreau, FREEDMEN IN
THE *SATYRICA*, p. 117).

The problem begins with their names: Roman citizens have a *praenomen*,
a *nomen*, and (in this period) usually a *cognomen* as well, like "Lucius
Annaeus Seneca." But nobody in the *Satyrica* except (ironically) Trimalchio
and some of his friends has that name form; almost everybody has a single
Greek name, which would make them either Greeks (in terms of Roman
law, *peregrini* – foreigners) or slaves. Is none of them, then, a Roman citizen?
This makes a difference in what would have been contemporary readers'
expectations about their sexual behavior.

Is Giton a slave? If so, his body is the sexual property of his owner, and he
has no honor to be besmirched. The besmirching of Giton's honor is a running joke in the book, but is it a joke because Giton is a slave or because he
is a slut? Significantly, the word *puer* in Latin can mean both "beloved boy"
and "slave boy." In all three rented-room episodes, it seems that Ascyltos

feels he has some claim on Giton, and in the last episode he actually puts up a reward for Giton's return and calls him a "runaway" (§97). On the other hand, Encolpius seems to have no legal power to make Giton stay: can either of them have legal title? Ascyltos's reward notice specifies Giton's age (16) and gives a physical description ("curly-haired, soft, pretty"): real runaway slaves had notices like that, and Giton here fits the ideal of the slave boy. Yet Giton's service is described ambiguously: sometimes he "attends to the duty of a slave" willingly (§26.10), sometimes unwillingly (§91.1), and on the ship of Lichas and at Croton he, along with Encolpius, pretends to be a slave (§102, §117). At Croton the two even swear the gladiators' oath to Eumolpus – an oath designed to convert free men into bodies consigned to display and death (§117.5–6). Slaves could not swear oaths; but then Encolpius and Giton are cowards, not fighters – this is another joke. Then again, in the second rented-room episode, Ascyltos says Giton should have freedom "at least in choosing his *frater*" (§80.5). In Encolpius's subsequent rant, both figures attacked are said to be freeborn: the second was to have taken on the man's toga, which Roman citizen boys did on reaching puberty; more problematically, the first is said to have been (or become) both free and freeborn by means of sex crime, a joke which implies that this figure was not really freeborn. And the second figure is implied to have acted as a woman for sexual use in a slave prison – not a usual place to find a free person. In this hall of mirrors, the only sure thing is Giton's fickleness.

What about Ascyltos and Encolpius, then? Both seem clearly to be free in the extant novel; are they not Roman? This would place them outside Roman morality. Are they freed slaves? This would imply a history of sexual use by former masters. However, if they are freed slaves, they (like Trimalchio) would have full Roman names; and, seedy as their past appears to be, we hear nothing of any former servitude. Rather, as students of rhetoric, they behave like young freeborn men; again, in the episode of the stolen cloak, they plan to go to court in a way not open to non-citizens (§13.4). Hermeros complains that Ascyltos acts like an arrogant member of the elite, even an *eques* (§57.4), among his freed-slave fellow guests. Eumolpus's hired servant Corax says he is no less "free" than his traveling companions (§117.12), who include Encolpius and Giton. On Lichas's ship, Eumolpus makes a great fuss about the sufferings of the "respectable freeborn" Encolpius and Giton (§107–8). On the other hand, Lichas then begs Eumolpus not to strain credulity (§107.10). Threatening vengeance against his betrayers, Encolpius begins, "Either I'm not a man or free" (§81.6) – but this is another joke, since Encolpius's virility is immediately due for yet another fall. When

Encolpius uses the standard terminology of a Roman divorce in telling Ascyltos to leave (§79.11), this is not because they had been legally married. Both the sexual and social status of all three characters seems mischievously indeterminate in the novel; they are living outside the law.

Eumolpus, too, acts like a Roman citizen – certainly he is free. In the tale of the boy of Pergamum (§85–7), he depicts himself as on the staff of a Roman provincial official (§85.1). This story, like any joke, tells a lot about sexual norms and expectations in what Eumolpus calls "the use of beautiful males" (§85.2): he expects the boy's parents not to trust him, he expects the boy to be unwilling to have sex with him, he hopes the boy will take a bribe, and he finds that the boy is not only willing but, in the end, eager to have sex more times than Eumolpus can manage. On the final night Eumolpus at first forces the boy, who is described as *male repugnanti*, "hardly fighting back" (§87.3). The story follows the standard three-stage structure of jokes, with a progression of sexual acts: first kissing, then feeling the whole body, then "the highest pleasure" (§86.3), "intercourse full and desirable" (*coitum plenum et optabilem*, §86.4), "joy" (§87.3). The joy is not specified, but the boy is said to be "fully mature and of an age yearning to have it done to him (*patiendum*)" (§87.7). It is worth thinking about where this story expects a laugh – what this story aims to teach the reader: philosophers (§85.2) and teachers lust after their students, no matter how prudish they appear; anal sex offers the ultimate pleasure; "no" means "yes"; boys are sluts, go ahead and try (cf. §140.11; see also Morgan, PETRONIUS AND GREEK LITERATURE, p. 40).

But this is, after all, just Eumolpus boasting; within the narrative, the main characters are rarely successful in bed. Their haplessness is often expressed by showing them to be defective in manhood and/or overmatched by women. In the orgy, Encolpius, Ascyltos, and Giton square off against Quartilla, her maid, and a young girl (§19.5); Encolpius and Ascyltos are intermittently assaulted by *cinaedi* (§21.2; §23.2–24.5). The first of these fragmentarily "struck us with his butt-cheeks twisted open and stained us with the smelliest kisses"; the second sings a song calling on his fellow *cinaedi*, slobbers on Encolpius with "the most unclean kiss," (vainly) grinds away at Encolpius's genitals so hard that he sweats off his makeup, and then "switches horses" and pounds Ascyltos with his kisses and buttocks. Quartilla, attracted by Giton (§24.7), arranges a mock wedding between him and the 7-year-old girl in her entourage (§25–6). Similarly, both Encolpius and Giton on Lichas's ship find themselves with fake slave tattoos on their faces and with heads shorn of hair and eyebrows; after fighting ineffectually, Encolpius pouts about his lost beauty and is jealous of Giton's cuddling with

Tryphaena (§113.5–9). At Croton, Eumolpus, who is pretending to be gouty and infirm, needs his servant to help him have sex with Philomela's daughter, while Encolpius tries and fails to have sex with her son (§140.11). All these scenes present behavior rarely seen elsewhere in Latin literature: the orgy itself (despite modern ideas of Rome), Quartilla's orchestration of it, the assault by *cinaedi*, the mock wedding of a girl Encolpius thinks too young "to be able to accept the law of womanish passivity" (§25.3), and Eumolpus's ingenious evasion of his (feigned) handicap.

Women

Women play only minor roles in the extant *Satyrica*, and the novel uses them mainly to express the common Roman stereotype of women as sex-crazed (Richlin 1992a: 173–7, 202–7, 215–19). The most typical episode is the tale of the widow of Ephesus (§111–12), told by Eumolpus on the ship of Lichas – appropriately so, since Tryphaena herself is described as less than virtuous; the story, ironically, makes her blush (§113.1). The moral of the story, as in the tale of the boy of Pergamum, is that no man should hesitate to approach even those deemed most chaste. Lichas's wife has been seduced by someone (§106.2). Circe likes to have sex with the most abject men she can find, while her slave Chrysis will only have sex with *equites*, an inversion of female norms which Encolpius finds "monstrous" (§126.5–11). Old women drag Encolpius to the brothel (§6.4), beat up Eumolpus (§95.8), and practice magic on Encolpius in order to restore his sexual potency (§131, §134–8), magic which paradoxically makes him a sexual victim through a sort of anal rape. Women's supposed tendency to commit adultery even features occasionally at Trimalchio's dinner party, with the shrewish wife of Glyco (§45.7–9), an unnamed freedwoman (§53.10), and the beautiful Melissa (§61.6).

Slave sex

What the dinner party does show in abundance is the sexual norms for slaves and freed slaves. Almost the first thing Encolpius and the reader notice about Trimalchio is the slaves who accompany him: long-haired boys (*capillati*, §27.1) and his pet boy (*deliciae*, §28.4). Both types belong to the category of male slave sex objects; the long hair of slave boys forms part of the beauty praised in erotic poetry (Richlin 1993: 535; for example, Martial

12.49.1), and naturally Trimalchio's dining room is staffed by *capillati* (§34.4, §70.8), as well as by boys from Alexandria in Egypt, proverbially beautiful (§31.3, §68.3). Both Hermeros (§57.9) and Trimalchio (§63.3) describe themselves as having started out as *capillati*; Trimalchio is so depicted in the mural that greets his visitors (§29.3). The ugliness of Trimalchio's *deliciae* is thus a joke (§28.4, §64.5–6); compare Trimalchio's description of his former master's *delicatus* (§63.3), called both a "pearl" and a *catamitus* (a term derived from "Ganymede"; see also Vout, THE SATYRICA AND NERONIAN CULTURE, p. 104). Habinnas has one, too (§67.12). One "pretty" boy is set free by Trimalchio (§41.6), another is kissed by him, leading to the climactic fight with Fortunata (§74.8–10, §75.4).

What this perhaps felt like to the slave himself is suggested by Trimalchio's important comments in his autobiographical speech towards the end of the dinner:

> "When I came from Asia I was the size of this here lampstand. In fact, every day I used to measure myself next to it, and so I'd get a beard on my beak faster, I smeared my lips with lamp oil. Still I was the toyboy (*deliciae*) of the Mister for 14 years. It's not disgusting, what your owner orders. But me, I was satisfying the Mrs, too. You all know what I mean." (§75.10–11)

The appearance of a beard is the conventional sign of the end of a boy's attractiveness to an adult male (for erotic poetry, see Richlin 1992a: 34–5, 275–6); Trimalchio is eager for it to appear, and his 14-year span of sexual service would have carried him well past the normal 12-to-18 eligibility period. His appropriation of the young citizen male's ritual dedication of his first beard hair (§29.8; cf. another slave at §73.6) thus has a double meaning. The tone of "it's not disgusting" is defensive – this is precisely the stigma the freed slave bears – and Trimalchio's open telling of this story is part of his awfulness. As for his sex with his owner's wife, he first brings it up when telling Scintilla "we know how you [married women] are" (§69.3), and says it led to his relegation to the family's plantation – a conventional punishment in Roman comedy, as being a removal from hopes of manumission (see also Verboven, A FUNNY THING HAPPENED ON MY WAY TO THE MARKET, p. 138). In the story of Glyco's wife, the financial manager who had sex with her is given by his owner, Glyco, to be eaten by beasts in the arena; Echion, the freedman speaker, comments, "How did the slave do wrong, when he was forced to do it?" (§45.7–9). When Hermeros tells his life story, he claims that he bought his slave-spouse (*contubernalis*) "so no one could wipe his hands on her hair" (§57.6; cf. §71.2); but the word "hair" is a conjectural addition to the text, based on Trimalchio's actions (§27.6), and perhaps what is at stake here is the desire to control the body's sexual integrity. Circe's "monstrous" preferences are precisely for men whose bodies are owned and/ or dirty from physical labor, or on display for pay (§126.5).

Although Fortunata never tells her own story, we hear it from various narrators. She is first introduced as having once been somehow tainted (§37.3), and is called *lupatria* – probably derived from *lupa*, "she-wolf," the slang for whore (§37.6). Trimalchio brags that she is a great dancer and can do the *cordax* (§52.8), an erotic dance, though no respectable woman would dance at all. Sure enough, when drunk, she wants to dance (§70.10); fighting with her, Trimalchio calls her a belly-dancer and says he took her off the auction block (§74.13). On the other hand, she is presented as a loyal wife and shrewd housekeeper, to whom it means a great deal to share Trimalchio's tomb, and the ever-frank Trimalchio makes it clear that they sleep together (§47.5; 75.9). Both she and Scintilla express jealousy of their husbands' erotic attentions to male slaves (§67.11, §68–9, §74.8–10), a dynamic of which we find real-life traces in Hellenistic marriage contracts (Lefkowitz and Fant 2005: 90), along with literary parallels (Juvenal 6.268–85). The faint suggestion of an erotic relationship between Fortunata and Scintilla (§67.11) was augmented by Fellini in his film of the novel.

The character of slaves' erotic relationships puts them all, with Encolpius and his friends, outside the law. They live in a world very different from any Roman ideal: Eumolpus hopes to be believed when he claims his putative slaves have spent his money on a shared girlfriend (§105.3); Niceros speaks with great fondness of his relationship with Melissa when both of them were still slaves – and she already had a *contubernalis* (§61.6, §61.9). The novel appears to give the reader a window into that world, otherwise visible mainly through the inscriptions freed slaves put on their tombstones (Joshel 1992, and Hope, AT HOME WITH THE DEAD). But how much would the author of the *Satyrica* have known about how slaves felt? See Andreau, FREEDMEN IN THE *SATYRICA*, for the problem of reading the freedmen, and INTRODUCTION, p. 9, for the general problem.

The penis as hero

To some degree, the *Satyrica* is the story of the adventures of Encolpius's penis, in the domain of the appropriate god. That Encolpius and his friends have offended the god Priapus is told them by Quartilla (§17.8); both she and Oenothea (§134.8) seem to be priestesses of Priapus. Priapus speaks to Lichas in a dream (§104.1), claiming responsibility for Encolpius's return. When Lichas recognizes Encolpius by his genitals (§105.9) they still seem to be in working order, but this is no longer the case when Encolpius reaches Croton. He tells Circe that he is the victim of witchcraft – certainly Roman curse tablets often attack body parts, including the genitals – and undergoes various magical treatments. Many of these are attested elsewhere, but not the leather phallus rubbed with pepper and nettles inserted into Encolpius's anus (§138.1–2). Elsewhere Encolpius attributes his condition to the wrath of Priapus (§139.4), who is himself a sort of personified penis; his sacred bird, the gander that Encolpius kills, along with the ostrich Encolpius promises in recompense (§137), are both phallic in shape and appear as such in Roman jokes and graffiti. Thus it makes sense for Encolpius to make a long speech to his penis (§132.7–14), while the plot is moved along by the display of the genitals of both Giton (§24.7, §108.10) and Ascyltos (§92.7–11). An edible Priapus even appears at Trimalchio's dinner, complete with a lap full of squirting fruit (§60.4–6), and "penis" seems to be the intended insulting answer to Hermeros's riddles (§58.8–9). As the riddles hide, or do not, a penis, so the novel plays hide-and-seek with Encolpius's; in one of the last extant scenes, Encolpius displays his restored self to Eumolpus (§140.12–13).

Literary sex, or, Encolpius in literatureland

One problem with taking the *Satyrica* as a document of Roman sexuality is that the text is refracted through numerous literary lenses, each of which comes with sex/gender conventions of its own. As a Roman comic text, the novel has a job to do that sets it in the company of comedy (more Plautus than Terence), verse satire (Lucilius, Horace, Persius, Juvenal; see Panayotakis, PETRONIUS AND THE ROMAN LITERARY TRADITION), Greek and Latin epigram and lyric poetry (Catullus, Horace, the *Carmina Priapea*, Lucillius, Nicarchus, Martial), and all sorts of invective, from graffiti to gossip to Cicero's courtroom speeches (Richlin 1992a). Jokes derive their power from the breaking down of inhibitions, from saying what people are trained not to say from childhood; comic texts invert and dirty moral ideals (Freud 1960). The connection between food, sex, and death at Trimalchio's dinner is a basic element of what, since the work of Mikhail Bakhtin, has been known as the "carnivalesque" (Bakhtin 1968; Stallybrass and White 1986; cf. Gowers 1993): fun with dirt. Despite all this pleasure, readers should bear in mind that jokes establish norms much as laws do, coercing their targets but telling nothing directly about them; misogynistic humor, for example, tells not about what women did but about what women faced, or how culture constructs "women."

However, this is not all the *Satyrica* is doing. First of all, it has its own favorite mode of exposition, an unusual one: voyeurism. Film theorists starting with Laura Mulvey (1975) have recognized the connection between modes of looking, narrative structure, and sexual curiosity; they base their work in part on Freud, an approach that was taken already by J. P. Sullivan in his important study of the *Satyrica* (1968a). Quartilla tells Encolpius that he has seen what he should not have (§17.4); this transgression is repeated when Quartilla and Encolpius spy on the sexual play of Giton and Pannychis (§26.4), when Encolpius and Giton watch Eumolpus being beaten up (§96), and when Philomela's son watches Eumolpus having sex with his sister (§140.11). Laura Mulvey says that "sadism demands a story"; arguably, the whole of the *Satyrica* constitutes a sort of spying on things usually unseen, with Encolpius serving as the plot's whipping boy, much as Apuleius's *Golden Ass* would spy on the Mediterranean underworld through the eyes of a donkey. The text uses the novel form and the first-person narrator as does a first-person-shooter computer game, placing the reader in the midst of the action – while continually reminding the reader that this first-person narrator is a gullible fool, always taken in by what he sees (see Slater, READING THE *SATYRICA*). The fragmentary state of the novel augments this effect for the modern reader, who, without any final plot trajectory, is more free than the book's first readers to shop for pleasure in the text.

In addition, the *Satyrica*, though briefly – at least in the extant text – participates in the longstanding Roman debate about gender and rhetorical style (Gleason 1995; Gunderson 2003; Richlin 1997; Rimell 2002). Although the opening speeches by Encolpius and Agamemnon portray rhetoric mostly in terms of food, Encolpius does speak of "chaste oratory" (§2.6), and complains, "You have brought it about that the body of oratory has been stripped of its sinews" (§2.2) – for the sexual sense of which compare Circe's dirty joke, playing on the common, obscene sense of "sinews" as "male genitals" in Latin (§129.5). Roman rhetorical theorists in this period divided oratorical style into "Attic" (pure, virile, simple) and "Asiatic" (fancy, effeminate, overblown), and wanted both the body and speech of the ideal rhetorician to be manly; that this opening speech is made by Encolpius turns out to be a joke, as we read on. The *Satyrica*'s simple, direct Latin falls well onto the Attic side of the divide, and the little poem that follows Encolpius's address to his penis defends the novel as "pure" in diction (§132.15; see Slater, READING THE SATYRICA, p. 28). Moreover, the poem suggests that purity paradoxically consists in sexual frankness and clarity. It does not help readers know what to think when we reflect that all the students and teachers of rhetoric and literature in the novel are corrupt, and none is a model of moral behavior or masculinity (a joke that would be picked up by Lucian in the second century AD; see Richlin 1992a: 283, 285–6, 290). The novel, turning itself into an exploding cigar, suggests that the study of literature goes along with bad behavior. Eumolpus seduces his student; Encolpius goes directly from the rhetorical school to a brothel.

And thereby Encolpius steps into a sort of literary funhouse, in which the action takes place not so much in a Roman world as against a painted backdrop of a Roman world. One set of backdrops comes from the rhetorical schools themselves, from the practice speeches known as *controversiae*: the brothel Encolpius enters is the setting for many (see, for example, the elder Seneca, *Controv.* 1.2); Agamemnon tries to tell Trimalchio about one practice speech on the common topic "a poor man and a rich man were enemies," and Trimalchio turns it into a joke (§48.5); Lichas's ship echoes the pirate ships that often feature in *controversiae* (§101.4); the speeches about Eumolpus's corpse make farfetched arguments just like *controversiae* (§141.9–11). What is at stake in rhetorical brothels and pirate ships is usually the chastity of a beleaguered maiden or the life of an embattled protagonist, and Encolpius, Giton, and Ascyltos find themselves cast in both roles.

Similarly, and as has often been argued, Encolpius and Giton parody the stock hero and heroine of the Greek romance (on the latter see Bakhtin 1981: 84–110; Konstan 1994). This novel substitutes for the usual chaste maiden and stalwart young man Giton (not at all chaste) and Encolpius (a deluded coward who repeatedly misinterprets Giton's behavior and loses him because he is too weak to fight for him). The shipwreck scene in which Encolpius and Giton tie themselves together to face death could have come straight from a Greek romance, along with the novel's many staged suicides and fights, partings and reunions. The substitution of a man/boy pair for a boy/girl pair is probably meant to be funny in itself; women are not so interesting to the author of the *Satyrica* (contrast *The Golden Ass*), and the novel evinces a camp aesthetic (on which see Cleto 1999, Wooten 1984) both in finding pederasty funnier than male/female sex and in making it central. Although, as David Konstan points out (1994: 115–16), man/boy pairs appear in the Greek romances too, there is a strong and parodic cross-gender component to Giton's character, as in Ascyltos's memorable line: "If you're Lucretia, you've found your Tarquin" (§59.5). The gender roles of these and other characters are partly determined by roles already set up in a genre that is romantic rather than comic, and this is part of what makes them funny: Giton as damsel in distress, Encolpius as daring hero. (For an alternative view on the question of the relationship to the Greek novel, see Morgan, PETRONIUS AND GREEK LITERATURE, p. 40.)

Moreover, the line about Lucretia and Tarquin imports a high drama of Roman chastity (see Val. Max. 6.1.1) into a decidedly low scene. The text continually emphasizes the squalor of the action by having characters describe it in lofty terms: so Giton compares the brawl between Encolpius and Ascyltos over himself to the battle between the sons of Oedipus for control of Thebes (§80.3), and Encolpius contrasts his own thwarted love with the loves of the gods he sees depicted in an art gallery (§83.3–6). Petronius's Philomela pimps her children; the Philomela of mythology, having been raped by her brother-in-law, helped murder her nephew. Many have seen caricatures of elements of Plato's *Symposium* in Trimalchio's dinner, and the tale "The Boy of Pergamum" (§85–7) certainly plays with the lofty ideals of Socratic love, as does Giton's snippy remark to Encolpius invoking the *Symposium* (§128.7; see further Morgan, PETRONIUS AND GREEK LITERATURE, p. 38). Most of all, the *Satyrica* delights in mock epic. The *Odyssey* comes up repeatedly, from the wrath of Priapus (instead of Poseidon) to the romance of Circe and Polyaenus; Giton hides under the bed like Ulysses under the ram in the cyclops' cave (§97.4–5, §98.5); Encolpius is recognized by his genitalia as Ulysses was recognized by his scar (§105.10); Encolpius addresses his impotent penis as Ulysses addressed his heart, in an episode stuffed with epic and tragic language, even scraps of poetry (§132.7–14). Lichas is compared to the cyclops Polyphemus (§101.5, 7). The old woman who guides Encolpius into a brothel looks, for a second, like the divine guide of Aeneas in Book 1 of Virgil's *Aeneid* (§7.2); the widow of Ephesus and her maidservant replay the roles of Dido and her sister Anna from the *Aeneid*, complete with quotations (§111–12); the brother rhetoricians are Agamemnon and Menelaus; Encolpius mourns the death of that part of his body in which he was once an Achilles (§129.1). Although the text has a complicated relationship with epic in other ways, notably in Eumolpus's poetry, it is important to realize how much the novel distorts epic gender to create comic gender, and creates pleasure by making epic sexual. When Tryphaena speaks a poem in epic style on the part played by *amor* in strife (§108.14), the reader is being asked to take sex seriously – by a most unreliable speaker. For more on the relation to epic, see the chapters by Morgan, Panayotakis, and Vout.

The novel also directly incorporates erotic genres, especially love poetry (§79.8; cf. §126.13–18) and the Milesian tale (on which see Morgan, PETRO-NIUS AND GREEK LITERATURE, p. 45). Two of the main extant examples of this story form are the tales "The Boy of Pergamum" (§85–7) and "The Widow of Ephesus" (§111–12), both bawdy. Moreover, there are repeated references in the text to mime, a form of (not silent) drama popular in Rome from the republic onward (§19.1, §80.9, §94.15, §106.1, §117.4; on the theatre, see also Panayotakis, PETRONIUS AND THE ROMAN LITERARY TRADI-TION): in its original form, it involved both male and female actors, impro-visation, and bawdy plots. The poem in the second rented-room scene draws an analogy between the action of the novel and the action of a mime and suggests that nothing is what it seems, that the text is a screen (§80.9).

It seems possible, then, that the characters' peculiar names in fact are pen-names, as it were, tying them to genre fiction: the characters in Greek romances have Greek names, as do many characters in Roman comedy and some figures in Roman satire; hence, so do the characters in the *Satyrica* (see INTRODUCTION p. 11 for translations). Their social and sexual status, then, depends as much on generic norms as on social ones; they are living outside the law because they are living outside the real world, on pages in a book. On the ship of Lichas, Eumolpus disguises Encolpius and Giton with ink, writing on their faces, and that is just how this book works.

But, with all this, it's worth remembering Christopher Isherwood's famous line, "You can't camp about something you don't take seriously" (1954: 125).

Outlaw Sex

The *Satyrica* has a long history as a banned book, and readers today should realize that this has affected what has been thought about the characters' sexual behavior, and vice versa. Histories of Latin literature from the nineteenth century well into the twentieth routinely identified the main characters as Greeks and/or freed slaves, perhaps because of a strong wish not to associate their sexual behavior with Roman citizens. The influential nine-teenth-century Roman historian B. G. Niebuhr believed the novel to have been written in the third century AD, which again would dissociate these escapades from classical Latin literature and history. To give them credit, the handbook writers did not completely conceal the existence of the *Satyrica*, as they did with other highly sexual texts; but they very rarely discuss the content of any part of the novel except Trimalchio's dinner, and to this day there is no readily available student text of the whole novel in Latin.

Circulation of the novel even in Latin was a problem from the beginning; the humanist Pierre Pithou joked in 1565 that he kept his copy "in jail" but would make it available to other learned men (quoted in Reeve 1983: 296), and Gaselee's history of the text (1910) is full of early scholars' qualms about publication. Yet the Latin text itself existed in more than two dozen editions before the *Cena* was even found, with the first French translation in 1643 (pre-*Cena*) and the first English translation, by William Burnaby, in 1694. The book was available to interested readers; Lord Byron used a phrase from the tale of the boy of Pergamum, *coitum plenum et optabilem* (§86.4), as code when he wanted to write to his friends about sex with boys (Crompton 1985: 127–8, 152).

Although, as shown by Harrison in this volume, the *Satyrica* (especially the *Cena*) has widely influenced English literature, translations of the novel, often billed as "unexpurgated," still belonged to the world of pornography well into the twentieth century. A version of 1708 by various hands ("Mr. Wilson, Mr. Burnaby, Mr. Blount, Mr. Tho. Brown, Capt. Ayloft, and several others," [Wilson et al. 1708]) features a frontispiece showing both human and human/satyr couples, and a man vomiting (see figs 5.1 and 5.2). The Preface to this edition excuses the project by listing other ancient authors who "describe vice in lively language." Translations were often privately printed, some incorporating deluxe erotic illustrations, and include a bizarre American version by Calvin Blanchard (1866), who compares Nero to "the Ex-Vice President of the C.S.A."; a 1902 version attributed to "Sebastian Melmoth" (that is, Oscar Wilde), reprinted in Chicago in 1927 with illustrations and in New York in 1930 (Melmoth 1902); a privately printed, limited edition (1927) translated by Jack Lindsay, with illustrations by Norman Lindsay, reprinted in 1944 (Lindsay 1944); and a translation offered in 1933 (anon.) with illustrations by the brilliant art deco artist Jean de Bosschère, who also illustrated the plays of Aristophanes (on sex-related issues in translating Petronius, including the highly obscene forged fragments, see Roberts 2006). Many more can be found in the standard Petronius bibliography (Schmeling and Stuckey 1977). Such editions were either

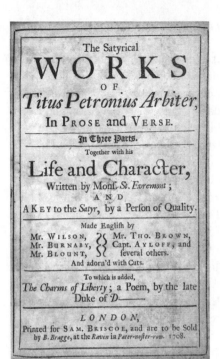

Figure 5.1 Title page from *The Satyrical Works of Titus Petronius Arbiter in Prose and Verse* (London 1708). (Photo: courtesy of The Bodleian Library, University of Oxford, from the copy held at shelfmark Douce P. 135.)

Figure 5.2 Frontispiece from *The Satyrical Works of Titus Petronius Arbiter in Prose and Verse* (London 1708). (Photo: courtesy of The Bodleian Library, University of Oxford, from the copy held at shelfmark Douce P. 135.)

hard to find (not in your public library or neighborhood bookshop), or very expensive and produced for a limited list of subscribers; editions in Latin existed in college and university libraries, but then you had to be able to read Latin pretty well to understand them.

The first generally available translation of Petronius did not appear until the twentieth century (Michael Heseltine's 1913 Loeb translation). As usual with translation series, erotic authors were among the first titles launched in the Loebs; it is notable that, when the Modern Library reprinted the Burnaby translation in 1929, they chose C. K. Scott Moncrieff to write the Introduction – a friend of Wilde and associate of the Uranian poets. The *Satyrica* did not appear in an edition practical for student purchase until the paperback version of William Arrowsmith's translation in 1960. Students reading this book for a course should realize that they are part of a brief moment in history when it has been possible for a lot of people to read this text, and a much briefer moment when it has been possible for it to be taught to students. Ask yourself why that has been so, and whether this book might not be lost again. Sex is not an incidental part of this novel. Nor is it an incidental part of history: "And what the people do, the candid tongue relates" (§132.15).

Further Reading

J. P. Sullivan's study (1968a) remains important for an understanding of voyeurism in the *Satyrica*; for visual theory, a good starting place is Laura Mulvey's (1989) collection of essays, which includes her 1975 piece and adds second thoughts. The literature on visual theory in textual analysis grew to enormous size in the 1990s: for an introduction to the theory of the pornographic with applications to antiquity, see Richlin (1992b); for visual theory and ancient material culture, see Kampen (1996) and Clarke (1998).

Why is sex funny? The work of Mikhail Bakhtin (1968) is fundamental to an understanding of Western ideas of what is funny about the human body; Bakhtin's perhaps excessive optimism about the cultural impact of these ideas was modified by Peter Stallybrass and Allon White (1986). Freud's *Jokes and their Relation to the Unconscious* (1960) also takes a more pessimistic view, aligning humor with hostile urges in the human psyche. Why was sex funny to the Romans? *The Garden of Priapus* (Richlin 1992a) presents an overview of Roman erotic, satiric, and invective texts, including the *Satyrica*, that leans toward the pessimistic. For context, readers are strongly recommended to consult two excellent sourcebooks: on women, Lefkowitz and Fant (2005); on homosexuality, Hubbard (2003). The most recent translation of the *Priapea* is Hooper (1999). Important recent studies of sex and gender in the *Satyrica* include Konstan (1994; in the general context of sex in the ancient novel), McGlathery (1998), and Rimell (2002; on language and the body); on translating ancient erotic texts, see Roberts (2006).

6

The *Satyrica* and Neronian Culture

Caroline Vout

When betting on the date of the *Satyrica*, the smart money is on late in the reign of Nero. As the Introduction to this volume has explained, its author, Petronius, is now routinely aligned with the Petronius of Tacitus's *Annales*, one of Nero's courtiers, who killed himself in AD 66 (see INTRODUCTION, p. 5). Once this link is established, allusions to the Neronian writers Lucan and Seneca, and to Nero himself, are identified throughout – both bolstering, and gaining credence from, the Tacitean association. This chapter is not about to argue with this: the combination of external and internal evidence, mutually dependent though they are, makes the odds as good, if not better, than for other options. But it is going to think hard about what to do with our winnings. Even if additional evidence were to turn up tomorrow to prove that the text is not Neronian, what follows demonstrates how our reading of Petronius is informed by comparison with other imperial authors.

Dating (alone) does not lead to fulfillment; it can often overly dictate a way of reading as the critic overlooks the obvious in favor of a forced parallel. Appendix A of Kenneth Rose's influential book (1971) – to which the popularity of a late Neronian date owes so much – lists some of the most forced, when it collates what Petronian scholars from the seventeenth century onwards have read as allusions to Nero, the bulk of them in the description of Trimalchio's dinner party, or *cena*. So, for example, the four "runners" (*cursores*) who accompany his litter at §28.4 are put next to the *cursores*, number unspecified, who Suetonius claims always traveled with the emperor (*Nero* 30.3). What sounds desperate in isolation assumes extraordinary power when used in conjunction with other "parallels" between the two texts (the golden boxes in which Trimalchio and Nero store their first beards at §29.8 and Suet. *Nero* 12.4 and so on) – as though providing an explanation or map of Petronius's enigmatic and now fragmentary journey. Many are the scholars who have been attracted by the idea of reading Trimalchio as Nero (for example, Walsh 1970: 137–9), and of interpreting the narrative he dominates as critical or parodic of reality.

Safer are those scholars who have moved beyond word for word, or Trimalchio/Nero "parallels," to explore what they see as common themes in the worlds of Nero's empire and the *Satyrica* as a whole, not just the *Cena*: the emphasis that they each place, for example, on artifice, theatricality, and doublespeak. For these, it is not a matter of direct influence, one text on another (or, in the case of Suetonius, who we must remember did not write his life of Nero until early in the second century, his sources' influence), so much as of formative and fruitful intersections between the worlds that shaped them – an overwhelming sense that the *Satyrica* could not have been written at any other time. This frame-shift, subtle though it may seem, frees Petronius up by acknowledging that his text is multi-directional: it is not that Trimalchio is Nero, for this would be to simplify both, but that they are painted using a similar palette, as is Eumolpus, the poet of the piece, who is as much Nero as he is Lucan. Seen like this, any Neronian context accorded to the *Satyrica* informs us not about reality, but about ways of representing reality in a given period.

The aim of this chapter is to pursue the implications of this conclusion. Catherine Connors's recent book on the *Satyrica* (1998) is exemplary in its sophisticated analysis of how the *Satyrica*'s poems collide with its prose and, beyond this, with modes of representation common in Neronian Rome. My mission is far more modest in scale as I concentrate first on one short passage of the prose itself, from the *Cena*. Close reading will show, step by step, how the search for "intersections" between texts reveals the processes of their telling and the make-up of Trimalchio's and Nero's tyranny. By this I do not just refer to intersections with the world of Nero, but also with other Roman worlds, from republican literature to funerary ritual and the triumph, which crowd together with the former to stress the dangers of treating "Nero" in isolation. We will then contextualize the *Cena* with recourse to further brief sections of the *Satyrica*, expanding our field of vision to encompass other kinds of representation. The hope is that, even if the text could be proven to be Flavian or later, the resulting chapter still serves as a lesson in how to read Petronius and imperial culture.

Close Reading

§27.6. *exonerata ille vesica aquam poposcit ad manus, digitosque paululum adspersos in capite pueri tersit ...* [text breaks off]

§28. *longum erat singula excipere. itaque intravimus balneum, et sudore calfacti momento temporis ad frigidam eximus. iam Trimalchio unguento perfusus tergebatur, non linteis, sed palliis ex lana mollissima factis. tres interim iatraliptae in conspectu eius Falernum portabant, et cum plurimum rixantes effunderent, Trimalchio hoc suum propin esse dicebat. hinc involutus coccina gausapa lecticae impositus est praecedentibus phaleratis cursoribus quattuor et chiramaxio, in quo deliciae eius vehebatur, puer vetulus, lippus, domino Trimalchione deformior. cum ergo auferretur, ad caput eius cum minimis symphoniacus tibias accessit et tanquam in aurem aliquid secreto diceret, toto itinere cantavit. Sequimur nos admiratione iam saturi* [...]. (Text: Smith 1975)

§27.6. He emptied his bladder, requested water for his hands and then after barely wetting his fingers, wiped them on his slave's head ... [*text breaks off*]

§28. It would take too long to extract each individual detail. Basically, we entered the bath, and once hot and sticky, immediately took refuge in the cold pool. Already Trimalchio had been steeped in oil and was being rubbed down, not with towels but with large rectangles made from the softest wool. All the while three masseurs were drinking Falernian wine under his nose and, as they argued, spilt a lot of it. Trimalchio claimed that they were drinking his health! From here, he was rolled in a scarlet cloak and placed on a litter, preceded by four runners wearing military decorations, and a go-cart which carried his favorite, an aged boyfriend, half-blind, uglier than his master Trimalchio. Anyway, as he was carried out, a musician with miniature pipes approached his head and, as though whispering something secret in his ear, played for the entire journey. We followed, already stuffed with admiration [...].

In this extract from the beginning of the *Cena* episode, Trimalchio well and truly lives up to his initial description as *lautissimus homo* at §26.9 (*lautus* meaning both "wealthy" and "washed"). He has washed his hands and wiped them (*tersit*) on the hair of his slave, and then bathed and been rubbed down (*pallis ex lana mollissima tergebatur*), before being packaged up for delivery to his dinner. The Greek root of the word for the coat in which he is wrapped (*gausapa*) and the effeminacy which still pervades it from its only other outing in the text – worn by the *cinaedus* ("man who likes to be sexually penetrated") who molests Encolpius and Giton at Quartilla's "orgy" (§21.2) – combine with the softness of the woolen towels to smother Trimalchio's masculinity. *Mollitia* ("softness") is a standard signpost in Latin literature of unmanly and thus un-Roman behavior. But camp is not the word's only charge. By far the best-known usage of the word *gausapa* in ancient literature is in Horace's *Satires* 2.8, commonly known as "Dinner with Nasidienus," where a slave is described (l. 11) as wiping the table with such an object (*gausape purpureo mensam pertersit*) in an adaptation of a line from the earlier satirist Lucilius (l. 598, ed. Warmington). These echoes – made more resonant by the *tergo* refrain and by the fact that the masseurs are drinking Falernian wine as Nasidienus does – whet the reader's appetite for the dinner to come, equate almost the steeping (*perfusus*) and rolling (*involutus*) of Trimalchio with foodstuff. This equation becomes more tempting when we consider that later (§38.15) *gausapa* is used adjectively to describe how the wild boar was served (*apros gausapatos*) at the undertaker's dinner parties.

But it is going to be a while before the reader is admitted to the dining room, literally and metaphorically. No sooner does Horace's satire surface, than it fades again, as the litter (*lectica*) on which Trimalchio is carried is further qualified, so as to lose its platter-like potential. For a moment, both it and the mention of Trimalchio's *deliciae* and *puer* are sufficiently informed by the effeminate connotations of the passage to point us towards Suetonius's account of the *puer* Sporus (*Nero* 28), whom Nero castrates, marries, and carries with him in a litter (*lectica vectum*). But the kissing that we find there and in the later *Augustan History*, which portrays the Emperor Commodus and his favorite, Saoterus, in a similar vein (SHA, *Commodus* 3.6), is wanting: instead we have the oxymoron of an "aged boy" relegated to a separate cart (*chiramaxium*). Whereas normally in Roman literature *pueri* are so beautiful as to attract attention, sometimes against the spectator's will, here the description repels us. If we do look, the boy is half-blind (*lippus*) and thus barely able to return our gaze – just as the desired literary parallel fails to meet expectation. Read like this, he is made emblematic, programmatic even, of the reader's thwarted recognition.

Suddenly, however, the boy is also forgotten as Petronius pans back to Trimalchio and to his transferal from the baths for a final time (*cum ergo auferretur*). In the *lectica* with him, we are told, is a *symphoniacus* ("musician") who plays the pipes for the entire journey. Others (for example, Gagliardi 1984) have emphasized the funerary connotations of this "carrying out" – a layer of meaning which I would not want to ignore, and which suits the context of Petronius's use of *gausapatus* later, as well as the obsession with death that pervades Trimalchio's dinner and Roman dining more broadly (see Hope, AT HOME WITH THE DEAD). The corpses of wealthy Romans were borne on *lecticae* and accompanied by musicians. A late republican relief from Amiternum in Abruzzo, now in the Archaeological Museum of L'Aquila (Kleiner 1992: 104–5), encapsulates this nicely in its depiction of the deceased on a couch, reclining as though at table, attended by flute-players.

But the fact that Trimalchio's musician is in the chariot with him and so close, "as though he were secretly saying something in his ear" (*tanquam in aurem aliquid secreto diceret*), potentially points in another direction. Why this odd aside here? One answer would be that it conjures up an image of the triumphant Roman general, who is honored for his campaigns overseas. He would process through Rome in a chariot (*currus*), accompanied by a slave whose job was to repeat to him that he was mortal. What would equating slave and *symphoniacus* achieve? It gives more emphasis to the *phalerae* ("military decorations") of the runners, and tempts us to read *currus* for *lectica* (a move made for real in the above-mentioned *Augustan History*'s appropriation of Nero and Sporus, where Commodus and Saoterus are in a *currus*) and the scarlet cloak for purple. It also perhaps lends more weight to the viewer's admiration expressed in the next line. Although the distance between the baths and the house is presumably modest, the reference to the "entire journey" reminds us that a *gausapa* was also a blanket worn while traveling, thereby turning this trip into an expedition. Much of what follows in the house is more Roman imperial and urban than the rest of Encolpius's picaresque escapades. While funerary connotations already suggest a shift in the narrative from one world to another, triumphal soundings further specify this shift: they signal the reader's arrival in Rome-scape, even though the protagonists are still in Campania.

Any mismatch between this passage and a possible triumphal paradigm (and there is admittedly none of the usual vocabulary) has potentially more mileage than the mismatch between it and Horace's poem or the Sporus anecdote. Elsewhere in this volume, for example (p. 171), Shelly Hales compares the description of Trimalchio's autobiographical wall-painting that follows our passage (§29.3–6) to the monumental reliefs on triumphal arches. The only other text in which *phalerae* are worn by those running beside chariots is the *cursores* passage from Rose's appendix (Suet. *Nero* 30.3), which I discussed earlier. But, unsurprisingly by now, that section of Suetonius offers no further parallels. Rather, it is his account of Nero's triumphal procession into Rome after his athletic victories in Greece in AD 67 (*Nero* 25.1–2) that fits better. Many of the buzz-words of Petronius's passage (*gausapa, phalerae, chiramaxium, symphoniacus*) are Greek in origin, while the action takes place near Naples, which serves as the point of departure in Suetonius's description. In a later version of this procession (Dio Cass. 63.20), which appears to be based on the same source as

Suetonius, Nero is accompanied not by a slave but by a musician, as in Petronius – a lyre-player. Back with Suetonius, the birds, ribbons, and sweetmeats thrown to the crowd are more in keeping with Trimalchio's dinner than the stereotypical triumph.

As Edward Champlin notes, however, in his recent book on Nero (2003: 231), not only is this triumph of AD 67 unusually Greek, but it is "ostentatiously not a triumph." It is certainly more "try-hard" or self-consciously performative than most, in that it uses the chariot in which Augustus himself had ridden and has the emperor's attendants loudly proclaim that they are "soldiers of his triumph." It is as though they feel the need to convince, as well as to flag the fact that this is "role-play." The fact that the procession is as far from any model as Petronius is from his already dilutes and enriches the essence of the prototype. Such a charge could, of course, be directed against any triumph: the general's status as *triumphator* demanded that he "walk the walk," but with sufficient flair to secure real cheers from a crowd who might otherwise be merely "going through the motions." As with all rituals, its meaning, and potential emptiness, lay in reproduction. More specifically, Mary Beard (2007: 85–92) has recently drawn attention to the fact that the evidence for a slave in the triumphal chariot with the general is less concrete than we might expect. For Jerome, for example (*Ep.* 39.2.8), the companion is simply that, a *comes*, a rather elastic word that can be used to gloss a multitude of categories from "friend" or "comrade," through "follower" or "devotee," to "attendant" or "soldier." Not only that, but it seems to be part of the tradition almost to experiment with his identity. In a relief showing the triumph of Titus, from his arch in the forum (see, for example, Kleiner 1992: 187–8), he has become a "she," a winged Victory, whose acclamation already points to Titus's apotheosis in the attic panel. Elsewhere, early in the third century, Philostratus (*V S* 488) describes how the Emperor Trajan once set the orator and philosopher Dio Chrysostom next to him "on the golden chariot in which the emperors ride in procession when they celebrate their triumphs in war, and often he would turn to Dio and say, 'I do not understand what you are saying, but I love you as I love myself.'" It would seem that the "companion," and other familiar triumphal baggage, had long lent themselves to distortion.

But the triumph accorded to Nero is extreme sport. He is victorious not over foreign peoples but over musicians, poets, and playwrights, epitomes of high culture rather than barbarians. His version is not only extravagant but explosive – both of the triumph and of the more modest descriptions which we usually associate with athletic victors (so destructive that Suetonius notes how the arch of the Circus Maximus through which he passes is caused to fall down). As Beard argues, this is one of several descriptions, not only by Suetonius and Cassius Dio but also by Tacitus, which exploit the familiarity of the language of triumph to highlight both the dissonance of Nero's reign (for example, at Tac. *Ann.* 14.13, when the people watch Nero returning to Rome after murdering his mother, "as they do at triumphs"), and the extent to which he is a "misfit." Misappropriating the model speaks louder than replicating it: so too with Petronius. Beard goes on to claim (2007: 271) that these quasi-triumphs raise the question of how "triumph-*like* a ceremony has to be before it counts as a triumph," and so reinforce as much as they "parody" the Roman-ness of Roman institutions. The issue is similar in the *Satyrica*. Its author asks: how close does this or any section of my text have to be to a supposed source for it to be read as a meaningful allusion?

Petronius's readers would understand what was being asked of them. This is Rome as it approaches the end of the Julio-Claudian dynasty, a place in which reproduction no longer suffices; where the script is so well known as to encourage the trafficking of oblique references, half-lines, refraction, and bricolage; where an emperor and his audience are most vocal at the points of departure. By grafting Horace *Satires* 2.8 onto reminiscences of Sporus and the triumph (in its various shades), as well, perhaps, as Roman funerary ritual, Petronius is contributing to this "hall of mirrors" – not "commenting on" Roman society and its failings so much as "reveling in" them. To say that he is here or elsewhere "parodying" Nero isn't the half of it – for that would be to imply that one were the original and the other the copy. Rather, he is exposing the complex ways in which Neronian culture is constructed and deconstructed. Emily Gowers (1993: 37–9) has drawn attention to other instances in Latin literature, some of them within Trimalchio's dinner itself, where descriptions of food are invested with triumphal imagery. The frequency of such a link should increase the chance that our multiple echoes were heard, and that the whisperings of Trimalchio's companion prepared the reader not only for the dinner's musical theatre, but for its obsession with mortality.

"It would take too long to extract each individual detail" (*longum erat singula excipere*), warned Encolpius at the start of this section. Usually this is read as an admission of the narrator's inadequacy. But instead we might read it as encouragement to rise to the challenge and draw out the details that are there – as far as we are able. Trimalchio's transferal from the baths on a litter counterbalances the procession at the end of his dinner

(§78): triumphal and funerary marches frame the eating, and the implications of this eating, in two different processions (*pompae*) (see Gagliardi 1984, and also Bodel 1999a, for a clear introduction to ring composition in the *Cena* more generally). It is as though events come full circle, since, before this, Trimalchio, Encolpius, and Giton leave the dining room for another brief sojourn in the baths (§72) – or almost full-circle. "You are wrong," warns the porter, "if you think that you can leave by the door you came in" (§72.10). It is as though they and the characteristics that they (and we) thought were known are changed by the experience.

Suetonius is not unaffected by this realization. His composition is also informed by post-Neronian sources which attempted to capture the emptiness of Nero's rule on paper, and by the need to make the many aspirations attributed to Nero in contemporary accounts symptomatic of his eventual failure. For even Nero was once admired: his tutor Seneca, for example, initially praised him as a latter-day Apollo and his rule as a new golden age to rival that of Augustus (Sen. *Apocol.* 4). His activities would no doubt have angered people anyway, but perhaps not as overwhelmingly as they did once he was assassinated in AD 68 and it became clear to his successors that they should distance themselves from him. Suetonius and Cassius Dio are part of this distancing tradition: as soon as Nero is cast as the tyrant *par excellence* there is no going back. He must dance to the tune of earlier tyrannical types such as Herodotus's Xerxes, King of Persia. All emperors have had to play the part of Augustus up to a point (especially the Julio-Claudians, the legitimacy of whose rule depends upon drawing dynastic links to him, Julius Caesar, and Venus), in their honorific titles, the style of their portraiture, even, according to Suetonius, the chariots in which they ride in triumph. But Nero's aping is now viewed as fake instead of flattering – or rather as too self-conscious or professionally acted to be convincing ("What an artist the world is losing!" are the memorable words which Suetonius [*Nero* 49.1] attributes to him just before he dies). When he sings tragedies on stage, says Suetonius (*Nero* 21.3), his mask is often fashioned in his own features, while for up to 20 years after his death, pretenders pop up in the east of the empire assuming his identity. The Nero of such sources celebrates his fictiveness, is no more real, in a sense, than Trimalchio.

It is against this literary melee that the many references to Nero catalogued in Rose's appendix (1971), and indeed Tacitus's description of Petronius's suicide (see Hope's final paragraph, AT HOME WITH THE DEAD, p. 159), need to be read. Discovering, for example, that a gladiator by the name of Petraites (mentioned twice by Trimalchio at §52.3 and §71.6) is attested as active in Neronian Rome cannot satisfy, beyond suggesting a *terminus post quem* for the *Satyrica*'s authorship (cf. INTRODUCTION, p. 5). Petronius himself warns against being so literal when he has Trimalchio mix what is often read as an allusion to Nero's Golden House (§77) with the words "when Scaurus came he preferred staying here to anywhere else." While scholars hunt for a Neronian Scaurus to complete the picture, and find a couple of possibilities in the shape of centurion Maximus Scaurus (Tac. *Ann.* 15.50) and A. Umbricius Scaurus, a manufacturer of fish-sauce from Pompeii (Castrén 1975: 232, and Hales, FREEDMEN'S CRIBS, p. 170), the most glaring contender remains Marcus Aemilius Scaurus. Republican he may be, but still a celebrity whose house and theatre, which he built for his aedileship in 58 BC, were so lavish as to become a metonym for luxury (Plin. *HN* 34.36, 36.4–8, 36.48–50, 36.113–15). What does it mean for this legendary millionaire to spurn his own villa for that of a freedman? One answer is that it attempts to dissuade the reader from equating the *Cena*, or its influence, with any one period. The *Cena* is not a text about Nero's Rome so much as a text which alerts us to the artifice or ingredients involved in representing Roman imperial culture, especially perhaps Neronian culture. Any similarity between it and Suetonius's sources is not necessarily a matter of direct impact, but one bred of diffusion.

Beyond the *Cena*

I want now to examine briefly how the complex relationship outlined above, between the world of the *Satyrica* and the representation of Roman imperial culture, seeps from the *Cena* into the rest of Petronius's narrative. For, if Nero is Trimalchio, then he is also, elsewhere in the text, Eumolpus the poet, and perhaps also, almost, the ship-owner Lichas, and our narrator Encolpius. "If Rome was Troy reborn," writes Catherine Connors (1998: 87), "any time the Romans looked at or thought about Troy, they were at some level implicated in considerations of their own city's and eventually their emperor's relations to the distant epic past." The city which Petronius's Circe inhabits, Croton, may well be "a self-consciously fictional space," an "underworld" even (Rimell 2002: 153), but it is also "a very (if not, the most) ancient city, and once the first in Italy" (§116.2), and – as the destroyer in 510 BC of the city of Sybaris (more of a metonym for wealth and luxury than M. Aemilius Scaurus) – one which is often read as a measure of Rome's immorality. In other words, it is no less a version of Rome than Trimalchio's house, as mythology and history converge in a vortex.

Before reaching Croton, Encolpius, Giton, and the poet Eumolpus must escape (via) a shipwreck which is to kill the ship's owner Lichas (§99–115). It is an odd scene, made odder by the fact that earlier encounters with Lichas, alluded to in this episode, do not survive (see Verboven's very different treatment of the episode, A FUNNY THING HAPPENED ON MY WAY TO THE MARKET p. 133). By now, Lichas is furious with Encolpius, and consequently described by Eumolpus as both a "Hannibal" and a "Cyclops." He is from Tarentum (mod. Taranto) in southern Italy, a city with a long history of opposition to Rome. Lichas is, therefore, resolutely inscribed as an implacable enemy of Rome as well as a fabulous and flesh-eating monster, whose most famous incarnation is Homer's Polyphemus. Again, Roman history and Homeric epic collide as Encolpius develops his role as Odysseus (alluded to throughout but confirmed at §127.7 where Circe addresses him by the same epithet [*Polyaenus*] as is used at *Odyssey* 12.184; see further Morgan, PETRONIUS AND GREEK LITERATURE, p. 32, and Panayotakis, PETRONIUS AND THE ROMAN LITERARY TRADITION, p. 56).

"Imagine that we have entered the cave of the Cyclops" (*fingite nos antrum Cyclopis intrasse*) exclaims Eumolpus (§101.7). It is a strong image and one which Victoria Rimell (2002: 129) has argued transports the reader back to what she claims are prior attempts at a similar conjuring trick – to the hellishness of the *Cena* and the cave-like Trojan horse of Eumolpus's *Troiae Halosis* (§89 v. 7). It is also the case that Eumolpus's initial assessment of Lichas as a modest man with "several estates and some slaves in business" makes him potentially similar to Trimalchio. What Rimell does not mention, however, is that Philostratus, writing at the end of the second/beginning of the third century AD, twice uses the image of entering the Cyclops' cave as an indictment of the terror involved in being in the presence of the emperor. On the first occasion, a philosopher called Philolaus of Citium runs into Apollonius of Tyana on his way into Rome and warns him against proceeding further due to Nero's intolerance of philosophy: "Suppose you die after your arrest and Nero eats you raw before you have seen any of his acts? That will be a higher price than Odysseus paid when he visited the Cyclops" (*V A* 4.36.3). On the second occasion, Apollonius himself says of his impending imperial meeting, "and yet Odysseus went into Polyphemus's cave" (*V A* 7.28.3). This reference is clearly meant to remind the reader of the earlier encounter and to underline Domitian's reputation (emperor from AD 81 to 96) as a second or "bald" Nero, as Juvenal famously calls him in his fourth satire (Juv. 4.38).

Regardless of the chronology of the two texts, Philostratus's image highlights the potential of reading Lichas like an emperor. The vocabulary used for his captaincy and steering of the ship, *navigii dominus, qui regit* ("the owner of a ship, who steers") is suddenly made more meaningful. *Dominus* can mean "sovereign" or "despot" as well as "owner," and the verb *rego* can refer to ruling. Such a "ship of state" metaphor as it is called, in which the governance of a city is compared to the command of a naval vessel, is very common and deployed, for example, by Suetonius (*Nero* 46) to describe the failure of Nero. And it is not just the literary record that is relevant. On the ceiling of an artificial grotto in the midst of Nero's Golden House is an octagonal mosaic showing Odysseus handing wine to a seated Cyclops. It is one of several Odysseus and Polyphemus groups to have been found in imperial villas, including sculptures at the villas of Claudius at Baiae and Domitian at Castelgandolfo and, most famously, at a cave in Sperlonga, long attributed (on the basis of very little evidence) to Tiberius. With or without Sperlonga, Sorcha Carey must be right when she writes (2002: 56) that these concrete re-enactments, "marked space out as imperial."

Presumably these emperors hoped that any identification inspired by this artwork assimilated them to Odysseus (hence my suggestion at the start of this section that even Nero and Encolpius might be equated). But they were not so powerful that they could control the minds of their subjects. They were the hosts after all, "like" Trimalchio, "like" the Cyclops. Though channeled, readers ultimately stake their own claims, investing in what the emperors have declared cultural currency. In this way, the overlaps between the *Satyrica* and other sources, such as they are, pertain not to one emperor so much as the construction of *the* emperor (in Juvenal, Philostratus, and in his villa decoration, Nero is Domitian). One wonders how many parallels between Trimalchio and Domitian or Trimalchio and Commodus one would find, if the consensus were that the *Satyrica* were Flavian or Antonine? Reference-spotters have long noticed a possible parallel between Trimalchio's exhortation to his guests not to restrain from belching and farting (§47.4) and Suetonius's report that Claudius (emperor directly before Nero, from AD 41 to 54) had contemplated passing an edict pardoning anyone who broke wind at dinner (*Claud.* 32). One of the reasons scholars countenance this is that Nero's predecessor helps the case for a Neronian dating.

Even Eumolpus, who has been seen as a stooge for Nero's pompous poetics and whose verses on Troy and the civil war are often read in relation to Nero's own singing of the sack of Troy as his city burns beneath him (Suet. *Nero* 38.2) and to the literature of the Neronian writers Seneca and Lucan, speaks to the question of *imperium* ("power to command," "empire") more broadly. "The Roman conqueror now possessed the whole world, sea and land and the course of sun and moon. But he was not satisfied [*satiatus*]," exclaims Eumolpus (§119 vv. 1–3). He goes on to talk about "pleasure worn thin [*trita voluptas*] by everyday use." (v. 8) It is a while before we realize that he is referring to republican Rome, pre-Caesar and Pompey, but by then the link has been made not only to the Rome of the present but also – by virtue of the word *satiatus*, which is frequently found in the *Cena* and means "full of food" as well as "satisifed" – to our reading of the dinner. His words are about any conquering Roman and the conspicuous and corrupting consumption of empire. The past participle *trita*, from the verb *tero* meaning "to rub," is sometimes used in a sexual sense, body to body (hence its suitability with *voluptas*, "physical pleasure"), and sometimes in the sense of wearing out, or making trite by over-repetition. These connotations bind together to intensify the message of decadence.

Putting Nero in Context

Nero is only ever part of the equation – and not Nero the man so much as Nero the image – that was to become so crucial in defining the lowest limits of Roman *imperium*. This Nero is composed of, as much as he contributes to, a web of constructions that came to build a shifting but enduring impression of Rome and Roman power. In this way, he must be seen as integral rather than external to the representational field of which the *Satyrica* is part; not the answer to the text's problems, but a means of getting inside its construction. Once in there, there are no easy exits. Spotting an allusion can lead in several directions at once, adding rather than cutting a swathe through alternative meanings. Some routes will get us further than others, but all have the potential, even in disappointment, to expose the narrative's mechanisms. As they do so, they also remind us of what is peculiarly Roman about the text – in cultural as well as purely literary terms – by engaging with such institutions as imperial succession and the Roman triumph.

Further Reading

For the detailed arguments concerning the dating of the *Satyrica*, see the Introduction to this volume. Of the recent scholarship on Petronius, I would like to flag Connors (1998) as being particularly relevant to this chapter, as well as Roland Mayer's classic article (1982) with its emphasis on the recyclable nature of Latin literary culture. For Suetonius's *Lives of the Caesars*, a good starting point is the translation by Catharine Edwards (2000) with its useful notes and index, while Andrew Wallace-Hadrill's monograph (1983) offers what is still one of the clearest discussions. For a convenient edition of the *Life of Nero* in Latin, see Warmington (1999).

The extreme nature of Nero's reign lends itself to retelling and attempts at rationalization. Most sophisticated among recent studies is Miriam Griffin's *Nero: The End of a Dynasty* (1984). Also worthwhile – on the regime and the strategies adopted by those living under this regime – is Rudich (1993). Particularly formative for the above discussion of his image and reputation are Bartsch (1994), Elsner and Masters (1994), and Champlin (2003), as well as Henderson's difficult but rewarding article of (1989), revised for his later *Fighting for Rome* (1998). On the representation of imperial power more broadly, with an emphasis on the problems of repetition and succession, see Vout (2009), and on Roman imperial visual display, Elsner (1998). Explosive on the Roman triumph is Mary Beard (2007).

7

Freedmen in the *Satyrica*

Jean Andreau

Translated by Paul Dilley

Although Trimalchio's dinner, the *Cena Trimalchionis*, represents only about a third of the *Satyrica* (50 paragraphs out of 140 in total), to many it is what comes to mind when one thinks of Petronius's work. And when one thinks about this dinner it is the freedmen who stand out. But can the adventures of these freedmen, who are the characters of a novel, and what is more, of a *satura*, a Menippean satire, that is to say a story dependent upon other works and other literary genres, be taken as evidence for social history? This is clearly the central question, constantly posed and at the same time constantly frustrated: because there is no definitive solution. Such an author of fiction chooses the elements he needs as a function of his literary project, in the context of his period; he interprets them, he presents them according to his own ideas and preferences, and he can even distort them voluntarily – for example, in order to parody or caricature (Dupont 1977). But, among his literary objectives there is also the desire to make the reader feel a strong *effet de réel* ("sense of reality"): the author avails himself of settings taken from everyday life, and the freedmen form part of these settings. The descriptions of city life in the *Satyrica*, of tombs and funerary rites, of cuisine, of sexuality, and of ships and life at sea, bear witness to this very strong desire to transmit the impression of reality. Given these interpretations and this authorial creation, is the *Satyrica* much further removed from Roman life and society than the *Annals* of Tacitus or the *Letters* of Pliny the Younger, authors whose objectives and methods are, of course, completely different? To what extent does the *Satyrica* provide us with information about the freedmen of Italy in the first century AD? I do not believe that one can give a full and definitive answer to these two questions. It is certainly more valuable to consider the text as the expression of the author's views, and his representations, than as the reflection of a supposedly objective "reality." We must build up our interpretation gradually: analyze the details of the work, take account of literary genres and Greco-Roman traditions, and compare it to what we know from elsewhere. This, at least, is the method which I shall strive to follow here, in presenting a series of remarks about the freedmen in the *Satyrica*, but also about their relationships with other groups (slaves, freeborn plebeians, *equites* [those in the social rank below senator], and senators) and their place in the social hierarchy.

The first of these freedmen, the richest, and the one who dominates over all the others, is of course Trimalchio – Gaius Pompeius Trimalchio Maecenatianus. We can easily understand that Trimalchio has, by himself, been the object of specific studies, independent of other freedmen of the period, and that he is often considered as a social "type." Although we are dealing with a fictional individual, he is seen as the most illuminating example of the wealth of those freedmen in the first century AD who "made it" – but whose actual number is, however, impossible to quantify.

Among the diverse interpretations of Trimalchio's character, two in particular have been frequently discussed during the second half of the twentieth century. The first is that of Michael Rostovtzeff, which has been taken up, in its most important aspects, by John D'Arms. For Rostovtzeff, Trimalchio's character is a symbol of the economic expansion which Roman Italy had experienced and the changes in mentality which had come about alongside this expansion (Rostovtzeff 1957: 57–8 and 562 n. 18, and Andreau 1993). At the time when he became rich, his activity was above all commercial; conversely, at the end of his life, at the time of the *Cena*, he was living above all from the revenues of his estates and his lending activities. But these differences are not very important for Rostovtzeff, because, in general, he thinks that the important actors in the Roman economic prosperity of the time did not limit their activity to one sector of the economy alone. He thinks that they were dedicated above all to agriculture and commerce, while also indulging in financial operations, and that, to their way of thinking, agriculture and commerce went together. On the other hand, although Trimalchio was indeed a freedman, his legal status was not very important for the interpretation of Rostovtzeff. There were, he believes, those among the municipal elites and the *equites* whose activities and enrichment were entirely comparable to those of Trimalchio. Trimalchio was a typical representative of the "urban bourgeoisie," and this bourgeoisie was not constituted only of freedmen; without doubt, the freedmen were less respected than freeborn, but, from an economic point of view, they were not so very different.

Rostovtzeff's theses have been taken up, with some additional nuances, by D'Arms (1981: 97–120), although Paul Veyne strongly opposed them (1961; see also, to a certain extent, MacMullen 1974: 49–51 and 102–4). Veyne insists, to a much greater extent than Rostovtzeff, on the specific peculiarities of Trimalchio and the constraints of his legal status. Trimalchio, in his eyes, was not representative of all freedmen, because after the death of his patron he experienced a complete independence not enjoyed by the majority of freedmen. Furthermore, Veyne believes that in order to understand the mentality and life of freedmen, whether or not they are independent, it is necessary to situate oneself in a pre-industrial world, a world of strictly defined legal status, of personal connections, and of aristocratic values. The extraordinarily rich Trimalchio, who possessed immense estates in southern Italy, owed his wealth to the legacy of his former master, probably a senator. His commercial profits only increased this initial fortune – and it is to landed wealth that Trimalchio truly aspires. But this immersion in aristocratic values, if it is necessary, is not sufficient, because in the monarchies of modern Europe there was no class similar to freedmen. Certain freedmen enriched themselves, of course, but, in the eyes of Veyne, they are not *parvenus* ("[newly] arrived," that is, upstarts), because they will never "arrive." The bourgeoisie of the *ancien regime* (pre-revolutionary France) were able to become gentlemen; by contrast, argues Veyne, the freedmen of Rome were not true bourgeoisie, and if they lived in a world of gentlemen, they could never themselves become gentlemen. It is in this sense that Veyne writes that freedmen constituted an "aborted class," and that their destiny was "blocked," whether they were rich or poor: they themselves could become neither bourgeoisie nor gentlemen, and their children, if they had any, integrated themselves into the pre-existing social categories of Roman society.

Of the two interpretations discussed above, that of Veyne is in my opinion the more productive and closer to the truth, because it is more attentive to the different episodes in the life of Trimalchio and the connections which his life maintained with the legal and social background of the freedman's condition. That said, among the freedmen of the *Satyrica*, it is Trimalchio who most eludes social contextualization. Petronius situates the character, frames it, as it were, with vibrant details, in such a manner that the reader can associate him with a particular reality, known or experienced. But he makes a baroque personage of him, whose outrageousness and enormity explode every impression of social reality. The character of Trimalchio does not only caricature what is known about rich freedmen; he becomes a purely literary creation, inserted into a context deliberately presented as less fictional.

In the *Cena*, the master of the house is not the only freedman; far from it. At the beginning of the dinner Hermeros, who is sitting next to Encolpius, after speaking with him about Trimalchio and his wife Fortunata, makes two or three remarks about the other freedmen at the table, and provides some details about two of them, Gaius Pompeius Diogenes and Julius Proculus (§38). Later on, several guests join the conversation (from §41.10 to §46): Dama, Seleucus, Phileros, Ganymede, and Echion. In their intervention, Seleucus and Phileros mention an individual named Chrysanthus, whose funeral had taken place that same day (§42–3). The status of all these men is not indicated explicitly; but the surnames (*cognomina*) of several of them, such as Dama, Chrysanthus, Seleucus, or Phileros, are an easy clue for modern historians, because they were very frequently the names of slaves, of freedmen, or of their relatives (Solin 1971). The surname of Hermeros, who is *sevir augustalis* (official of the imperial cult) like Trimalchio and Habinnas, is similarly very indicative; moreover, Hermeros in no way hides his servile origins, and he is described as a co-freedman (*collibertus*) of Trimalchio, which implies that he had the same patron (§57–9.1). The interventions of Niceros (§61–2) and Plocamos (§64.2–5) follow.

Encolpius, Ascyltos, and Giton, three of the four principal characters in the extant novel, take part in the dinner, to which they have been invited (the fourth, Eumolpus, appears only after the end of the episode). In contrast to the names of the other guests, those of the four protagonists, although they are also Greek, are not the usual *cognomina* of freedmen, but rather conventional names recalling the traditions of mythology or literature (see also INTRODUCTION, p. 11). What is the legal status of these individuals? As Amy Richlin remarks in the present volume (SEX IN THE SATYRICA, p. 86), it is very difficult to respond to this question. As far as their place in society is concerned, the text contains confusing, even contradictory indications. At several points, Giton is considered a slave – for example, by Hermeros (§58.3–5); but later in the novel Eumolpus presents him, as well as Encolpius, as a young man, freeborn and honorable (*iuvenes ingenui, honesti*, §107.5). Evidently we cannot trust the words of Hermeros or Eumolpus – and it is not unlikely that Giton was a slave. For their part, Encolpius and Ascyltos were free (§81.6). But were they freeborn, or freedmen? We do not know. The tirade of Hermeros seems to suggest that Ascyltos was freeborn; the phrase at §81.4, on the contrary, seems to suggest that he was a freedman, while Encolpius was freeborn. But it is not clear. Were both freedmen? Or freeborn? Was Encolpius freeborn and Ascyltos a freedman? In any case, their individual names reveal nothing about their legal status. I wonder whether Petronius has intentionally refused to situate them socially, whereas he underlines the servile origins of the other guests at the *Cena*. The four protagonists would then be presented as living outside the framework of society (*extra legem uiuentibus*, §125.4), roaming from one city to another, and one milieu to another, without belonging to any. The dinner of Trimalchio is very much a place populated by freedmen. But one should not confuse it with the whole of the novel. We probably possess no more than one small part of the novel, which seems to have been very long, and we do not know what the lost parts contained (on the general problem, see Slater, READING THE SATYRICA). And, except for the dinner of Trimalchio, there is barely a mention of freedmen in the rest of the preserved text; unless I am mistaken, only one character in the later part of the text could be a freedman, the procurator Bargates, and even this is not certain (§96–7). The *Satyrica* in its entirety was probably not a work focused on freedmen. But, obviously, this does not lessen in any way the interest of the *Cena*.

It would be absurd to think that the *Cena* presents to the reader a complete range of the many types of freedmen, and of the problems which confronted them and their interests. That is not the point of this comic work of fiction. For example, there is no trace in the novel of imperial slaves and freedmen, that is to say, of those who worked in the administration or the exploitation and management of the properties of the emperor (agricultural and pastoral lands, mines and quarries, etc.). Neither do we see in the *Cena* freedmen working with or for their patron for a wage. In a general sense, there is scarcely any information about the relations between the freedmen present at the dinner and their former masters. There is some information about the relationships that they had with their masters while slaves, but not about those which they later maintained with their patrons. There is no mention, for example, of *obsequium* ("respectful behavior") or of *operae* ("assigned days of labor") or of specific norms which were imposed on freedmen in the areas of marriage or inheritance (Andreau 1993). I will return to this point.

Furthermore, all of the freedmen at the *Cena* take part in urban professions, that is to say occupations of commerce, manufacturing, and services. The fact that some of them possess land, or that they have bought it, because estates were the most obvious sign of social elevation, does not mean that they worked in this agricultural setting. Trimalchio, when he was a slave, was sent to the country by his master as a *vilicus* (overseer) and as a temporary punishment (§69.3), and, at the moment of the *Cena*, he possesses immense rural domains. But clearly he was not a man of the country; he was primarily an accountant, a financial administrator, before he dedicated himself to commerce. Echion, who is certainly much less rich, also possesses a property which he calls a *villa*, with buildings which he calls *casulae*. The word *villa* suggests a property of non-negligible extent, while *casulae*, small houses or farmhouses, lead one to imagine something more modest (§46.2). But, whatever his degree of wealth, he does not appear to be an *agricola* ("farmer"). He is presented as a *centonarius*, a word whose precise significance is a matter of debate. Either it is a civic rank, the *centonarii* having an official role in fighting fires (Ausbüttel 1982: 73–5, and Van Nijf 1997: 91), or else it is a profession, and we should understand a rag-and-bone man – that is to say, one who works with or deals in second-hand textiles (that is the solution chosen in this volume by Verboven, A FUNNY THING HAPPENED ON MY WAY TO THE MARKET, p. 130). The two interpretations are not mutually exclusive, and one can imagine that some of the *centonarii* engaged in fighting fires were at the same time engaged in the textile profession (Tran 2006: 10–11, 184, 517). In the case of Hermeros also, who paid to be freed (something considered entirely normal by many Latin authors), and who had been named *sevir* at no cost to himself, although he possessed lands which he bought himself (*glebulae*, §57.4–6), is it necessary to connect him to the world of the countryside? Nothing indicates that it is.

Julius Proculus was, for his part, in the business of funerary processions (*libitinarius*). Chrysanthus, who was buried on the day of Trimalchio's dinner party, was in commerce (*homo negotians*), unless it was a business of his brother (in §43.4, it is essentially impossible to determine who is engaged in the harvest and who in commerce). Ganymede's reflections on the price of bread appear to me to be typical of someone who lives in the city and does not have an agricultural income; the small houses (*casulae*) that he claims to possess are not necessarily in the country, and could very well be located in the city (§44). Finally, Echion mentions a certain Phileros, who was a lawyer (*causidicus*); and he never envisages directing his young slave Primigenius towards agriculture or animal husbandry. The professions which he wishes for him are all urban: hairdresser (*tonstrinum*), public crier (*praeco*), or advocate (§46, especially §46.7–8).

John Bodel has quite rightly remarked that Petronius does not leave any prospects to the freedmen whom he portrays: he presents them as without a future (Bodel 1994; see also Kleijwegt 1998). They associate almost solely with other freedmen (even if Agamemnon and the three main characters of the novel are invited by Trimalchio). And they do not have children capable of achieving a better social situation. Trimalchio, the richest and the most remarkable of them, is himself condemned to live in this closed world, without hope that his descendants might be able to achieve a better condition. This observation confirms that the *Satyrica* does not provide a complete panorama of the social group of the freedmen. In the "reality" of the empire, it was not so – contrast the senator cited by Tacitus who states that very many *equites* and the majority of senators were descended from freedmen (*Annales* 13.27.1–2)! A single phrase in the novel, which Trimalchio reports the perfumer (*unguentarius*) Agatho to have uttered, evokes this reality: "I advise you not to let your family perish" (§74.15). With these words, Petronius opens a window on a strong tendency for social climbing which the rest of the *Cena* seems to deny.

Let us return to the relationships which these freedmen maintain with their patrons. Trimalchio falls into the category of an independent freedman, because his former master is dead, and he died without an heir. But in the *Satyrica* there is practically no mention of the other freedmen's former masters. Were they all independent? Since they are, on two occasions, denoted as co-freedmen (*colliberti*, §38.6 and §59.1), we can ask whether they did not all have the same patron, the Gaius Pompeius who freed Trimalchio and bequeathed his inheritance to him. There is certainly at least one exception, Julius Proculus (§38.11–16), and it is true that we only know of one who carries the *nomen gentilicium* (family name) Pompeius – Diogenes (§38.7–10). But the very fact that the *nomen gentilicium* is not indicated is perhaps revealing: if all, or almost all, were possessed of the same name, it would not be necessary to mention it. If this hypothesis is correct, it modifies the idea of the dinner party that we can construct. Are we in fact concerned not with the social framework of the urban freedmen of the city in question (Puteoli?), but more specifically with a limited number of freedmen of a single, very rich patron? Trimalchio would have become the head of the pack, the leader, of these freedmen, after the death of the patron and his wife. If we find ourselves in the presence of people who know one another very well and are frequent associates this would, then, not only be because it is a question of freedmen, who are not in a position to associate with the freeborn (Veyne 1961), it would also be because those invited to Trimalchio's dinner party formed a single and unique *familia* – consisting of freedmen of the deceased Gaius Pompeius and of their own freedmen, slaves, and clients.

Such a hypothesis would perhaps contribute to explaining the manner in which the relationships between the freedmen and their slaves are presented in the *Cena*. If the *Satyrica* clearly does not provide a complete vision of the condition of slaves, one could argue, without paradox, that the slaves have more of a presence here than the freedmen (and, certainly, than the freeborn). Not only are slaves constantly mentioned in the course of the *Cena*, but they are also pervasive in the rest of the novel, and we encounter frequent allusions to slavery. There is mention of a slave workshop and fugitive slaves (§95.2, §96.5, §97.10, §105.11, and §107.4). We see a *servus publicus* ("public slave"), who accompanies the public crier, while Encolpius contemplates a disguise as black-skinned Ethiopian slaves (§97.1 and §102.13). Chrysis underlines the taste of an elite woman for slaves and nobodies (§126.1–11). During the course of the storm, faithful slaves save Tryphaena (§114.7). There are many more examples. Only one servant is not a slave, that is the barber who accompanies Eumolpus; his condition as a free wage-earner (*mercennarius*) is underlined in several places (§94.12–15, §99.6, §103.1 and §108.4).

Despite some occasionally spectacular incidents, the relations between the slaves and their masters are good or even very good, especially over the course of Trimalchio's dinner party (Canali 1987). In several instances, the master of the house demonstrates his understanding and indulgence for his slaves: for example, he delivers an emphatic eulogy of his cook (§70.1–7). When a slave commits an error, he allows himself to be persuaded not to punish him, which surprises some of the guests. And above all, he includes them in his jokes and entertainments. He even plays with their freedom, for example, when he frees the one named Dionysos in order to be able to say that he has freed the god Liber (§41.6–8), or when he frees the slave who has wronged him (or who, probably, has pretended to wrong him; §54). The most vivid episode is clearly that of the pig which appears not to have been gutted (§49). Even here, Trimalchio plays with his slave, the cook, and with the punishments that he could inflict on him. Furthermore, it is necessary to draw attention to the passages in which one of the guests, for example, Echion, speaks of his affection for his *deliciae* ("favorite"), for the closest of his *pueri* ("boys"). For Luca Canali, in the *Satyrica* the free and the slaves live in a sort of symbiosis and show themselves to be very much in collusion with one another. One could respond to Canali that it is a matter of trusted slaves, very close to their masters and, whether they wish it or not, often linked to them by sexual relationships. The situation would clearly be very different if we were being shown agricultural slaves or miners. Nevertheless, what the secretary (*actuarius*) recites about the estate that Trimalchio possesses at Cumae shows that things are a little more complicated. Certainly, the slave Mithridates was crucified, and for a reason whose extreme gravity could probably be doubted; and an *atriensis* ("door-keeper") was relegated to Baiae (§53.3 and 53.10). But the report also shows that there existed on these estates aediles who published edicts, marital unions susceptible to later dissolution, tribunals presided over by servants of the bedroom (*cubicularii*), and even wills by which some slaves would be able to disinherit their master Trimalchio (§53). We are clearly swimming in the full flood of fiction. It is all the same very strange that Trimalchio, who appeared so arbitrary and so focused on himself and his merest whim, has instituted or maintained such a non-legal, "juridical" panoply, in such a manner as to place his agricultural slaves in a kind of city within the estate. Pliny the Younger explains how he organized a system of wills for his slaves that was not dissimilar (Pliny, *Epistulae* 8.16); but Pliny clearly did not go as far as Trimalchio down this path, not by a long way.

For a modern reader, it is surprising that freedmen who have an elevated idea of themselves, like Trimalchio or Echion, do not hesitate to present themselves as former slaves and to talk about their servile past, a fact which in no way prevents them from being themselves owners of slaves and patrons of former slaves whom they have freed. Yet these attitudes, which one could easily take as an exaggeration in line with the comic and satirical character of the work, are also found on a number of funerary inscriptions – for example, on that of Marcus Sutorius Pamphilus, who died at Rome at the beginning of the empire, interred with his mother, his wife (a *colliberta*), his *deliciae* (a slave, who is probably his biological daughter), a co-freedman, and five of his freedmen and freedwomen (*CIL* 6.1892; Tran 2006: 468–70).

An historical parallel may be useful at this point: Pliny the Younger recounts the assassination of the senator Larcius Macedo, which took place around the year AD 100. A group of slaves, who were living with him in his villa at Formiae, attacked him when he was at the baths. They beat him and left him for dead on the scalding floor of his private baths; he subsequently regained consciousness, but died several days later (Plin. *Ep.* 3.14). Pliny considered Macedo to be an arrogant and cruel master, whereas he prided himself on being more humane (which did not prevent him from fearing such explosions of anger from slaves on his own account). He observes that Larcius Macedo was the son of a freedman, and that this did not stop him from being cruel: "He had too far forgotten that his father had been a slave – unless he remembered too well" (Plin. *Ep.* 3.14). Trimalchio and his co-freedmen did not conduct themselves at all like Larcius Macedo; they had not forgotten that they had been slaves, and at the same time this memory did not lead them to acts of cruelty, or at least not to such an extent. Is this because they were freedmen, rather than the sons of freedmen? Or because they were not senators? Or because they are characters in a novel?

Neither Agamemnon nor Encolpius nor Ascyltos nor Eumolpus represent Petronius; none of them is the spokesman of the author. Moreover, one of the characteristics of the *Satyrica* is that the author does not appear, that he is absent, concealed, as several philologists and historians have recently noted (Labate 1995a; Conte 1996a). Neither does it seem that these main characters represent the elite, despite what is sometimes asserted. They are instead transgressive characters, whose social context remains undefined. In my opinion, the elite are just as absent as the author. When Habinnas appears Encolpius takes him for a praetor, but Agamemnon corrects him (§65.1–7). The error of Encolpius and the words of Agamemnon show that neither Encolpius nor Habinnas are members of the elite. Eumolpus is the poet *par excellence*, and he represents a lettered culture which impresses Trimalchio, Hermeros, Echion, and the others but at the same time exasperates them, especially if *scholastici* ("rhetoricians," "learned men") like him flaunt their education (§56–8; Labate 1995a and 1995b). The terms which evoke the social elite, the true elite, are *eques* and the corresponding adjective, *equestris*. These terms are attested four times in the novel (§14.2, §57.4, §92.10, §126.10). The poem which Ascyltos recites is very revealing in this regard: even the *eques* who sits as judge is powerless against money (§14.2). And when Hermeros wants to silence Ascyltos's derision, he asks him, "*eques Romanus es?*" ("Are you a Roman *eques*?"). His point is that Ascyltos is not of a sufficiently high social rank to mock those of humble rank and those who have been slaves (§57.4). Even if you do not personally know the city's magistrates and notables, you name them and speak of them familiarly (§45); and you do not hesitate to criticize them, especially if they are aediles, and therefore charged with controlling the millers/bakers (§44.3–13). By contrast, the *equites*, who are not named, but to whom general allusions are made, are themselves emblematic of high society.

It is true that Encolpius and Ascyltos mock Trimalchio and his dinner party at several points, and that this attitude marks the distance between their own culture and the tastes and manners of the master of the house and his guests. But they do not always mock them, and they are entirely in agreement with Trimalchio on certain ideas, which are considered characteristic of the mentality of the freedmen, for example, on the power of money. It is common to emphasize those words which show that, for the freedmen, it is money alone that counts. But the poem of Ascyltos, which I mentioned above, speaks of nothing else; and the importance of money is reaffirmed in the last part of the text, when Encolpius has killed the goose and rectifies his wrongdoing by handing over two pieces of gold (§137.1–9). The superiority of money in comparison to law and culture is again proclaimed in this passage, and Encolpius and Oenothea do not appear to be in disagreement with the idea. It is not impossible that the *Cena* is a satire on the entirety of Roman life at the time, and not only on the world of freedmen.

Interpreting the *Satyrica* is extremely complex and cannot be based on only one strategy of reading. Freedmen occupy a central role in the dinner of Trimalchio, and it is true that one of the goals of the text is a satire on freedmen. But it is not possible to reduce either the entire novel or even the episode of the *Cena* to this. The *Satyrica*'s freedmen and slaves resemble, in more than one respect, those whom we find mentioned in other documents of the period, but it is not in any sense a work of "realism." It is a work of fiction, and multiple threads are entangled in this complex web.

Further Reading

There is an abundant bibliography on Trimalchio and the other freedmen of the *Satyrica*. In addition to the titles cited in this chapter, one might consult, for example, Bodel (1984) and (1989), Boyce (1991), Van der Paardt (1996), and Highet (1998: 119–34). To better understand their situation it is also necessary to study emancipation and freedmen generally, for which see Duff (1928), Treggiari (1969), Andreau (1993), and López Barja de Quiroga (1995). In addition, discussion of freedmen inevitably leads to discussion of slavery and slaves, to which are dedicated, for example, Buckland (1908), Bradley (1987), Thébert (1993), and Bradley (1994). On the slaves and freedmen of the emperor, some of whom managed his property, notably his estates, one should consult Weaver (1972). Finally, it is interesting to situate the commercial activities of Trimalchio in what is known about commerce in central and southern Italy in the first century AD; on this subject, see in particular D'Arms and Kopff (1980), as well as Morley (2007a), where one will find a complementary bibliography, and Verboven, A FUNNY THING HAPPENED ON MY WAY TO THE MARKET.

8

A Funny Thing Happened on My Way to the Market

Reading Petronius to Write Economic History

Koenraad Verboven

Petronius's *Satyrica* is a goldmine of data on occupations, sales, loans, investments, and all things we now think of as constituting "the economy." No work in Latin literature is so rich in information on the living economy of the first century AD as Petronius's *Satyrica*. Yet as a narrative source few are as complex. The story is fiction, a mixture of satire and slapstick comedy. Although Petronius's characters and situations are recognizably rooted in reality they are uniquely individual and clad in deforming stereotypes. If we want to use the *Satyrica* as a historical source on the Roman economy, it has to be interpreted with meticulous care. The "data" need to be scrutinized, filtered, and put in perspective before they can be accepted as "evidence." The effort can be strenuous sometimes, but is always rewarding. However distorted Petronius's scenes and characters are, they infuse life and color into the most dreary facts and figures.

A Rogues' Market and Commodity Culture

The episode of the stolen cloak is a good example to start with (§12–15). Encolpius and Ascyltos go to a street market to sell a precious cloak they stole in a previous (lost) episode. Here they encounter a peasant and a woman who come to sell a ragged tunic. Ascyltos recognizes it as his own, previously lost by Encolpius, in the hem of which he had hidden a number of gold pieces. Encolpius's idea of threatening the peasant with a lawsuit should he refuse to give back the tunic is rejected by Ascyltos. They are strangers in the town, no one would believe them. The courts are so corrupt that no judge would favor them without a bribe. So they decide instead to sell their precious cloak cheaply and buy back the old tunic. But when the peasant's wife inspects the cloak, she cries out, "Thieves!" Promptly Ascyltos and Encolpius grab the tunic and accuse the peasant of stealing their shirt. The market dealers gather round laughing. Some night guards (*nocturni*) are called in who insist that the matter be brought to court and the disputed items be deposited in their care. One of the dealers quickly volunteers as trustee. Predictably, neither party wants a lawsuit and the episode ends with the peasant throwing the ragged shirt in Ascyltos's face, grabbing the precious cloak, and both running off as fast as they can.

On the surface, the episode paints a bleak picture of how Roman law affected – or failed to affect – market practices. The story appears to confirm the lack of effective legal institutions, one of the prime structural conditions for economic development (Frier and Kehoe 2007). Closer analysis suggests a different reading. Ascyltos's assertion that they were strangers whom no one would believe makes sense in a world without passports or ID, but this reflects the limitations of the justice system rather than its defects. Although in theory Roman trials had to be initiated by the plaintiff (Johnston 1999: 112–32; Robinson 1997: 79–101), Ascyltos and the peasant are practically forced into litigation against their wishes.

The legal system reflected and enforced the overwhelming importance of social status in Roman society. Complaints by lower-class persons (*humiliores*) against aristocrats (*honestiores*) had little chance unless they were backed up by powerful patrons. Testimonies in court by aristocrats carried considerably more weight than those made by lower-class witnesses (Garnsey 1970). But this is not what Ascyltos is complaining about. His complaint relates to ordinary corruption. We have no way of measuring the degree of corruption in Roman courts. We may surmise that it was more common than in modern Western countries, but there is no reason to believe that it was as bad as Ascyltos suggests.

We have a fairly large number of writing tablets relating to legal proceedings preserved in Pompeii and Herculaneum (some drawn up in Puteoli (mod. Pozzuoli), where the episode of the stolen cloak may be situated; we shall come back to these tablets later on). Together with some inscriptions (particularly municipal charters, like the *lex Irnitana*), these tablets are direct witnesses of legal practice on a local level. Contrary to Petronius's novel they document an apparently effective justice system that allowed litigants flexible and reliable remedies (Camodeca 1999; Gonzales 1986; Rodger 1990).

Local courts were the responsibility of annually elected local magistrates. Litigation usually started with both parties accepting a *vadimonium* – a formal pledge that they would appear on an agreed date before the judicial magistrate. Sequestration of disputed objects, as in Petronius's story, was possible, but not obligatory in the case of a *rei vindicatio*, the procedure for restitution of property. If the defendant failed to appear he risked forfeiting his property to the plaintiff. If he duly appeared and denied the accusation, the magistrate consulted both parties on the terms of the case and the appointment of a judge. This two-step system, combining elected politicians, designated judges, and public hearings, limited the scope for corruption in ordinary trials. Roman cities were mostly small communities that loved gossip and rumor. The fact that judicial magistrates were elected politician-aristocrats, whose status (*dignitas*) depended on their reputation presumably helped to keep excesses in check (see Johnston 1999: 112–32; Robinson 1997: 79–120).

That being said, curiously absent from the cloak scene are the magistrates responsible for market affairs, the aediles. Their absence is well in line with the odd timing of the market (at dusk) and the doubtful nature and origins of the articles for sale. This is no ordinary market. It is a rogues' market in a rakes' story.

This rogues' market, however, is not an isolated oddity in the story. The material world in Petronius's novel is profoundly determined by market exchanges. The story is set in a commodity culture in which everything – goods and services – is produced, traded, bought, and sold for money: vegetables sold by an old woman on a street corner (§7.1), knives of Noric iron (§70.3), whores and rooms rented by the hour (§8), meals and lodgings (§81–2, §92, §95–6), bread (§44), houses and landed estates (§44.15, §53), books (§46.7), haircuts and shaves (§94, §103), funerals (§38.14), etc. Even the value of gifts is routinely expressed in money (§53).

Is Petronius depicting social reality – in his own distorted way – and whose social reality is it? (cf. the discussion INTRODUCTION, p. 9.) The *Satyrica* is not unique in the prominent role it attributes to commodities. Fergus Millar notes a similar picture underlying Apuleius's *Golden Ass* (Millar 1981: 72). Anyone reading Martial or Juvenal is likely to be struck by the variety of goods and services that could be bought and sold. Scholars increasingly interpret commodity consumption as a typical feature of the economy of the early principate. Greg Woolf describes commoditization and mass consumption as archaeologically detectable "markers" for Romanization in Gaul (Woolf 1998: 169–205; cf. Morley 2007a: 52–4; Wilson 2008). Bryan Ward-Perkins interprets the disappearance of mass-produced, good quality consumption articles as signifying the "disappearance of comfort" and the decline of Roman civilization (Ward-Perkins 2005: 87–120).

This "modernizing" view of the Roman economy is strongly opposed to the "old orthodoxy" of the 1970s and 1980s, when leading scholars under the influence of Moses Finley emphasized the primitiveness and non-market character of ancient economies (cf. Scheidel and von Reden 2002). In many ways these new views are a welcome correction to the often holistic views of what is called the primitivist school. We should beware, however, of the anachronism involved in describing Roman society as just a "commodity culture." The existence of commodity markets is not enough to allow us to conclude that the Roman economy was a market economy. Even if commoditization was a profound characteristic of urban life, only a minority (20 percent?) of Romans lived in cities. Weekly trips to sell vegetables on the urban market hardly suffice to turn a peasant into a market-oriented, rural entrepreneur. The political elite mostly consisted of large landowners whose dependence on markets was relatively limited. Gift-exchange and political redistribution (mainly through the provision of grain for the city of Rome – the *annona* – and army supplies) remained important alternatives to market exchange. Autoconsumption by peasants and large households always remained an important ingredient of the ancient economy (Meickle 2002: 243; Morley 2007b; Saller 1982; Verboven 2002; Whittaker 1985).

These realities, however, are largely absent from the *Satyrica*, as if Petronius consciously cut them out of the picture. Martial or Juvenal differ substantially from Petronius in this respect. In their works, patronage and (instrumental) friendship are central themes (Cloud 1989; Saller 1983). Gift-exchange and instrumental friendship in the *Satyrica* are prominent only as instruments of manipulation and deceit in the Croton chapters (§116–41), where the practice of inheritance hunting plays a central role (on which see also Hope, AT HOME WITH THE DEAD p. 143).

The phenomenon of elite self-sufficiency appears to be illustrated by Trimalchio's obsession with producing everything needed for his extravagant dinner parties on his own estates. His determination, however, is a grotesque deformation of what Paul Veyne calls the favorite myth of antiquity: αὐτάρκεια (*autarkeia*), an existence fixed on the satisfaction of one's natural needs (Veyne 1979: 268–9; cf. Veyne 1961: 237; Finley 1999:109–10). Whereas autarky was traditionally associated with moderation, simplicity, and the avoidance of luxury, Trimalchio's autarky aims for excess as his natural way of life. Exotic luxury items were typically goods that even the greatest landowner had to buy. The epitome of such items in Petronius's time were articles imported from Arabia and the Far East. Pliny the Elder, writing a decade or less after Petronius, claims that the value of these imports totaled 100 million sesterces (*HN* 12.84). Yet Trimalchio's exotic luxuries were produced on his own estates. He ordered Indian mushroom spores rather than mushrooms and his pepper was home grown (§38.1–4).

Go to School and Get a Good Job

The social corollary of commoditization is professionalization. The *Satyrica* abounds with "working-class" characters whose social identity is defined by their profession. Almost all are freedmen, with the notable exception of Eumolpus's servant Corax, a freeborn barber who hired himself out as a servant (*mercennarius*, §103.1, §117.11).

The link between freedmen and economic occupations is confirmed in inscriptions and monuments. Up to 78 percent of funerary inscriptions in Rome that mention the deceased's profession are set up in commemoration of slaves or freedmen (Joshel 1992: 47). This is not a faithful reflection of social reality but betrays the need to compensate for social discrimination (see also Hope, AT HOME WITH THE DEAD, p. 153). Professional success was the only way for most freedmen to achieve social standing. Accordingly, they were proud of their expertise and talent and felt respect for hardworking professionals (Joshel 1992: 76–91; Petersen 2006: 114–16).

The occupations practiced by slaves and freedmen were infinitely varied. There was virtually no profession that was not practiced by slaves. Inevitably, this often required a high degree of schooling and training. The freedmen in the *Satyrica* value education a lot, but not the idle cultural learning of the elite (although they appreciate the status attached to that). They prefer a practical education that teaches them profitable skills and crafts.

The fresco picturing Trimalchio's life shows Minerva – goddess of learning and crafts – as his childhood patroness (§29.3). He was bought on the slave market as a young boy and trained in calculation as an accountant (*ratiocinator*). Eventually he was made *dispensator*, the chief steward of his master's patrimony, which was the highest position a slave could achieve in a household. Trimalchio's own *dispensator*, Cinnamus, illustrates the wealth and power these men wielded (§30).

Primigenius, the "pet boy" of Echion the ragman (*centonarius*; cf. Andreau, FREEDMEN IN THE SATYRICA, p. 119, for an alternative interpretation of the term), attended the classes of a public teacher and was given extra lessons at home by another tutor. Echion bought him some books on law, hoping that he would get the taste and become a lawyer, because "there is a lot of money in that" and it would help him manage his master's household and business (cf. Juv. 14.191–4). If the boy was resistant, Echion was determined to make him learn a trade; that of a barber perhaps, or an auctioneer, or a barrister, for "learning is a treasure and a trade [*artificium*] never dies" (§46.3–8).

Exaggerated as Petronius's characters may be, they exemplify two basic realities: that training and schooling could make the difference between poverty and comfort; and that masters were not opposed to educating their slaves. The latter is not surprising, because it was a necessary precondition for entrusting specialized tasks to slaves and "upgraded" their market value. Cato the Elder made a business of training slaves to sell them for a profit (Plut. *Cat. Mai.* 21.6; Booth 1979; Forbes 1955).

Of course, not all skills could be learned at school. Hard work and a business instinct could be equally important. Chrysanthus started from scratch but died leaving a fortune in cash, which he made as a businessman in wine. Presumably he grew rich buying grapes on the vine, a well-attested, lucrative, but risky practice (§42–3; cf. Erdkamp 2005: 120–34). Pliny the Younger describes how the *negotiatores* ("business men") who had bought up his vintage ran into financial straits when the harvest failed and they found they had bid too much (*Ep.* 8.2.1).

Contrary to what Echion (§46) and Hermeros (§58) suggest, intellectual skills too could be "commercialized." Encolpius and Ascyltos had been making a living from their *scientia litteris* (learning) (§10.4–7), although their schooling and "expertise" was probably more basic than those of the rhetorician Agamemnon or the poet Eumolpus. Petronius paints a less than commendable picture of these "professional" intellectuals. Their talent is mediocre, their high-flown words and ideals are betrayed by their dubious morals, and they flock like parasites around the wealthy. But inscriptions and literary texts confirm that teachers, orators, and poets could and did sell their services, and sometimes even gained great wealth through it

(Bonner 1977: 146–62). The famous grammarian Q. Remmius Palaemon, who taught Quintilian and Persius, was first employed in his master's textile workshop. He learned his letters together with his master's son when he was appointed to accompany him to school. After Palaemon was freed he gained recognition as one of the best *grammatici* of his time, despite his arrogance and depravity. Suetonius claims that he made 400,000 sesterces a year from his school, while he also invested in textile workshops and expert viticulture (*Gram.* 23).

An alternative path, much preferred by *literati*, however, was patronage. Literary patronage is prominent in the works of authors like Martial, Juvenal, Horace, and others, but it is conspicuously absent in the *Satyrica*. This is well in line with the general absence of the aristocracy in the novel (see Andreau, FREEDMEN IN THE *SATYRICA*, p. 123, on this). The talent of Petronius's characters was too mediocre to be courted by elite patrons, even though it sufficed to earn them an invitation to Trimalchio's party and duly impressed the barbarous Bargates (§95–6). Eumolpus explains his shabby appearance by saying that he was a man of letters of the kind that "the rich were accustomed to hate" (§83.7), although he had (so we are told) once accompanied a quaestor to Asia – *stipendio eductus*, "led on by a salary" (§85.1) – a privilege reflecting perhaps Catullus's journey to Bithynia in the retinue of its governor C. Memmius in 57 BC (Catull. 10 and 28).

Petronius's would-be intellectuals remain outsiders to the world of the aristocracy, but this does not prevent them from looking down upon Trimalchio's lot. Echion, who notices this, is not impressed. Agamemnon and his companions may be culturally educated, but economically they are a poor bunch. The "professor" should come to Echion's *villa* some time to admire the "little property." They could eat some fresh country produce and Agamemnon could meet Echion's *deliciae* ("darling") whose prosperous future is assured (§46, compare also Hermeros's invective at §57–8).

The scene is a beautiful example of status dissonance, a typical phenom-enon of complex stratified societies such as the Roman, where social position is determined by various criteria: birth, gender, ethnicity, wealth, education, talent, life-style, etc. (Hopkins 1974: 105–6; Verboven 2007: 860–1). Ideally, high social rank depends on and implies the conjunction of different criteria. Status dissonance occurs when persons of lower rank become upwardly mobile and acquire some positive criteria attached to high social rank, but continue to lack others. Thus, Trimalchio's set rank high on the wealth criterion, but low on the cultural (and birth) criterion. Agamemnon's group rank (relatively!) high on the cultural criterion, but low on the wealth (and birth) criterion. While the former compensate for their lack of education by overemphasizing their wealth, Agamemnon compensates for his poverty by overemphasizing his education and rhetorical skill. He does so discretely at the dinner party, but quite emphatically in his discussion with Encolpius on the decay of eloquence and the loss of literary taste (§3–5). Both groups, however, lack the composure of true *homines liberales* ("men born to freedom") – that ill-defined quality that distinguishes a respectable man from an upstart and which derives from the seemingly natural and unconstrained manners of one who has assimilated all relevant status criteria as an inseparable part of his social identity.

Big Business

In peacetime truly grand fortunes were made primarily in maritime trade. The exceptional profitability of commerce was generally acknowledged (Paterson 1998). Lucilius spontaneously thinks of maritime trade when his friend Seneca suggests that he knows a fast way for him to become rich (Sen. *Ep.* 119.5; cf. Cic. *Tusc.* 5.86; *Fin.* 5.91; Juv. 14.192–209). Trimalchio's decision to sell his master's estate and go into business mirrors the protagonist of Plautus's *Mercator* (*The Merchant*) who sold his father's farm to buy a ship and gathered a fortune in trade (*Merc.* 64–74).

Roman aristocrats considered commerce unworthy and base (Joshel 1992: 63–9; Morley 2007a: 82–5). The legal ban on senators owning merchant ships, which dated back to the late third century BC, remained in force until late antiquity (Livy 21.63.3–4; *Digest* 50.5.3; *Pauli Sententiae* (Leiden) 7–11). Livy claims the law was voted through because profit-making was deemed unworthy (*indecorus*) for senators. A background in business did not legally exclude a person from becoming a municipal council member, but it was considered *inhonestum*, "shameful" (*Dig.* 50.2.12). Cicero asserted that it was not by nature that the Carthaginians were treacherous, but because they were a trading nation (Cic. *Leg. agr.* 2.95).

Of course, these views are not shared by Trimalchio, who takes great pride in the fortitude he displayed in the face of his initial bad luck (§76.4–5). Lichas too is described as a *homo verecundissimus* ("a most moderate man" [§101.4]). Monuments and inscriptions commemorating businessmen confirm these positive self-images, but reflections of respectability enjoyed by wealthy merchants are found also in elite authors. Cicero describes them as "wealthy and honorable men" (*Verr.* 5.154). He is especially lenient towards wholesale traders who withdraw from trade to become large landowners (*Off.* 1.150–1), as Trimalchio eventually did, although he retained some interests in seaborne trade (§39.8). Lichas from Tarentum (mod. Taranto) also invested part of his profits in landed estates, while he continued to run his trading house (*familia negotiatorum*) and to sail and conduct his business personally (§101.4).

However, maritime trade was also dangerous (Morley 2007a: 29–30). Like Trimalchio's first five ships on their maiden voyage, Lichas's ship, despite its robustness, was wrecked in a storm and its owner drowned (§114). Stories of shipwrecks are common in the ancient sources. The description of the misadventure and wreckage of the ship which brought St Paul to Italy in Acts 27 is a well-known and elaborate example (cf. also Synesius of Cyrene, *Epistulae* 5). In AD 62 a storm destroyed 200 ships in the port at Ostia (Tac. *Ann.* 15.18.3).

The dangers involved in maritime commerce constituted an additional reason why elite authors were apprehensive. As in most agricultural societies, Roman aristocrats were predominantly risk-averse in their economic strategies. "It is true that it is sometimes better to seek wealth through trading, if only it would not be so dangerous" (Cato, *Agr.* praef. 1; Kehoe 1997 and 2007: 549). Merchants are censured for their audacity and irresponsibility in the face of danger, driven by avarice (Cic. *Fam.* 16.9.4; Juv. 14.256–302; Hor. *Carm.* 3.24.35–44; 29.58–64; *Sat.* 1.4.29–32). Trimalchio, on the other hand, presents his way of dealing with risk as strength of character and, again, his self-admiration is not without parallels in elite opinions. Although "bent on danger and calamity," the merchant is "strenuous and industrious," according to the elder Cato (Cato, *Agr.* praef. 3; cf. Cic. *Leg. Man.* 18).

This curious mixture of wealth and respectability, moral impropriety and admiration, betrays the apprehension felt by Roman elites and their protégés for the potentially disruptive effects of trade on social order. Independent freedmen are well attested, and talented and lucky traders had good prospects for improving their social status (Garnsey 1981; Verboven 2007). Eumolpus laments that merchants, soldiers, flatterers, and adulterers gathered wealth, while men of genius were never rich (§83.10). Similarly scornful comparisons are found in Columella (*Rust.* praef. 7–10), Martial (1.66), Juvenal (14.193–5), and many others. The complaint is illustrative of the social criticism that growing trade provoked. Their servile background may have prevented upstarts like Trimalchio from ever truly arriving

(Veyne 1961; see also Andreau, FREEDMEN IN THE SATYRICA), but they were unmistakably knocking at the door for their children to pass.

Nevertheless, we should not be duped. Although aristocrats were rarely personally active as traders, they did invest through their slaves and freedmen, and in this way controlled more of ancient commerce than they cared to admit (D'Arms 1981; Pleket 1983). The silence of the *Satyrica* in this respect is again illustrative of Petronius's non-elite focus.

The late republic and early empire witnessed an unprecedented increase in commerce, which in the eyes of many was bound up with the essence of the empire itself (Paterson 1998). The Mediterranean is littered with ancient shipwrecks that testify to the flourishing of maritime trade. The peak which this reached in the period between the first century BC and the second century AD would not be matched again until the sixteenth century (Morley 2007b: 571–3). The Roman Empire experienced a moderate growth over the first two centuries AD that may have doubled or tripled GNP (Saller 2002; Kehoe 2007: 543–50; Lo Cascio 2007: 619–20).

Strictly speaking, however, shipwrecks and archaeological distribution maps document movement of goods, not trade. The question of what drove these movements has been hotly debated. Dick Whittaker argues that market demands were not a decisive factor. What prevailed in his view were political motives (supplying food to the populace and the army) and the social preoccupations of large absentee landowners, who ordered the produce of their estates to be brought "home" to supply their extended families (including slaves) and to enable them to indulge in gift-exchange and public benefactions. The backbone of Roman commerce would therefore have been a command and moral economy (Whittaker 1985). This view has been sharply criticized (Paterson 1998) and has now given way to a much more varied model, relying heavily on New Institutional Economics, in which market forces, political interventions, and gift-exchange are intertwined (Bang, Ikeguchi, and Ziche 2006; Scheidel, Morris, and Saller 2007).

The *Satyrica*, however, shows few signs of a command or moral economy. Although Trimalchio aims to be self-sufficient and poses as a public benefactor, Petronius clearly does not intend us to believe that his fantastic wealth was used primarily to feed and clothe his *familia* ("household") or to be distributed to his fellow citizens. Neither is there any reason to suppose that when he was still a merchant Trimalchio sold only the produce of his own estates, or that Lichas did so. Clearly Petronius's focus is on commerce, not on distribution or gift-exchange.

Money Makes the World Go Round

Trimalchio survived to enjoy the fortune he made as a merchant. The "30 million sesterces" he expected to leave when he died are the proverbial expression of a millionaire's fortune (cf. §45, §76, §88, §117; Duncan Jones 1997; Scheidel 1996). The golden bracelet he dedicated to Mercury as a one thousandth part of his profits weighed 10 pounds of gold, which puts the total of his profits at 10,000 pounds of gold, the equivalent of 42 million sesterces, or 42 times the wealth required to be a senator in this period. The sum is of course grossly exaggerated, in line with his supposedly immeasurable landed estates (§67.7).

When Trimalchio had amassed more wealth than his entire *patria* (his home city) possessed he retired and started lending at interest to or through his freedmen (§76.9; see D'Arms 1981: 103). Interest-bearing loans were a common investment among upper-class Romans. According to Seneca, an aristocratic fortune typically consisted of a handsome slave staff, a beautiful urban residence, large landed estates, and much money put out at interest (*Ep.* 41.7). Pliny the Younger claims that he was almost wholly in real estate, but he had some money out on interest (*Ep.* 3.19.8).

By an amazing stroke of luck, we have 127 documents on writing tablets dating to AD 26–61 preserved from the archives of a private credit enterprise. The tablets were discovered in a wooden chest found near Pompeii, but document business conducted in Puteoli (mod. Pozzuoli). The enterprise was run by a freedman's son, C. Sulpicius Faustus, and his freedman C. Sulpicius Cinnamus, and was later inherited by Faustus's brother C. Sulpicius Onirus (Andreau 1999: 71–9; Camodeca 1999; Jones 2006).

The Sulpicii were moneylenders and credit intermediaries (*faeneratores*), who specialized in extending loans and sureties to maritime traders. Whether they were also deposit bankers (*argentarii*) is disputed, but they certainly provided services as middle men, channeling funds from a variety of investors (from centurions to senators and imperial slaves) to long-distance maritime traders. Petronius's expression <per> *libertos faenerare* (§76.9) suggests that Trimalchio used or set up credit enterprises like that of the Sulpicii to invest part of his fortune.

The Roman commercial economy could not function without credit. Any sizeable business enterprise relied on credit. Seneca admitted that "if you want to do business you need to borrow" (*Ep.* 119.2). Inevitably this entailed the risk of bankruptcy. Several tablets of the Sulpicii document insolvency trials and the sale of securities and mortgages. One of Trimalchio's guests, C. Julius Proculus, made a fortune as an undertaker, but when his luck turned his partners left him to the mercy of his creditors and he was forced to auction most of his luxury goods and mortgage the rest (§38). Another semi-fictitious example of a businessman going bankrupt, Damasippus Mercurialis, is found in Horace's *Satires* (2.3). He was a dealer in real estate and art who incurred heavy debts at the Ianus Medius – the place where Rome's moneylenders and brokers convened.

To Live Off the Land

Despite its apparent complexity, Petronius's economy remains rooted in agriculture. In the ancient world, even in the most urbanized environment, the rhythm of the economy was determined by the seasonal fluctuations of agriculture. Roman cities, like their Greek counterparts, were very sensitive to their food supply. It was the prime responsibility of local magistrates and city councils to take adequate precautions to ensure the supply. They were not always successful (cf. Erdkamp 2005; Garnsey 1988; Rickman 1980). At the time of Trimalchio's *cena*, we are told, a year of drought had caused food prices to surge (§44–6). One of the guests, Ganymede, worries that he will have to sell his "little dwellings" (*casulae*). He accuses the aediles of colluding with the millers and bakers, and of accepting bribes from them – a familiar complaint, which typically ignores the responsibility of the landowning elite and of wholesale merchants, who manipulated food prices through speculation and hoarding (Bang 2006: 71–4).

The dependency of the ancient economy on the land went far beyond the provision of food. Landed estates supplied important raw materials, such as wool, leather, and bone. Clay-beds, and the ceramic and brick industry attached to them, were often part of landed estates (Kehoe 2007: 559–66). Property (landed and urban) was both a token of status and a safe investment, and thus doubly appealed to the *nouveaux riches* (Finley 1999: 95–122; Garnsey and Saller 1987: 44–5). Like Lichas and their host, the businessmen at Trimalchio's table owned landed and urban property. "Let me take you to my humble farm and we will find some good stuff to eat despite the drought," says Echion to Agamemnon (§46.2).

Trimalchio inherited large estates from his former master, which he initially sold to finance his trading ventures, but subsequently bought back and expanded (§67). His Cumaean estate alone would have yielded 500,000 *modii* of grain (c. 4.3 million litres; §53.2), half the amount needed for the monthly imperial distributions in Rome. One of his estates, Trimalchio claims, touched the confines of Tarracina (mod. Terracina) and Tarentum. He was now hoping to buy Sicily, so that he could sail to Africa along his own lands (§48.3); yet if he could succeed in acquiring Apulia he would be satisfied (§77.3).

Clearly these claims are ridiculous, but the theme of concentration of landownership is common in the literature of the early empire (Garnsey and Saller 1987: 66–71). In 8 BC, the freedman millionaire C. Caecilius Isidorus – like Trimalchio a former businessman – died leaving 60 million sesterces, 4,116 slaves, 3,600 ox-yokes (enough to work 360,000 *iugera* of arable land – over 90,000 hectares), and over a quarter of a million cattle (Plin. *HN* 33.135).

Concentration of ownership does not imply that the estates merged into vast ranch-like properties suitable only for extensive cattle-raising or cereal farming. Pliny the Elder thought that *latifundia* (large estates) had caused the ruin of Italy (*HN* 18.35), but archaeological survey shows the persistence of small and medium-sized farms and plots. Farm tenancy was a common feature in Italian agriculture. Columella recommended the leasing out of estates that were too distant to be visited regularly (*Rust.* 1.7.6–7). For landowners who preferred not to rely on tenancy, the most common type of rural enterprise in the late republic and early empire was the *villa rustica* – a moderate-size enterprise run primarily by slaves, producing cash crops for urban markets. *Villa* agriculture could not function without additional hired labor at peak periods. Significantly, the 4,116 slaves left by Isidorus were not enough either to farm the 360,000 *iugera* that his oxen could plough, or to herd his cattle (Garnsey and Saller 1987: 66–71; Kehoe 1997 and 2007: 553–7).

Estate agriculture of any type in Italy was market-oriented and was expected to yield a surplus in cash. Trimalchio's Cumaean estate would have brought in 10 million sesterces (§53). Remmius Palaemon, the grammarian, once bought a neglected estate near Nomentum for 600,000 sesterces and hired a famous freedman viticulturalist, Acilius Sthenelus, to (re)plant it with vines. Eight years later the harvest was sold for 400,000 sesterces with the grapes still hanging on the vine (cf. Chrysanthus, above), and Palaemon sold the estate to Seneca for 2.4 million sesterces (Plin. *HN* 14.48–51; cf. Plin. *Ep.* 6.30).

Slave exploitation is the norm for the management of large rural estates in Petronius's world. On Trimalchio's Cumaean estate, 70 slave children were born in a single day (§53.2, the figure is obviously grotesque). Hired rural labor is absent from the novel. Trimalchio himself had been sent off as *vilicus* ("overseer") to an estate by his master as punishment for sleeping with his mistress (§69.3). This was a flagrant (and comical) deviation from sensible estate management as described by the agronomists. Columella advises his readers "not to appoint an overseer from that sort of slaves who are physically attractive, and certainly not from that class which has busied itself with the voluptuous occupations of the city. [...] A man should be chosen who has been hardened by farm work from his infancy, one who has been tested by experience." An illiterate slave is better than a literate one, "because, not knowing his letters, he is [...] less able to falsify accounts" (*Rust.* 1.8.1, trans. H. B. Ash). It hardly seems possible to find a more anti-Trimalchio image than this. Petronius will have known Columella's work, and it is tempting to think that the lines about Trimalchio's stewardship were written with these words in mind.

Conclusion

Using Petronius's *Satyrica* as a historical source for the Roman economy requires close critical reading and a constant adjustment through, and comparison with, other sources. The novel is not situated in a fantasy world, but the scenery is as distorted as Petronius's characters. Nevertheless, I hope to have shown that with proper care the data on economic reality woven into the story can be filtered out and used to substantiate our views on the Roman economy in the age of Nero.

Further Reading

Kloft (1994) and Schnur (1959) offer general studies on the reflections of economic reality in the *Satyrica*. Veyne's study of Trimalchio (Veyne 1961) is a classic and indispensable to understanding how this fictitious character relates to historical reality. It is well worth reading it together with the long chapter on "The 'Typicality' of Trimalchio" in D'Arms (1981: 97–120). Love (1991: 160–5) offers an interesting Weberian analysis.

    Booth (1979) shows how Petronius's novel documents the education of slaves in Roman society. Bonner (1977) provides a good introduction to education in ancient Rome. Those who want to know more about Roman law may start with Johnston (1999). Joshel (1992) gives a good basis for understanding how professional occupations helped to construct social identities in ancient Rome. Finley (1999) is unavoidable if you want to study the ancient economy, although many of its basic ideas are now abandoned or disputed. Scheidel and von Reden (2002) offer a good reader of articles and papers on the ancient economy to supplement and correct Finley. Scheidel, Morris, and Saller (2007) is the best recent survey available on the ancient economy. Morley (2007a) is a good general introduction to trade in classical antiquity. D'Arms (1981) gives fascinating insights into the organization of Roman commerce. De Ligt (1993) offers a thorough analysis of periodic markets and fairs. An excellent introduction to all aspects of banking and money-lending is Andreau (1999). Garnsey and Saller (1987: 83–103) provides a quick introduction to questions concerning food supply and the risks of famine. More thorough studies on the subject are Rickman (1980), Garnsey (1988), and Erdkamp (2005). On land-holding and agriculture, Garnsey and Saller (1987: 64–82) is a handy quick introduction. Pleket (1993) is helpful to put Roman agriculture in a comparative perspective.

9

At Home with the Dead

Roman Funeral Traditions and Trimalchio's Tomb

Valerie M. Hope

Introduction

> *Man's life alas! Is but a span,*
> *So let us live it while we can*
> ($34.10, trans. Sullivan 1965, used throughout this chapter)

Trimalchio wants his guests to seize the day, to eat, drink, and be merry. Ever eager to present himself as a generous and gregarious host, Trimalchio serves the best wine, stressing that it is a superior brew to that consumed by the previous day's guests. For Trimalchio wine is one of life's delights, something that makes human existence, short as it is, bearable; and, since death marks the end of such pleasures, life must be lived to the full. To add visual emphasis to his words Trimalchio plays with a silver skeleton, twisting its joints into various lifeless poses.

Petronius, through Trimalchio, may well be reflecting and parodying the musings of serious philosophers on the meaning of life and death, but Trimalchio's light-hearted perspective also finds ready parallels in Latin inscriptions and Roman art. Epitaphs could talk to the living, noting how the deceased had enjoyed life and urging the reader to do the same for soon they too will be no more: "While I lived I drank freely. You who live drink!" urges one old soldier in his epitaph (*CIL* 3.293). Dinner parties and banquets with their over-indulgent characteristics were also a favored venue for *memento mori* (reminders of mortality), with images of death, such as the skeleton, adorning cups and mosaics (Dunbabin 1986; Dunbabin 2003: 132–5).

Were the guests and diners supposed to give their mortality serious consideration? Or to "read" these images as tongue-in-cheek justifications for excess? Either way it suggests that in the first century AD death and the dead could be integrated into Roman life in ways that can seem alien from a modern Western perspective. Indeed the *Satyrica* is peppered with references to the dead, the dying, and funeral customs. Fake suicides, fickle widows, ghost stories, legacy hunters, and funeral plans provide *topoi* (traditional themes) and stories within the story.

One of the highlights of the *Cena* is Trimalchio's description of his desired tomb (§71). This piece of fiction, a tomb that never existed, has become one of the most famous and enduring of Roman monuments. The short passage is a gold-mine for anyone interested in Roman commemorative practices and funeral traditions, and also for those investigating freed slaves and their presence and presentation in Roman society. Little has been written on these subjects without reference to Trimalchio and his tomb. So why has this imaginary tomb become so influential? What is its real value in the study of funerary monuments in Roman society, especially among freed slaves? And what else does the *Satyrica* reveal about Roman attitudes to death and the place of the dead in Roman society?

Death, Dying, and the Dead

Death dislocates the deceased and the bereaved from their usual roles in the social structure, placing them in a marginal or liminal state. The deceased person has left the world of the living, but the corpse is still present; at the same time the bereaved are isolated, marked out by dress and behavior, and excluded from full participation in the community. Rituals help to guide and structure behavior through this problematic time, ultimately serving permanently to separate the dead from, and to reintegrate the bereaved with, the living. In the Roman world the deathbed, the funeral, grieving for the dead, and remembrance of the dead were all governed by expected and established conventions. In short there were right and wrong ways, ideals and counter ideals, for death, disposal, mourning, and commemoration. Petronius's *Satyrica* provides many insights into these expected conventions, and often challenges the associated ideals.

In his home Trimalchio ostentatiously reminds himself, and others, that life is short: a clock in the dining room and a trumpeter tell him how much longer he has to live (§26.9); among the images in the entrance hall are the three Fates spinning the threads of human lives that can break at any time (§29.6); Trimalchio even claims to know from astrology that he has precisely 30 years, four months, and two days to live (§77.2). All this is designed to exhibit Trimalchio's educated tastes, that he has engaged with philosophy, mythology, and astrology, and that, as a wise man, he is prepared for death. There is no doubt much intended irony. On the surface, Trimalchio has thought, it would seem, of everything: his tomb, his epitaph, and even the details of his funeral. Yet, in focusing on worldly things Trimalchio neglects the moral and spiritual preparations which were the characteristics of the truly wise man. Trimalchio appears to have faced his mortality and accepted death, but in reality he struggles to look beyond his own lifetime and achievements; his thoughts about death remain grounded in the material world of the living, not in the spiritual world of the dead.

It has been suggested that Trimalchio is obsessed with death (Arrowsmith 1966: 306; Cameron 1970: 338; see also Bodel 1994: 237), his house and feast being filled with allusions to it. In addition to the more obvious motifs (as noted above) scholars have suggested that the biographical wall-paintings in the house are reminiscent of tomb decor (Bodel 1994); that aspects of the *Cena* recall funereal gladiatorial games (Saylor 1987); that the labyrinthine features of his house, and cries such as "You can't leave by the same route you arrive" (§72.10) recall the terrain of the underworld (Newton 1982: 408–9; Courtney 1987; Bodel 1994: 239; and Hales, FREEDMEN'S CRIBS, p. 167); and that, overall, the visit of Encolpius and entourage to Trimalchio's home recalls literary descriptions of visits to Hades (Newton 1982; O'Neal 1976; Bodel 1994: 239), especially that of Virgil's Aeneas (*Aen.* 6; see further Morgan, PETRONIUS AND GREEK LITERATURE, p. 35). Why does Petronius play with so many deathly associations? Courtney has noted that it is as if those present at the banquet are "experiencing a kind of living death" which cannot be disguised by the trappings of luxury (Courtney 2001: 117). Bodel has argued that Petronius is creating a comic underworld predominantly occupied by shady and shadowy freed slaves (Bodel 1994: 251). Trimalchio's house becomes "a mausoleum, a home of the dead" (Bodel 1994: 243), filled with people who are free but not freeborn, who in many ways are isolated from the wider community and have struggled hard in life to compensate for their servile past (for status dissonance see Verboven, A FUNNY THING HAPPENED ON MY WAY TO THE MARKET, p. 131). Death was the ultimate threat that would annihilate the reputation and achievements for which these freed slaves had struggled so hard.

Trimalchio's near obsession with death may take literary, artistic, and philosophical motifs to an extreme, but all good Romans were supposed to confront their mortality and at the very least compose a will. In reading his will aloud Trimalchio wishes to bask in what he perceives will be future glory, "So my household will love me now as if I were dead" (§71.3). The last will and testament could be perceived as a mirror of a man's character (Plin. *Ep.* 8.18.1); this was the Roman's last word on the living, a place to comment on friends and sometimes even enemies. This is parodied when Trimalchio is left nothing in some of his workers' wills; he is omitted with praise and complimented out of necessity (§53.9; for Petronius's own will see below). In Latin literature wills were often associated with human greed and the stereotype of the shameless inheritance hunter (for example, Plin. *Ep.* 2.20; Hor. *Sat* 2.5; Mart. 2.26, 5.39, 12.56; Champlin 1991: 87–102; see Verboven, A FUNNY THING HAPPENED ON MY WAY TO THE MARKET, p. 128). In the *Satyrica*, the inhabitants of the Italian town of Croton are described as either inheritance hunters or the victims of inheritance hunters: "There is nothing but corpses being pecked and crows pecking them" (§116.9). Of course, Encolpius and gang fit right in and try to dupe the inheritance hunters by pretending to be wealthy, even testing people's greed by tying receipt of bequests to eating the flesh of a dead man (§141.2–11). Crucial to the process of inheritance hunting was the prospect that the wills of the wealthy could be changed regularly; the living testator took power by controlling and thwarting the expectations of the heirs. Trimalchio wins favor, and hopes to gain continued good service from his household, by reading his will, but he would have many opportunities to change his mind if he were to live the further 30 years predicted by the stars (§77.2)!

A good Roman needed to put his estate in order and accept his fate; then he could meet death calmly and resolutely. A good death was to die at home, in bed, of old age (but with mind still fully intact), with one's nearest and dearest to hand to catch the last breath with a kiss (Hope 2007: 93–6). We can note the end of the Emperor Augustus who, according to his biographer Suetonius, died peacefully in his own bed aged 65 uttering some apt and witty final words, with his wife Livia present (Suet. *Aug.* 99). In a world of high infant mortality, frequent epidemics, wars, and malnutrition, and with inadequate pain relief, we may question how many people achieved such a dignified and peaceful end. Petronius parodies the ideal in the description of Chrysanthus, whose funeral one of Trimalchio's guests has just attended. Chrysanthus lived to 70 or more, had made a fortune, had enjoyed himself while alive, kept a good head of hair, and maintained his sexual appetite

(§42–3). Whether Chrysanthus was a good man and prepared for death (he was actually done for by some weird diet!) is of little importance here; what affects the quality of his death is the quality of his life spent earning and enjoying the pleasures of the flesh.

In Latin literature it was often more telling if an individual failed to achieve a good end. Dramatic deaths might be unexpected, enforced, or involve violence and corpse abuse. Several times Petronius's leading characters cheat what would have been unpleasant and dishonorable deaths, allowing play with, and inversion of, idealized death scenes. In the failed suicide attempt of Encolpius and Giton the suicidal despair of the lovesick, who cannot even manage to kill themselves successfully, is mocked (§94.8–15). This is far removed from, and parodies the theatricality of, the ideal noble suicide bravely met in the face of real adversity (Edwards 2007; Hill 2004): think of Brutus after the battle of Philippi (Plut. *Brut.* 52–3) or the enforced suicide of Nero's tutor, the Younger Seneca (Tac. *Ann.* 15.63–4). Death at sea was also often perceived as a bad death, especially since the corpse might be left unburied (for example, Hor. *Carm.* 1.28; Virgil *Aen* 6.150–80). Giton and Encolpius fear this fate as the ship goes down, tying themselves together and hoping that some stranger might eventually bury them (§114.8–13). They survive the wreck, but Lichas does not and suffers the final indignity of being disposed of by his former enemies (§115.7–20).

Lichas's death introduces the subject of the acceptable disposal of human remains. After the shipwreck Encolpius speaks over the drowned body, questioning why it is so important to be buried or cremated: whether flesh is consumed by water, fire, earth, or beasts it all amounts to the same thing (§115.17–19). The final sequence of the *Satyrica*, which explores cannibalism, also plays with and inverts the ideals associated with decent disposal of the dead (§141), creating a shocking image of irrational people so obsessed by greed and wealth as to consider committing one of the ultimate sins (for philosophical discussions of cannibalism see Hook 2005). Such a horror was far removed from the norm of decent disposal; cremation was widely practiced at this time, and inhumation, in the story of the widow of Ephesus, is described as a Greek custom (§111.2). In popular tradition the soul would only rest in peace if disposed of properly – an ideal also challenged by the superstitious tale of the body-snatching witches (§63). Abandoned bodies, unburied corpses, and rotting flesh are dehumanizing and, in Roman society, dishonorable: man's care for the dead is an element of what separates him from other species. Yet that care and attention also entails a nonsense, identified by serious philosophers and echoed by Encolpius, that people, even those who dismiss the afterlife, act as if the dead still have sensation and would care about the fate of their remains (Lucr. 3.870–93; compare Lucian, *Luct.* 21). To accept death is to accept the total annihilation of the self and the dissolution of the body and all sense of personal identity; such acceptance was a challenge that could defeat even the best of ancient philosophers. In the *Satyrica* the reader is made to wonder whether preparations for their own death, be they philosophical, spiritual, or practical, really matter. Trimalchio is perhaps an extreme satire of all this misguided pre-death preparation, pursuing deluded, desperate, and ultimately pointless plans for self-perpetuation, the final example of which is his tomb (see below). The imaginary tomb of Trimalchio is a folly to man's vanity. Can any tomb, any construction of man, survive the test of time (compare, for example, Hor. *Carm.* 3.30; Ovid, *Met.* 15, 871–9)? Besides, was the cemetery the best place to perpetuate one's reputation? The werewolf story at the *cena* suggests a seedier side to the cemetery, where the grand aspirations of tomb owners are subverted by late-night adventures and superstition (§62). We can note, as well, in the tale "The Widow of Ephesus" the juxtaposition of tombs and the dead with criminals and sex; the bodies of the dishonorable are exposed in close proximity to the tombs of the honorable (§111–12); the cemetery and the dead are placed on the edge of town and respectability, more forgotten than remembered, so Petronius would have us believe.

If the dead were to survive in any fashion it was through the living, Individuals might plan, via will or personal instruction, for tomb, burial, and funeral, but it was the survivors who were in control, whose interests came first. If the dead primarily only exist in the memories of the living, they need someone to remember them, and in the first place to mourn them. Poor old Lichas lacks any family mourners and misses the accustomed displays of grief, except for those of his enemy Encolpius who, despite previous animosities, steps up to the mark and offers a generalized lament on the fate of man (§115.12–19). In Roman society the genuinely bereaved were expected to behave in a certain way, to give visible and audible expression to their loss. When Trimalchio imagines he is dead and reads his will, his household take on the expected maudlin behavior of the bereaved (§71.4). Later, in Croton, Encolpius and Proselenos, made glum by Encolpius's impotence, are described as like mourners who have been visiting a new grave (§134.7). Women in particular were supposed to give expression to grief, to have disheveled hair, tear at their cheeks, and make dramatic gestures. Chrysanthus's wife is criticized for not putting on a good enough show of grief (§42.7). At the other extreme is the widow of Ephesus, who is so devoted to her husband that she is prepared to go to the grave with him (§111.1–5). Petronius is stereotyping female behavior and playing with male anxieties: if a woman cried too little she was unfeeling, maybe even unchaste; if she cried too much this might also be a sign of subterfuge. The author may also be tapping into current debates about how one should mourn in public and the differences between elite and popular expectations for the bereaved. We can note how Seneca the Younger had complained that the *plebs* lacked dignity in grief, weeping and throwing themselves off couches in a theatrical fashion when mourning their losses (*Ep.* 99.16). By contrast, the elite, especially elite men, were expected to show restraint and a "stiff upper lip"; but in doing so they might be judged as lacking in humanity. Witness the alleged negative reaction to the imperial household's mourning at the death of Germanicus, at least according to Tacitus (*Ann.* 3.2–3). How one mourned in public was open to evaluation and possibly wilful misinterpretation by onlookers and commentators: to cry too much was showy and false; to cry too little was to be unfeeling. Indeed, grief in the *Satyrica* tends to be artificial or misplaced, creating laughter from tears: the show of grief for Lichas is not heartfelt, that for Trimalchio is not genuine since he is not yet dead; and the behavior of the grieving widows is also questioned.

The last task that the living survivors perform for the dead, or at least the physical remains of the dead, is to organize and attend the funeral. The dead may seek to control events by will or instruction, but the execution of their wishes lies in the hands of the living. In the *Satyrica* funerals match and thus parody lives. Lichas's funeral is a basic one from necessity; as a drowned man removed from family and friends he is lucky to be disposed of at all. This can be contrasted with the good send off received by Chrysanthus: he was carried out in style on a bier covered in gold cloth with a decent show of mourners, the ranks of whom were swelled by ex-slaves (§42.6). Trimalchio also envisages a funeral with all the trappings for himself: a fancy shroud, wine, perfumes, and trumpet players (§77.7–78). The enactment of Trimalchio's funeral may be parody and a suitably ironic way to end the *Cena*, but it provides an ultimate example of *memento mori*, which finds a real parallel. Seneca the Younger tells us that a certain Pacuvius, the governor of Syria, used to be carried out every day after dinner as if a corpse in a funeral procession to cries of "He has lived! He has lived!" (Sen. *Ep.* 12.8). All this hints at the tensions and contrasts in funerals, and death in general, between the need for decency, restraint, and serious behavior on the one hand, and on the other the display, grandeur, and even frivolity of the living. Funerals could have a party element: those attending might expect to be impressed and well entertained. Subsequent commemorative events might also be more fun than sombre. Habinnas arrives at Trimalchio's house already drunk after attending a feast held nine days after a death. Some wine had been poured onto the bones of the dead, while the living had dined in extravagant style, which reflected well on the nearest and dearest of the dead (§65–6). Funerals are more for the living than the dead, unless, of course, you are Trimalchio, always seeking to blur the boundaries between life and death.

Death, how the living planned for death and reacted to and even celebrated the deaths (and lives) of others, can be viewed as a recurring theme in the *Satyrica*. The work is far from macabre, but it does challenge some of the ideals and behavior associated with the dead, dying, and the bereaved, and engages with some of the contentious issues surrounding how one should mourn for and remember the dead. Petronius often promotes a rational attitude to death by parodying the irrational (see Walsh 1974: 187). In terms of the narrative structure death also acts as a focal or turning point in the *Satyrica*. There are three important death scenes, imagined and real, those of Lichas, Trimalchio, and Eumolpus, that all challenge the ideals of a good death. The "deaths" of these supporting characters close major sections of the narrative and may serve to emphasize the death-oriented, underworld experiences of the narrator (Bodel 1999a: 48). In the *Satyrica* death is never far away.

A Fictional Tomb

A mainstay in Trimalchio's preparations for his death is the planning of his tomb (§71.5–12). Trimalchio argues that the tomb will bring him "life after death," and the design very much represents a retrospective view of his life as lived, rather than a prospective view of the life hereafter. The tomb symbolizes Trimalchio's achievements. It becomes a way of advertising and even creating a success story, and thereby, in some ways, cheating death, or at least it is an attempt at cheating death. For those, like Trimalchio, who had risen from little, who believed in the here and now, their earthly legacy may have been more important than the prospect of any life to come. To get it right, to ensure that the tomb told the desired story, one needed to take matters into one's own hands. Instructions might be left in a will, if the heirs were to be trusted to follow them, but a safer option was to commission the monument while still alive (Plin. *Ep.* 6.10). This may well be Trimalchio's intention: the description of the tomb is preceded by the reading of his will. The latter prompts Trimalchio's musings, and later he indicates that the will should contain provisions to protect the tomb. However, overall, the level of detail employed in the tomb description would be ill-suited to an actual will, few surviving examples of which contain exact details about tomb structure and decor (Champlin 1991: 171). Besides, Trimalchio directs his comments at Habinnas, a fellow freedman and monumental mason, as if the project is already underway, or at least being planned. Habinnas is instructed to build the tomb and to bring it to life. Trimalchio justifies his attention to detail by arguing that tombs should be better equipped than the houses of the living, since they will be occupied for much longer. Trimalchio's tomb is to resemble a house, which is somewhat ironic since, as noted above, his house resembles a tomb (Bodel 1994: 243).

The overall impression of Trimalchio's tomb is of something large, grand, and elaborate. Trimalchio does not specify what form it is to take – whether it is to be a round tomb, square tomb, tower tomb, or chamber tomb; whether it is to mark just his burial or that of others also. The precise architectural and functional details matter less than the total impression. We can, however, identify certain central elements. The tomb is to be big: a hundred feet facing the road and two hundred back into the field. Latin epitaphs often contained dimensions indicating road frontage and the depth, although most were considerably more modest than this. Trimalchio may be intending the plot to serve for both his tomb and a tomb garden, especially since he wants various fruits and plenty of vines around his ashes. The fruits and vines may be a reference to offerings that are to be made at the grave, but there is evidence for small orchards and vineyards attached to tombs, the produce from which could be used to support the upkeep of the tomb (Jashemski 1979: 141–53; Toynbee 1971: 94–100). The tomb is also to include a sundial, which should be so positioned that all can read Trimalchio's name. The sundial plays once more upon the motif of the passage of time, the importance of getting on with life before time runs out. But in providing his tomb with an amenity function, Trimalchio is, above all, promoting his own remembrance by encouraging the casual passer-by to read and keep his name alive. Trimalchio also plans to have a guard to protect his tomb from the same passers-by, to prevent people fouling the site. The cemetery and its tombs, as noted above, could easily be subverted and abused.

Trimalchio's tomb was, then, to be large, surrounded by orchards and gardens, to incorporate a clock, and have a guard for protection. Much of the rest of the description focuses on the sculptural and decorative elements. The first thing Trimalchio mentions is a statue of himself, although it is unclear whether this was to be displayed on the exterior or interior of the tomb and whether he was to be depicted standing, sitting, or reclining (Whitehead 1993: 302–4). Nevertheless, it is likely that he intended this portrait to be a central element in the design, which was to be complemented by other visual props: a puppy, wreaths, scent bottles, and images of a gladiator. A little later Trimalchio mentions additional images: ships in full sail, and a scene of himself sitting on a platform, wearing the robes of office and five gold rings, distributing money to the people. Then, recalling that he had once paid for a public dinner, Trimalchio suggests adding a banqueting scene and a view of the whole town having a good time (see Donahue 1999). The next set of proposed images reflects the more personal, private, and familial side to his life, as Trimalchio adds a statue of Fortunata with a dove and her dog and his favorite little slave. Finally, Trimalchio pictures some wine jars, including a broken one with a slave weeping over it. Taken as a whole, the selected images suggest Trimalchio's tastes, wealth, and interests: everything from his love of gladiators, family, and wine to his preoccupation with enjoying life's pleasures before it is too late. The proposed decorative scheme also shows Trimalchio in various guises: as a leading citizen, businessman (the ships – see below), office-holder, public benefactor, host, husband, and master. On the one hand, the images can be viewed as promoting the richness of his life, underlining that personal identity was often multifaceted; on the other hand, the varied images deprive the monument of a unity of message, almost suggesting a crisis of identity.

The visual dimensions of the tomb are to be complemented by the verbal in the form of an inscription. It is worth remembering, however, that Latin epitaphs incorporated a strong visual dimension: an epitaph would have been integrated with, rather than separated from, the overall design, and it would have been understood to some degree even by the illiterate or semiliterate since words could act as pictograms, and inscriptions were often formulaic (Woolf 1996: 28). Indeed, one of Trimalchio's guests notes that he can only read stone-cutters' capitals (§58.7). The first thing which Trimalchio wishes to be inscribed is "This monument does not go to the heir" (§71.7). This statement, often abbreviated to the initial letters *HMHNS*, was a relatively common statement in Latin epitaphs, but it normally came at the end of the inscription rather than at the beginning! Trimalchio has earlier indicated, in the reading of his will, that Fortunata is to be his heir (§71.3); Trimalchio has no children, no blood descendants, and therefore this tomb is to be for, and to remain focused upon, him for all time, which reflects the centrality of Trimalchio in his house (see Hales, FREEDMEN'S CRIBS, p. 170).

The titular epitaph, supplied at the very end of the tomb description (§71.12), sums up Trimalchio's modesty, honors, wealth, and learning. It incorporates common epigraphic conventions such as an emphasis on the name of the deceased, titles, and posts held, and uses formulaic statements such as *hic requiescat* ("here lies") and *vale* ("farewell"), but these are combined with far from standard comments on the extent of Trimalchio's fortune, his refusal of honors, and the fact that he had never listened to a philosopher. These unusual and immodest claims add a comic twist and remove the epitaph from the norm (Bodel 1999a: 43). The sense of distortion is compounded by the omission of a reference to Trimalchio's freed status and by the inclusion in his nomenclature of some famous names from Rome's past, Maecenas and Pompeius. Trimalchio uses the epitaph to lay claim to wealth and esteem, while distancing himself from the pursuit of honors and learning. D'Arms suggests that the epitaph evokes "equestrian grandeur," recalling leading men who had rejected honors for the pursuit of leisure or business interests (D'Arms 1981: 112). Despite the epitaph's claim to faux modesty, on the whole the different elements of Trimalchio's identity compete for attention, just as in the pictorial images intended for the tomb.

It is a challenge to visualize what this fictional tomb would have actually looked like. The passage is often a stream of unstructured thoughts that are not developed or integrated into a whole. Trimalchio is perhaps not quite sure or confident in what he wants, and at certain points seems hesitant (Whitehead 1993: 311). We can imagine that this is not the first time he has had this conversation with Habinnas, and that on each occasion he adds or removes a detail. Indeed, later on, after an argument, he scraps the portrait of Fortunata (§74.17). The description of the tomb is suggestive of the process of negotiation between client and mason, with the end result being a product of Trimalchio's wishes and Habinnas's abilities. The illustration of this process is perhaps one of the tomb's most interesting qualities. However one reacts to Trimalchio's tastes and requests, there remains something human and understandable about the way in which, in Petronius' depiction, Trimalchio thinks aloud, often hesitantly and almost in a childlike fashion, about how he might or should be remembered. He is not sure that he has got things right: does the epitaph, for example, do him justice?

Petronius draws the reader into the uncertainties and insecurities that shape Trimalchio's life (see Beard 1998: 98).

Petronius piles up motifs and funeral clichés to create an unimaginable monstrosity: a tomb that pulls out all the stops in a haphazard fashion. Yet the description still remains believable, largely because it envisages different elements of the tomb design at work and to some extent complementing each other. The tomb uses various dimensions to communicate: it involves the visual, textual, spatial, and sheer scale. The reader can picture the tomb appealing to the senses: sight (images, words, sundial), hearing (if the epitaph were read aloud), taste (wine, fruits), and smell (perfume, gardens, fruit). It also stimulates varied emotions: love for family; sadness and tears; passion for fighting gladiators; happiness in the enjoyment of food and largess; and pride in achievements. For these reasons the description creates a powerful image: even if one cannot quite see how all the elements might come together their variety is tantalizing. Anyone and everyone can build Trimalchio's tomb in the mind's eye; and for those familiar with surviving Roman funerary monuments and epitaphs it has its roots in reality, and can even cease to be a fantasy.

Real Tombs and Real People

Trimalchio's tomb is a fiction, but there are thousands upon thousands of tombs and epitaphs that do survive from the Roman world. Most of these are now fragmented and decontextualized: we have epitaphs without tombs, sculpture without epitaphs. This is one reason why Trimalchio's description is so important, because it enables us to imagine, even if somewhat incoherently, that the original clients and creators of these monuments did picture epitaphs and images working together. Where tombs, and whole areas of cemeteries, are well preserved we can begin to reconstruct the fuller dynamics of tomb construction and the interplay of the available communicative dimensions at which Petronius hints.

Roman cemeteries were located on the edge of settlements, beyond the town walls; they often had an elongated appearance as tombs lined the roads leading into the towns and cities. One of the first and last things a visitor would see would be the tombs of the dead. Road frontage could be important, and tombs could appeal to the passer-by with epitaphs that addressed the viewer, eye-catching decor, and impressive scale (see fig. 9.1).

Figure 9.1   Tombs fronting the road at the Nocera Gate necropolis, Pompeii. (Photo: Hope.)

At first reading, Trimalchio's tomb may seem ridiculous, but Petronius is clearly toying with the realities of tomb design and cemetery function. To what extent can we understand the relationship between Petronius's fiction and real tombs? Is Petronius drawing on a specific repertoire of real tombs and real people?

On one level we can easily find parallels for many elements that Trimalchio requests for his tomb. The very act of self-commissioning a monument, planning and ordering your tomb in advance of death, was not uncommon. Many epitaphs include the phrase *vivus fecit* indicating that the tomb had been "built while (the commemorated person was) still alive." As noted above, elements of the proposed titular epitaph also echo surviving Latin epitaphs, and examples of tomb gardens, guards, and even sundials can all be found (Whitehead 1993). The decorative elements, the statues, portraits, dogs, wreaths, gladiators, ships, and scenes of largesse are all well attested in funerary art (Whitehead 1993; Donahue 1999). To take one example, the image of the ship: ships could be used in tomb decor as a reference to the journey of life, death being equated to the safe harbor at journey's end (fig. 9.2); but the ship might also symbolize earthly pursuits, a career as a sailor or ship-builder, or a more general allusion to trade by shipping (fig. 9.3). Some time after the description of his tomb, Trimalchio reveals that he made his money through the shipping trade (§76.3–8). So on Trimalchio's tomb the ship emblem may refer to business pursuits, the completion of life's jour-ney, or indeed encompass both meanings (cf. fig. 9.2). What this example illustrates is that the decorative motifs employed by Petronius draw upon a repertoire taken from real tombs, although most real tombs were decorated with considerably fewer images than Trimalchio requests.

Aspects of the tomb design may find ready parallels, but is Trimalchio's tomb underpinned by a social reality? It has long been noted that funerary commemoration, epitaphs, markers, and tombs, appear to have appealed to, and have been set up to and by, freed slaves more than any other social group. More freed slaves were commemorated in epitaphs than members of the freeborn populace, and they often employed specific decorative motifs such as relief portraits (Kleiner 1977; Kockel 1993; Wrede 1981; Zanker 1975). These preferences have been related to the marginal status and often precarious position occupied by the freed slave; a freed slave had achieved a dramatic change in his or her legal status but was still marginalized and stigmatized by a servile past (cf. Verboven, A FUNNY THING HAPPENED ON MY WAY TO THE MARKET, p. 131); a freed slave may have been particularly conscious of the family – children and spouses – that had been denied to

Figure 9.2 Tomb 43, the Isola Sacra necropolis, Portus. The black-and-white mosaic at the entrance to the tomb depicts the Portus lighthouse flanked by ships in full sail. The Greek motto reads "Here is the end of our work." The mosaic recalls the maritime connections of the town (and possibly the tomb founders) and simultaneously marks the completion of life's journey. (Photo: Hope.)

Figure 9.3 The tombstone of Publius Longidienus, a ship-builder, Ravenna. (Photo: Hope.)

them as slaves and stood now as symbols of the foundation of a new citizen family (Taylor 1961; Mouritsen 2005). Funerary monuments and epitaphs allowed this social group to mark and celebrate their successes and achievements; in the cemetery the freed slaves had a freedom of expression denied to them elsewhere; here they could create their identity unfettered by elite expectations and prejudices. By contrast, among the elite of the early empire we can trace some negative opinions about tombs and extravagance at death. Seneca the Younger requested that he be given no funeral (Tac. *Ann.* 15.64); the tomb of the Emperor Otho endured because of its modesty (Tac. *Hist.*

Figure 9.4 The funerary altar of Gaius Calventius Quietus, an *augustalis*, the Herculaneum Gate necropolis, Pompeii. (Photo: Hope.)

2.49; Suet. *Vit.* 10); Frontinus declared his name would live if he deserved it: a tomb was unnecessary (Plin. *Ep.* 9.19). Studies of tomb architecture also suggest that after the construction of the mausoleum of Augustus, in Rome at least, the elite could not compete in the funerary sphere. The elite looked to their houses and home towns as arenas for display, and in general more modest, introverted tombs became the norm from the early first century AD onwards (Eck 1984; Bodel 1997; von Hesberg 1992).

Trimalchio, it would seem, then, is deliberately being set up, albeit in exaggerated form, as a crass ex-slave swimming against the tide of elite good taste. The message would seem to be: the bigger and showier the tomb the more inadequate the man. Indeed, there are tombs and freed-slave commissioners that so closely parallel aspects of Trimalchio's tomb and life that they can appear to make the fiction real. Pliny the Elder tells of a certain Clesippus, a freed slave who owed his success, like Trimalchio, to his former owner's favor; he prospered and built a large tomb, of which fragments from the grandiose epitaph survive (Plin. *HN* 34.11–12; *CIL* 1².1004; Bodel 1989; cf. Pomeroy 1992). We can also note the tombs of several *augustales*, priests of the emperor cult, of which Trimalchio claims to be a member: for example, the tomb of Lusius Storax from Chieti, which depicts gladiatorial contests reviewed by magistrates; or from Pompeii the altar tombs of Gaius Munatius Faustus, with a depiction of a scene of largesse, a ship in full sail, and an honored double seat at the theatre, and that of Gaius Calventius Quietus (fig. 9.4) with a double seat and oak wreaths (Whitehead 1993; Kockel 1983).

However, relating Trimalchio and his fictional tomb to this contemporary material may not be so straightforward. It can be tempting to look at a surviving tomb, be reminded of Trimalchio, and then draw conclusions and make assumptions about those commemorated – but, in looking for a "real" Trimalchio, there is a danger of circular argumentation. Lauren Hackworth Petersen has cautioned against "Trimalchio vision," and the risk that we impose Trimalchio onto the material evidence while forgetting that he is a satirical literary construct (Petersen 2006). The famous tomb of the baker Eurysaces in Rome, for example, decorated with a frieze of baking and a striking design of cylinders, which have been interpreted as grain measures, bread ovens, or kneading machines, could be considered as idiosyncratic as Trimalchio's design (fig. 9.5). Here we have Trimalchio's tomb in the flesh, a freed slave being showy and grandiose. However, the parallel between Trimalchio and Eurysaces is underpinned by the assumption that Eurysaces was a freed slave when there is no clear

Figure 9.5 The tomb of Marcus Vergilius Eurysaces, Porta Maggiore, Rome. (Photo: Prag.)

evidence to prove this to be the case. In comparing Eurysaces with Trimalchio we risk overlooking that in itself Eurysaces' tomb suggests that he was wealthy and successful and may have been widely respected (Petersen 2006: 84–122). When we are looking at real tombs, Trimalchio's tomb may mislead us, encouraging us to set up a false polarity between the tastes of the elite and the tastes of freed slaves, and leading us to overlook the fact that the elite were only a minority within Roman society and that the non-elite were not all ex-slaves.

Trimalchio's tomb needs to be treated with caution, but as a literary construct the tomb would only work in Petronius's day if it bore some resemblance to reality. It would be foolish to disregard the possibility that Petronius is revealing some truths about cemetery culture and about the types of people who set up tombs and the decorative motifs they preferred to use. Not all these people may have been freed slaves, they may not all have been claiming or saying the same things about their place in society, but tombs were a vivid and relatively accessible form of communication that appealed more to some groups than to others.

Conclusion

The *Satyrica* is not ostensibly about death and dying, tombs and the cemetery, but it is suggestive of how people coped (or did not) with the sense of their own mortality, how they faced death, how they planned for death, how death shaped lives, and how in life and in death individuals negotiated their position in society and constructed their identities. The *Satyrica* does not reflect an exact image of social realities and conventions, but it does play with people's fears and insecurities in a world where death was very much a part of life.

Trimalchio's tomb is important because it is a rare literary example of a tomb. We have plenty of real tombs, but few ancient accounts, descriptions, and interpretations of them. So, although it is exaggerated and parodic, it has been influential in how Roman tombs and the Roman cemetery are interpreted. Trimalchio's tomb provides insights into the relationship between commissioner and stonemason, the rationale behind the pre-death planning of monuments, and about the process of self-fashioning and self-presentation. There is a danger, however, that this one literary text may become too influential in how we view thousands of surviving tombs and funerary monuments. Petronius's insights are invaluable, but they do not provide a blueprint with which to interpret every tomb or the behavior of all freed slaves.

To end this discussion of the *Satyrica* and death we cannot avoid noting Petronius's own demise – if, that is, we are to accept the author of the *Satyrica* to be the Tacitean *elegantiae arbiter* (see INTRODUCTION, p. 5). This Petronius laughed in the face of death (and the emperor) and challenged the conventions of the idealized good death, a tactful will, and an honorable memory. Forced to take his life by the Emperor Nero, in whose court he had served, Petronius inverted the stereotype of the elite (philosophically-derived) suicide by spending his last hours not in high-minded literary composition and philosophical discussion, but in eating, sleeping, listening to silly poems, and playfully chatting with his friends. In his will he did not flatter the emperor, but revealed Nero's terrible excesses and debauchery (Tac. *Ann.* 16.19). There is no mention of Petronius's funeral or tomb; and it is hard to imagine that these would have mattered much to him. In his death Petronius challenged elite expectations in different ways from those found in the *Satyrica*, but both his death and the work that was to be his lasting legacy highlighted central issues and ideals about living and dying in ancient Rome.

Further Reading

Whitehead's article (1993), which draws out many relevant parallels between surviving tombs and Trimalchio's tomb, is a useful starting point. Petersen's recent book (2006) takes a different approach, but places the tomb in a broader art-historical context. For the tomb in the context of the *Satyrica* and its death themes, see in particular the articles by Bodel (1994; 1999a). For a wider view of monuments, the cemetery, and funerary customs, Toynbee (1971) remains essential; and for a selection of relevant sources see Hope (2007). The cemetery and how monuments functioned on a street of tombs are usefully introduced by Purcell (1987) and Koortbojian (1996), while Carroll's book (2006) summarizes the content, role, and design of epitaphs. For the specifics of Roman wills, idealized death scenes, and Roman funerals, see respectively Champlin (1991), Edwards (2007), and Bodel (1999b).

10

Freedmen's Cribs

Domestic Vulgarity on the Bay of Naples

Shelley Hales

Vulgarity and Villas

Domestic space in the world of the *Satyrica* can be dangerous. As Encolpius discovers on his visit to Trimalchio's house, art can literally bite back. The end of the episode sees a slavering guard dog barking at them so ferociously that both Encolpius and Ascyltos end up in the fishpond. The painted dog they have encountered on the way in has metamorphosed into the snapping hound Scylax (§64). They have to be rescued by the hall porter, and the dog is pacified with some tasty morsels (§72), like Virgil's Cerberus, who guards the gates of Hades (Virgil *Aen.* 6.417–23). The allusion makes explicit that dining at Trimalchio's is a living hell.

The home in which Trimalchio entertains his guests is often seen as the height of ostentation and bad taste. Freedmen are characterized as men who come from nothing, make a fortune, and exhibit their wealth in their gaudy homes. Trimalchio's fake Corinthian bronze (§50), latest dining-room gadgets (§60), and autobiographical frescoes (§29) are the equivalent of the plasma screens, chandeliers, and gigantic portraits that are paraded in the homes of footballers and celebrities who invite the audience to tour their homes in life-style TV programs and magazines. What wouldn't Trimalchio give to be paraded in this way?

Another comparison might come from a documentary reviewed by Andrew Mueller, a *Guardian* journalist, in which the cameras instead toured the homes of tyrants and dictators from Ceausescu to Hussein. "I didn't realise you could spend a million dollars in Woolworths" ("The Guide," October 8, 2005). Here, by posing as an authority on style, the speaker dissolves the threat of political tyranny, genocide, and corruption by picking apart its perpetrators' soft furnishings. The only reaction of the

Figure 10.1　The Priapus in the vestibule of the House of the Vettii, Pompeii. (Photo: Sophie Fox.)

educated middle classes to the combination of new money, low class, and extreme power or profile is to accuse it of bad taste. The equation of freed-men and bad taste is apparently well attested in the archaeology of the Bay of Naples, on which Trimalchio's house is reckoned to have stood. The House of the Vettii in Pompeii, a lavishly decorated house, best known to visitors for its well-endowed Priapus weighing his large phallus against a big bag of cash (fig. 10.1), is usually thought to have belonged to Vettius Restitutus and Vettius Donatus, both known from their seals (Cooley and

Cooley 2004: 214–15), who are generally assumed to be freedmen brothers (Richlin also discusses the figure and phallus of Priapus, SEX IN THE SATYRICA, p. 83). The abundant use of fake marble, the overdressed garden, pornographic frescoes, and the friezes showing cute cupids involving themselves in various types of manufacture and commerce have all been seen to befit the aspirant misadventures of a pair of freedmen opportunists (Trimalchio, of course, has his own pastry Priapus, §60.4). The connections freely made between the Vettii brothers, Trimalchio, their status, and their perceived chronic taste have become so pervasive that it is precisely with this pairing that the most recent study of "freedman art" begins. Lauren Hackworth Petersen uses exactly this perceived relationship in order to begin the process of refuting the assumptions commonly made about freedman taste and the relationship between the archaeologically attested homeowners and Petronius's literary invention (Petersen 2006: 5–10; see Hope, AT HOME WITH THE DEAD, for the problems of this equation with regards to "freedman" tombs).

For any imagined vulgar freedman new to home improvement plenty of moralistic literature unwittingly provided hints on how best to pump huge amounts of cash into a luxury home. Seneca the Younger, the man who managed to have two (not mutually exclusive) careers as both the owner of some of the most splendid villas of his age and also the Neronian era's voice of the moral minority, relies on long-established traditions of moral rhetoric to denounce the luxury villas of his contemporaries: villas that feature roof gardens and bath houses built out into the sea (Sen. *Ep.* 122.8). Notorious villas like those of Lucullus (Plut. *Luc.* 39.3) apparently provided the model for Seneca's rage, and numerous villa remains around the Bay of Naples, tottering on terraces on mountain sides and teetering on bridges over the sea, seem to suggest that maybe he had a point (Lafon 2001; Edwards 1993). What made these buildings exceptionally luxurious was not their size or expense but explicitly their displays of transcendence over the natural world. As Pliny the Elder framed it, the definition of *luxuria* was a hubristic desire to overcome and subvert the laws of nature (for example, Plin. *HN* 9.139, 33.3, 33.64; Wallace-Hadrill 1990).

In this context, Trimalchio's town house (*domus*) hardly seems a contender. None of the crimes perpetrated by the elite are here: no evidence of lavish architectural design, no vaults, apses, or marbling, nor even sculpture. Look closer, though, and the same will to alter nature is there in substance if not in scale, even if all Trimalchio can manage is a hare that looks like Pegasus. This affinity might alert us to the fact that what might be laughable about the representation of Trimalchio's interior decor (and the Vettii's too) is not his vulgarity of taste, made inevitable by his low status, but a rather more subtle interplay with prevailing traditions of domestic display. By exploring the remains of the Vettii house alongside Petronius's description of Trimalchio's home, perhaps we might arrive at a more productive understanding of the relationship between the two and of their relationship to prevailing Roman traditions of domestic activity, architecture, and decoration. In doing so, the interconnections between those activities, architecture, and decor, and hence the relationship between the character and behavior of Trimalchio and the extensive description of his domestic setting, may also become more apparent.

Importance of the *Domus*

Throughout the evening, Trimalchio and his guests demonstrate their preoccupation with the acquisition of property. Trimalchio has built his house himself, one of his first moves after making his fortune (§76.8), and he has transformed it from a *cusuc* ("shack") to a *templum* ("temple") (§77.4). Diogenes has gone so far as to put up a public notice to let the world know he will be moving from his *cenaculum*, a room over a shop, to a *domus*, a town house (§38.10). They show all the more pride in these achievements because of the barriers in the way of achieving such a change in residence (Andreau, FREEDMEN IN THE SATYRICA, p. 118, discusses the implications of possessing different kinds of properties). One of Trimalchio's sayings is along the lines of "He who is born in a *pergula* (booth), doesn't dream of an *aedes* (house)" (§74.14).

The importance of property to these men can be explained on two levels. Firstly, there is the visible display of wealth, a stamp on the landscape showing the freedman's financial success. Secondly, there is the implication of social presence and belonging to the community. Throughout the text we are reminded that Trimalchio's residence is a *domus*, a word that connotes not just a town residence but associated traditions of domestic life and architecture. The *domus* was imagined as a seat for the *memoria* ("remembrance") of family life, a place made hallowed by the presence of the hearth, the spirit of ancestors, and the record of familial achievement. Inside, ancestor masks (*imagines*) watched over the next generation, admonishing and encouraging the *paterfamilias*, the living head of the household. The *domus* also provided the space wherein a family displayed itself to the outside world, home to a whole host of "public" functions, most importantly the morning *salutatio* ("greeting") and the evening *cena*. The *salutatio* was an essential element of the patron–client network that stimulated the economics and politics of Rome. Clients presented themselves to pay their respects, acknowledging their ongoing allegiance to their patron, while he reciprocated with the donation of *sportula*, a gift of food or nominal amount of money. The *cena* or *convivium*, the evening meal, was supposedly a more intimate affair to which the patron invited his friends and, as a treat, dependants to share a meal. Of course, it is the latter that allows our heroes to enter Trimalchio's *domus* and us to take a tour in order to observe how well it measures up.

Insularity of Trimalchio's *Domus*

The social importance of the *domus* is most famously expressed by the architect Vitruvius, who, at the beginning of the principate, went to some lengths to prescribe exactly how a house should be appointed so as to reconcile the *familia* ("household") with its civic surroundings and to allow the *paterfamilias* to undertake his social obligations with due dignity (Vitr. *De arch.* 6.5.1–2). Famous statesmen of the republic had decorated their homes with their hard-won military spoils (Cic. *Phil.* 2.68; Plut. *C. Gracch.* 15.1) and chose locations in Rome that dominated the landscape, so they could see and be seen by the whole city (Vell. Pat. 2.14; Wiseman 1987). Although most sources on the importance of housing come from the late republic, at a time when houses were potent political weapons, the importance of visibility as a marker of status and wealth persisted (contrast the invisibility, for example, of life in a crowded *insula* ["tenement block"], as in Martial 1.86). Family rituals of marriage, death, and coming-of-age included processions that traveled between private and public space. It is presumably in an attempt to achieve this kind of public platform that Trimalchio makes such a show of himself in the baths and starts the *cena* with a procession following his litter to his house (§28.1–5). (Vout, THE SATYRICA AND NERONIAN CULTURE, p. 105, discusses the triumphal overtones of this procession, further emphasizing Trimalchio's attempt to make a public spectacle of himself.)

Figure 10.2 *Cave canem* ("beware of the dog") mosaic in the vestibule of the House of the Tragic Poet, Pompeii. (Photo: Sophie Fox.)

Given that this procession leads us to Trimalchio's front door, offering Encolpius an opportunity to describe his first impressions of the house, it is striking that we learn nothing at all about the exterior, except for the doorway. On one level, this might simply be a reflection of domestic practices as we find them in the cities of Campania, where house facades are generally plain with few, high, small windows. There are various reasons for this lack of penetrability, including climate and, not least, as we can see from the *Satyrica*, the fear of low-lifes looking to move in on your property/wife/children (it was a common misrepresentation of the *domus* that guests might wander around at will: Vitruvius [*De arch.* 6.5.1] insists on it, although it is a gesture vigorously denied by more practical homeowners like Fronto [*Ep.* 5.1]). The tiny windows of Pompeian houses contrast with the tall doorways, often flanked by fake half-columns or, as in the case of the House of the Vettii, decked out with a memorable painting. Trimalchio's threshold is certainly well flagged: a brightly dressed slave shelling peas and a magpie in a cage to greet the visitors (§28.8–9). There is a strong sense of one-way traffic: a sign promises a good beating to any slave who tries to leave without permission (§28.7). In fact, it will be just as difficult for Encolpius to leave. Nobody ever leaves Trimalchio's house by the way they came in (§72.10). Trimalchio himself does not get out much, having to make a big deal of this year's two dinner dates (§30.3). The entrance is guarded by the big wall-painting of a dog (§29.1), a common feature of vestibule floor mosaics in Pompeii (most famously in the House of the Tragic Poet [fig. 10.2], which, like Trimalchio's, bears the useful advice *cave canem*, "Beware of the dog" [cf. Veyne 1963]). It is not clear whether the guard dog is intended to keep people in or out, perhaps reminding us again of the inescapable entrance to the Underworld (also on this allusion Hope, AT HOME WITH THE DEAD, p. 142, and Morgan, PETRONIUS AND GREEK LITERATURE, p. 35).

Layout of the *Domus*

Once inside, however, Trimalchio's house stops being usefully like the houses of Campania. Doorways into Pompeian houses tend to offer a straightforward view: in the House of the Vettii (fig. 10.3) we can see through the door into an *atrium* ("hall") and through to the back of the house with its beautiful peristyle garden filled with fountains, marble

Figure 10.3 The view from the entrance through the House of the Vettii, Pompeii. (Photo: Hales.)

furniture, and sculpture, including yet another well-endowed Priapus. Such views suggest an easy, symmetrical house in which we shall know our way around. But Encolpius's experience in Trimalchio's house is not so comfortable. As soon as he is over the threshold, he is bamboozled by the layout and content of the house. The entrance hall has an *atriensis* (an "entrance keeper," whose title derives from the *atrium*), but we appear to be in a peristyle, with a colonnade and even a troupe of athletes (§29.7). Throughout the visit, the guests rely not on their own knowledge of houses but on slaves who tell them which rooms to enter and how to do so (§30.5). We are kept similarly in the dark. It is only near the end that Trimalchio offers a quick résumé of his home's features (§77.4): it has four dining rooms (*cenationes*), 20 chambers (*cubicula*) in addition to one each for himself and Fortunata, and two marble colonnades (*porticus*). Unusually in a description of a *domus*, but, of course, in line with Trimalchio's preoccupations, he also tells us something about the slave quarters: upstairs he has a row of cubicles (*cellatio*) and a really good *cella* for the *atriensis* (Andreau, FREEDMEN IN THE SATYRICA, discusses the obsession of Trimalchio with slavery and the interactions between the freedmen at the dinner party, their former slave lives, and their own current slaves). We also get to see the private baths (*balneum*) (§73). The description implies a pretty big house (those houses in Pompeii with two peristyles, like the House of the Faun, are exceptionally grand), but it is a waste of time, despite previous attempts, to reconstruct Trimalchio's house. We are not supposed to be able to: it is, as Encolpius explains, impossible to articulate, a "new kind of labyrinth," a metaphor we will examine more fully later on (§73.1).

Memory and Autobiography

If we cannot make sense of the architecture of the house, can we do any better with its paintings? Once past the dog, Encolpius first sees a series of scenes depicting the life of their host, showing succinctly everything we will later hear related about Trimalchio. He is pretty much laid bare before we start. The fresco cycle charts his life from his debut in the slave market, learning accounting, and becoming a steward to being hauled up onto a tribunal (presumably as a *sevir Augustalis*, a freedman official of the imperial cult) by Mercury (Richlin, SEX IN THE SATYRICA, p. 90, notes the way in which the mural, through its written labels, like Trimalchio's later autobiography, draws attention to his sexual service as a young slave). Just in case we fail to get it, the artist has included written descriptions and has reinforced his point by calling on the gods to make cameo appearances: Minerva herself leads Trimalchio into Rome, Mercury helps him on the path to success, and Fortune with her cornucopia and the Fates spinning out his generous life thread share the dais with him (§29.3–6).

It is not at all unusual to find these deities called on by "tradesmen": Minerva and Mercury are ten-a-penny in paintings in *tabernae* ("shops") in Pompeii and, equally, some homeowners do not shrink from invoking wealth, whether via the Vettii's Priapus or simply a message in the floor (as in the entrance to House VII.i.46): "Well, hello profit!" The seal of Vettius Conviva included a *caduceus* (Mercury's wand). Art and autobiography might meet in other ways, such as the large mosaic jars (daubed with slogans: "The best sauce in town!") found in the *atrium* of a smart yard on the edge of town, complete with a spectacular sea view and private baths. Perhaps inevitably, it has been suggested that this is the home of the famous *garum* sauce (fish sauce) magnate of Pompeii, Scaurus (Cooley and Cooley 2004: 165–6). Sullivan (1986: 195) wonders if the Scaurus whom Trimalchio later namedrops as a house guest (§77.5) might be that very entrepreneur. This forms another good example of how we might choose to characterize the taste of someone who makes a living from processing pickled fish guts (Vout, THE SATYRICA AND NERONIAN CULTURE p. 109, offers some very different suggestions as to who this Scaurus might be; Andreau, FREEDMEN IN THE SATYRICA, p. 118, offers further discussion of the professions and statuses of the freedmen at the *cena*).

Trimalchio does not just invoke profit, he literally worships it as one of his household gods (§60.8–9). The Roman house was the focal point of a family's religious life. The household shrine (*lararium*) was home to the hearth fire of the *domus*, the household gods (*Lares*) and the familial *genius*, a common ancestral spirit that neatly avoided the specific deification of any one individual. Not for Trimalchio such ambiguities: his *lararium* features his own beard clippings (§29.8; see Richlin, SEX IN THE SATYRICA p. 90, on the sexual implications of these pubescent trimmings), and the golden statue that he and his guests venerate is of Trimalchio himself (§60.9). Having no offspring or ancestors, whether real or *imagine*-d (and no future: he has no children, no *familia* except his slaves), this *domus* has no *genius*, only the living owner (on the difficult status of the freedman with regard to his past ancestry and future commemoration, see also Hope, AT HOME WITH THE DEAD, p. 147; Andreau, FREEDMEN IN THE SATYRICA,

p. 120, emphasizes the importance that freedmen placed on their descendants, the lack of which further isolates Trimalchio).

This enforced self-reliance is often used to explain the self-referential mode of "freedman art" (Whitehead 1993; see also Hope, AT HOME WITH THE DEAD), but in appealing to the pedigree of autobiographical wall-painting, Trimalchio could point to Sulla, whose villa at Tusculum was sup-posedly decorated with images of his battle exploits (Plin. *HN* 22.12), demonstrating that the elite were just as much disposed to blowing their own trumpets in private space (Eck 1984; Prag 2006). Undaunted, Trimalchio's paintings likewise ape monumental relief sculpture, the kind that tells of military endeavor and civic panache and that we might more readily expect to see on the triumphal arches of Rome (Hölscher 2006). In these scenes, emperors are led into the city by Roma (helmeted like Minerva) and are accompanied on platforms or swept up to the heavens by Victory or *Aion* ("Time"), winged counterparts to Trimalchio's Mercury. Elsewhere in the house, he takes further opportunity to ape civic grandeur, hanging the rods and axes of magisterial office on the doorpost of his dining room (with the excuse of his dignity as *sevir*, §30.1), imitating men much grander than himself, whom he, in his studded ring and purple-striped napkin can only come close to emulating within his own home (§32; Vout, THE *SATYRICA* AND NERONIAN CULTURE, p. 105, discusses further the process of "playing up" to these grand, military roles).

Myth and Education

The next set of paintings that Encolpius sees, he has to get some help with: scenes from the *Iliad* and *Odyssey* with a further, seemingly more incongruous panel showing the amphitheatre games of Laenas (§29.9). An eclectic mix of high culture and low-class entertainment perhaps? Similar eclecticism occurs again in Trimalchio's choice of silverware, the decoration of which also includes Greek myth and Roman gladiators (§52.1–3). In fact, the wall-paintings of Pompeii demonstrate the same tendency: why on earth did one homeowner think that the amphitheatre riot of AD 59 would look good in his living room? Did he have some personal connection with the riot? Had he started it? Lost a relative? Did he admire the fighters, want to recall an event that had put his town on the map, or did he just love the amphitheatre?

More palatable to us, perhaps, are the panels of Greek myth, which may be supposed to reflect an owner's (and our own) cultural fluency and awareness of artistic tradition. The Vettii themselves fielded scenes of Pentheus, Pasiphae, and Ixion. And is it only we who are obsessed with the link or were the Vettii, too, told confidently by the decorators that their panel of the baby Hercules strangling snakes was a copy of an original by Zeuxis, one of the grandest Old Masters? The elder Pliny's *Natural History* (35.61–6) contains a brief description of the Zeuxis painting, vague enough to convince some of the close likeness of the Vettii's version. The desire to show off Greek mythology and to do so using Hellenistic templates is an exceedingly popular practice in Roman houses, in the minor arts as well as on the walls. Trimalchio attempts to parade his expertise throughout the party, mangling the myths on his silverware (§52.1–2). His house is properly appointed for the pursuit of such learning: he makes sure we know that he has (presumably much underused) Greek and Latin libraries (§48.4).

The reason for Trimalchio's excessive display is perhaps made a little clearer at this point. He is also all too well aware of the cultural and monetary worth of art itself. Posing as a connoisseur he likes to spout his knowledge: the history of Corinthian bronze, for example (§50). The socially loaded practice of appreciating fine art will be demonstrated later in the sequence, when Encolpius and Eumolpus muse on the paintings in a provincial art gallery that has a (suspiciously) impressive roll-call of featured artists: Zeuxis, Protogenes, and Apelles among them (§83–90). Eumolpus, taking on the role of tour guide, turns out to be as idiotic as Trimalchio, garbling the biographies of these artists, making the notoriously prolific and financially savvy sculptor Lysippos (Plin. *HN* 34.37) into a tortured artist dying in poverty over one statue (§88.5). An important feature of both their attempts at art criticism is their eagerness to stress the illusionistic effects of classical art, such naturalism being a quality we too admire (Elsner 1993). Eumolpus does not get it quite right when he says of the great classical Athenian sculptor Myron that his works were so good they captured the soul of their subjects (§88.5; in fact, this was said to be the one thing at which he failed), but he is groping for the common idea that Myron's statues were incredibly life-like. In the *Greek Anthology* there are plenty of epigrams that emphasize this quality: the cow that is so convincing it attracts the attentions of bovine admirers; the athlete who appears to breathe and strain on his starting line (*Anth. Pal.* 9.734; 16.54). Trimalchio, too, makes sure we know he can see naturalism when he sees it. Rounding up his misinterpretation of his cups, one of which shows what he insists is

Cassandra slaying her sons, he moves on to stylistic analysis: of the figures of the dead youths, he is moved to declare that their corpses are fashioned so skillfully, you would think they were alive (§52.1)!

Hunting

One popular aspect of domestic decoration that is conspicuously missing from Trimalchio's house is garden painting. The representation of the natural world, often in very unnatural places, was very popular. Hunting scenes, in particular, are seen all over Pompeii: animals hunt each other in the House of the Ceii, and humans hunt animals in the House of the Ancient Hunt. Very similar iconography surfaces in Trimlachio's dining room in the form of embroidered couch-covers that are brought in during the meal, depicting hunters carrying spears and nets: familiar accoutrements for the none-too-sporting Roman hunt (§40.1). The embroidered representation of the hunt is not the end of the theme – in a few seconds hounds, hunters, and even a (ex-) wild boar are coursing round the dining couches. The theme is enacted by the household as the dish itself, the dead boar, recreates its own autobiography and, in effect, turns up to its own funeral, just as Trimalchio will try to do later on. This piece of theatre is reminiscent of other reported dinner scenes, particularly a much earlier example reported by Varro (*Rust.* 3.13.2–3) to have taken place at the villa of Hortensius, where a slave played the part of Orpheus, whistling up a whole host of animals.

The episode, including these often overlooked antimacassars, brings together all elements of the *domus*: the space of the dining room, the decor that embellishes it, and the behavior of its occupants all become caught up in the same pursuit. Some clue to the overlap is provided by the slave responsible for all the horrid party food: Daedalus, a man who can make a pigeon out of lard (§70.2), is deliberately meant to remind us of the mythic Daedalus's role as master inventor of craft, of space (most obviously the labyrinth to which the whole *domus* will shortly be likened; cf. Morgan, PETRONIUS AND GREEK LITERATURE, p. 36), and also of naturalistic art. According to Diodorus Siculus (4.76), Daedalus was the first artist to create statues that were so life-like they could move, that is to say that he was the first to invent naturalistic art (to make life out of marble) and so to achieve the effects held in such high esteem by Eumolpus and Trimalchio.

Theatricality

The effect of the merging of these elements is that reality and representation seem to collide repeatedly in Trimalchio's house (Slater 1990: 57). At one point, as Encolpius is served by singing slaves, he cottons on to what is happening: "You would think you were in the chorus of the pantomime not the *triclinium* [dining room] of a *paterfamilias*" (§31.7). It is not difficult, in reading through the episode, to see many links to the theatre and other spectacles. On one level there is the actual theatrical entertainment, singing, acting, acrobatics; on the other there is the "staged" nature of all the events during the meal, which draw on sets, props, and actors for effect. Many critics have recognized Trimalchio's domestic set-up to be essentially theatrical, and several articles have demonstrated that such performances are typical of the ritual of Roman *cenae* (for example, D'Arms 1999), where host and guests play up to their social roles. Here we move from theatre to "theatricality," a mode of behavior and of representing the world. Such "putting on" has come to be closely associated with ideas of Neronian decadence and insincerity (Bartsch 1994; Leach 2004: 114–21), qualities which then are seen to be mirrored in the *Satyrica* (the effect of circular argument as to the text's "Nero-ness" again coming into play; see Vout, THE SATYRICA AND NERONIAN CULTURE, for a sophisticated analysis of the relationship between Neronian Rome, the Petronian text, and this theme of theatricality).

As much as this theatrical turn suits the literary construction of the *Satyrica* (Courtney 2001; Panayotakis 1995), the idea of the theatre was perennially popular in Roman houses, so much so that Vitruvius (*De arch.* 7.5.2) mentions it as a standard theme of interior decor. Alongside scenes that seem to show plays in production, many commentators have viewed paintings, like that on a wall from the House of the Labyrinth showing a colonnade receding behind curtains into the distance (fig. 10.4), as "theatrical": huge painted sets, which seem to show cityscapes or sanctuaries opening up behind the "real" wall. Much ink has been spilt on considering how accurate these sets are, pondering which real theatres they could have been copied from, and even using these paintings to recreate Roman theatres (Lehmann 1953; Little 1971). More recently, though, a link has been made between the "stagey" paintings and the "theatrical" nature of domestic behavior. Such fads are not confined to the Neronian period and not even to Pompeii; the best discussion of theatre scenes in Roman houses is actually about mosaics in Antioch (Huskinson 2002–3), but is incredibly useful in showing how

Figure 10.4   A wall of the 'Corinthian *oecus*' in the House of the Labyrinth, Pompeii. (Photo: Hales.)

domestic interiors merged with the use of space, just as Trimlachio's hunt spills off his soft furnishings into the dining room. The apparent collapse of representation and reality is a nice way of understanding the painting in the House of the Labyrinth too, where real columns in the room mirror the pretend ones in the fresco.

In Trimalchio's house, space, art, and behavior are all brought together to create an atmosphere of confusion and disorientation. In fact, Pompeian interiors seem to aim at similar effects. Ironically, the House of the Labyrinth (named after the mosaic labyrinth in a neighboring room to the one examined here) is, again, a good example. The room we have been discussing is visible in the distance, straight ahead from the front door. Once inside, however, the viewer is encouraged to look anywhere but back outside as the overpowering paintings on the three surrounding walls envelop you and draw you into their colonnades and precincts. The plan of the house, which seemed simple and uncontested on the way in, becomes much more immersive once inside. Like Trimalchio, the owner of this house has used artifice to make a labyrinthine pretend world in what is actually a rather straightforward house.

If these spaces have anything to do with the theatre, it is not because they copy real theatres, but because domestic art and space, like the theatre, seem to evoke different worlds, transporting the viewer to a world beyond normality (and Trimalchio's guests are certainly beyond that). In exploring Greek tragic theatre, Rehm has adopted a term from Foucault with which to name this kind of space – it is a "heterotopia," a world outside normal conventions that, by virtue of that distance, can be critical of those conventions (Rehm 2002: 19–34). The term might sound scarily like a word Trimalchio has garbled in one of his declamations, but its meaning is actually not too hard to grasp: what it could mean for us is the potential of domestic space and decor to fashion a space beyond the everyday outside world which allows hosts and guests the chance temporarily to escape that world and reinvent themselves. Domestic art creates a fantasy world where the boundaries of normal life are called into question.

Reality and Fantasy, Deception and Naturalism

Of course, unlike the more naïve viewers of art and spectacle in the *Satyrica*, most party-goers in the House of the Labyrinth were not fooled by the *trompe l'oeil* (lit. "deceives the eye," that is, illusory) architectural vistas opening around them. Even though they are deliberately painted to look real, guests were not regularly gashing their heads trying to walk through the painted gateways. Encolpius is clearly a fool, and his friends realize it, for nearly breaking his leg in trying to escape the painted dog (§29.1–2).

The bruised Encolpius raises an important point. When you consider the ridiculousness of being scared of a painted dog then the whole idea of mistaking art for reality seems pretty silly. All of a sudden it is not just that Trimalchio manages to bumble his go at art criticism by seeing life in corpses, but that he should see life in art at all. The very notion that art could/should be reality, an idea uttered not only by the characters but by such establishment figures as Pliny the Elder, is called into question. While Trimalchio and Eumolpus pontificate about life-like art, Petronius is having a laugh at their expense. Illusionism in art might be a high point of artistic endeavor but it is not the sole, or even main aim of the artist. Similarly, recognizing naturalism is only a preliminary viewing response (Bryson 1990: 17–59). The power of art lies precisely in realizing its artifice so it can break free from, or comment on, the constraints of reality. Apart from Encolpius's rookie response at the beginning of the evening, the spectators at the dinner party are constantly aware of the artifice of what they see. The further joke is that even while showing confidence in the life-like qualities of art to be a ridiculous position, the crew of the *Satyrica* are all too fond of bewailing the decline of that life-likeness and blaming the decadence of their age as the cause (§88; Elsner 1993).

In their criticism, as in their praise, the characters of the *Satyrica* echo perennial commonplaces of art appreciation. Indignant moralists-cum-art critics like Vitruvius likewise blamed an immoral present for a decline in art, a decline they saw manifested most clearly by a preoccupation with the unreal and fantastic. When he attacks the fantastic elements of contemporary wall-painting, Vitruvius suggests that, in turning away from reality, painters have turned from the "truth" (Vitr. *De arch.* 7.5.3–4; cf. Hor. *Ars P.* 1–5). Elsner understands this insistence on "realism" as a "rejection of subversion," of the "unreal and anti-realistic" (Elsner 1995: 57). In fact, in deriding the "unnatural," Vitruvius's criticism turns out to be not so far removed from Seneca's assessments of luxury villas, which also defy nature, reveling in artifice to experience new imaginative heights.

While we're sniggering at Trimalchio and Eumolpus, however, we might want to realize that the joke is also on us. Perhaps we too should consider our own imbecility for reading Pliny or Vitruvius at face value. Like Trimalchio, art historians have traditionally been preoccupied with naturalism, and it is not so long ago that attempts to explain the "decline" of naturalism in terms of moral decline finally died out. We still live with a legacy that dismisses post- or non-classical art – art that does not look as real as Myron's cow – as slightly soiled. In taking the representation of reality as the ultimate goal of art, Pompeian wall-paintings were similarly interpreted in terms of the reality they imitated: a stage set here, an art gallery there. But the joke of naturalism turns out to be in using illusionism precisely to create the fantastic and unreal. The frescoes in the House of the

Labyrinth are not simply theatres or sanctuaries, any more than the rooms of the mythic panels in the House of the Vettii are meant to copy civic art galleries. To privilege any one model is to miss the deliberate conflation of influences and their recycling into painting's own fantastic language.

The preoccupation with fantasy and the rejection of reality, and the somewhat ironic use of illusionism as a vehicle to portray that, is perhaps the best link between "real" domestic space and art and those of Trimalchio. Fantasy offers scope for invention and manipulation. The extent to which Trimalchio's fantasy takes a hold on his guests is shown throughout the *Cena*: the painted dog mistaken for a real one (and then becoming the real Scylax by the end) and the labyrinth from which they cannot escape. His whole household is activated to keep it all going: slaves, food, art – none are what they seem, and his audience has no choice but to humor him as it waits for the emergency services to arrive.

As much as this argument might seem in danger of making Trimalchio a sophisticated master of domestic space rather than a vulgar upstart, there is still plenty of room for going wrong. The power of wall-painting and domestic space in impressing guests and visitors lies in the fact that fantasy is limitless. Only Trimalchio would dull the fantasy by making it explicit, by only seeing the possibility of faking reality. While most other homeowners create fantastic concoctions of other worlds, most of Trimalchio's fantasies are of himself. Neither is he willing to let the viewer's imagination run with the images they see. By over-explaining his paintings and cups, just as he does all his jokes and party turns, he closes down all ambiguity (Tanner 1979: 52–6). The stamps that flaunt the weight of the silver (§31.10) and his insistence on weighing Fortunata's jewelry (§67.7) show off his wealth but also expose its limitations.

Conclusion

Trimalchio's *domus* is a sealed box in which he can be king of his castle. His aspirations, through impotence, are turned inwards. His authority can only exist within this *domus*-gone-wrong, within the fantasies he creates through manipulation of the visual world around him (Andreau, FREEDMEN IN THE SATYRICA, p. 119, also stresses the insularity of Trimalchio and his circle of friends). And perhaps this really shows the disaster of Trimalchio's *domus*. The whole point, to repeat the phrase, of heterotopic space is that its other-worldliness only works as a temporary retreat from reality. Domestic space provided spectators with space in which to reconfigure themselves for their grand entrance back onto the public stage. The cleverest players are those who manage somehow to play off the two worlds, to legitimate fantasy with reality and bolster reality with fantasy. The Trimalchios of the Roman world mishandle their relationship with their art, putting themselves directly into the display and trapping themselves in their own private, solipsistic worlds. Trimalchio's whole existence is wrapped up in his house; in fact he only really exists on the walls of the house (or on the reliefs of his tomb). His house; does not partake of the social penetrability for which the *domus* was designed: his guests are fellow freedmen and just as impotent outside each other's walls. This, of course, is why Trimalchio looks forward to his funeral and lives in a house that has become a kind of tomb (Bodel 1994). Death will allow him to get his public memorial (see the chapter by Hope, AT HOME WITH THE DEAD). Meanwhile, these enervated men must stay in locked rooms: as Ganymede says, men are lions at home, foxes outside (§44.14). Once Encolpius and crew escape, we know full well that they will never find their way back. Like the Phaeacians in the *Odyssey* (and see Vout, THE *SATYRICA* AND NERONIAN CULTURE, and Richlin, SEX IN THE *SATYRICA*, for some more Odyssean parallels), whom Poseidon punishes for hosting Odysseus by throwing up rocks around their island, the reward for Trimalchio's hospitality to these particular lost travelers is to disappear forever.

Further Reading

For a general introduction to different types of Roman housing, see Barton (1996). Wiseman's (1987) influential article demonstrates the importance of the *domus* in providing a public face for its owners. Edwards (2003) has a useful chapter on the morals of building. Wallace-Hadrill (1994) has done most to pursue the sociological importance of domestic space and decoration, swapping emphasis from the literature of Rome to the archaeological remains of Pompeii and Herculaneum (see also Hales 2003). Petersen (2006: 123–62) addresses assumptions of freedman taste in interior decor.

Discussions of Roman domestic art have shifted over the last decades from formal analysis to more interpretative modes. Bryson (1990) and Elsner (1995: 49–87) provide exciting ideas about wall-painting's tendency to fantasy and subversion. Leach's (2004) major study of wall-painting is the first to break away from traditional, formal categorization and includes a whole chapter on the theatrical style. The turn to see theatricality as a

Neronian phenomenon comes from Bartsch (1994). Huskinson's (2002–3) article on Antioch mosaics is very useful for explaining the relation between theatre, decor, and theatrical behavior. She draws on several discussions of the relation between theatrical spectacle and dinner parties, by D'Arms (1999), Jones (1991), and Rosati (1983/1999), all of whom (the last exclusively) draw on Trimalchio's dinner party.

A good example of traditional attempts to reconstruct Trimalchio's *domus* can be found in Bagnani (1954). Later discussions of the building and its art play much more with its role in reflecting wider themes of the episode. On Trimalchio's home as the Underworld see Bodel (1994). Elsner's (1993) article offers an inspiring analysis of the later episode of Encolpius and Eumolpus in the art gallery and discusses its relation to contemporary practices of viewing and describing art.

11

Petronius's *Satyrica* and the Novel in English

Stephen Harrison

Introduction

Though scholars hotly debate the point at which the novel emerged (or re-emerged) in Europe as a recognizable literary form (cf. Doody 1996), that date is sometimes placed (for example, by the influential McKeon 1987) in the second half of the seventeenth century, the very period in which the fullest version of the Latin text of the *Satyrica* was published (1669), to complete the work we have today, and in which the first vernacular translations appeared (for example, the English version of Burnaby in 1694). But the *Satyrica* had already excited novelistic imitation in English a century previously, in Thomas Nashe's colorful *The Unfortunate Traveller* (1594), a picaresque tale with a prosimetric frame and a wide range of literary pastiche and parody, which certainly shows the influence of Petronius (see Kinney 1986: 341–3, 357–8). In the seventeenth century some imitation of Petronius is evident in the Latin fictions of John Barclay (*Euphormionis Lusinini Satyricon*, 1603) and Walter Charleton (*Matrona Ephesia*, 1659), while in the eighteenth century Petronian material can be found in the earthier parts of the novels of Smollett (see below); but it was in the nineteenth century, when the novel in England reached its highest prestige and importance as a literary form, that the influence of the *Satyrica* and Petronius begins to be extensive. In what follows I shall trace the reception of Petronius and his novel through examining some fictional successor versions of one of its key episodes, the *Cena Trimalchionis*, and conclude by considering several novels (one written a century ago by a Nobel Literature laureate and two written in the last 30 years) in which Petronius himself and his novel appear as subject matter.

Dormice and Honey: The *Cena Trimalchionis* through the Novelistic Ages

Tobias Smollett, *Peregrine Pickle* (1751)

In Chapter 48 of Smollett's picaresque novel *Peregrine Pickle* (1751), the eponymous hero, visiting Paris, is invited by a fellow Englishman, a young physician named only as "the Doctor," to "an entertainment in the manner of the ancients." This points us to the world of Greece and Rome, and Smollett himself here alludes to the legendary Latin culinary writer Apicius and cites a line from Horace's last satire (2.8), the *cena Nasidieni*, the over-elaborate dinner with pretentious food-notes from the host given by Nasidienus at his own house. The Doctor indeed plays a Nasidienus role in Smollett's comic dinner, introducing a range of gross and luxurious dishes to his disgusted guests, but the figure of Trimalchio and the Petronian episode of the *Cena Trimalchionis* are also clearly laid under contribution. Some of the luxurious dishes are lifted from the excesses of the *Cena*: the pie of "dormice liquored with syrup of white poppies" plainly picks up the *glires melle ac papavere sparsos*, "dormice sprinkled with honey and poppy-seed" of §31.10, while the "sow's stomach, filled with a composition of minced pork, hog's brains, eggs, pepper, cloves, garlic, aniseed, rue, ginger, oil, wine, and pickle" recalls the apparently ungutted sow of §49.1 filled with prepared meats. Apart from the grossly luxurious food, a further Petronian element is clearly the hypocrisy of the guests: one of them, a French marquis, resists nausea to praise the soup:

> Peregrine […] asked the marquis how he found the soup. It was with infinite difficulty that his complaisance could so far master his disgust as to enable him to answer, "Altogether excellent, upon my honour!"

This is closely parallel to the insincere praise of Trimalchio's dinner from the guests Encolpius, Giton, and Ascyltos. Like the *Cena Trimalchionis*, Smollett's feast is full of slapstick incident, especially the moment when the painter Pallet (a caricature of the great Hogarth), physically shocked by tasting "the essence of a whole bed of garlic" in some poultry, upsets the whole dinner on his fellow-guests.

These allusions are part of a tissue of classical quotation in Smollett's novel, but the use of the *Satyrica* may perhaps indicate some consciousness of fictional precedents in Latin literature for the modern literary genre. The same can be said more firmly for two nineteenth-century appearances of the *Cena* in fiction, both in early historical novels, which also use echoes of Petronius as authentication for their Roman scene-settings.

Lord Lytton (Edward Bulwer-Lytton), *The Last Days of Pompeii* (1834)

Lytton's *The Last Days of Pompeii* (*LDP*), one of the most popular novels of the nineteenth century, narrates two luxurious banquets which both recall the *Cena Trimalchionis*, appropriately enough in a novel set in AD 79, close to the Neronian period then, as now, standardly assigned to the *Satyrica* (see INTRODUCTION, p. 5). In Book 1 Chapter 3, Glaucus, the Greek hero of the novel, gives a dinner at his house in Pompeii (a re-imagining of the House of the Tragic Poet) with elaborate service and musical accompaniment, though the elaboration is more in the setting and accoutrements than in the food itself, which is barely mentioned. The aedile Pansa shows off by bringing his own special napkin which outdoes those of the host:

> [...] young slaves bore round to each of the five guests (for there were no more) the silver basin of perfumed water, and napkins edged with a purple fringe. But the aedile ostentatiously drew forth his own napkin, which was not, indeed, of so fine a linen, but in which the fringe was twice as broad, and wiped his hands with the parade of a man who felt he was calling for admiration.

This clearly reflects (and caps) the description of the elaborate napkins provided by Trimalchio at §32.2. Similarly, Petronian pretensions about wine are echoed. In *LDP* Glaucus serves an ostentatiously labeled vintage wine and orders the slave to give its details:

> "Bring hither the amphora," said Glaucus, "and read its date and its character." The slave hastened to inform the party that the scroll fastened to the cork betokened its birth from Chios, and its age a ripe fifty years. "How deliciously the snow has cooled it!" said Pansa. "It is just enough."

This combines two elements in the *Cena*: the extravagant use of snow as a cooling agent (used with water not wine in Petronius, cf. §31.1) and the pretentious parading of a vintage wine through a label; the more or less plausible 50-year Chian in Lytton recalls, and makes more realistic, the somewhat fantastic century-old Falernian in Petronius (§34.6). Another descendant of the *Cena* in Lytton's novel is the meal described in Book 4 Chapter 3: "A fashionable party and a dinner à la mode in Pompeii," given by the hedonistic Diomed, who, like Trimalchio, is a rich merchant who "affected greatly the man of letters." Though Diomed, unlike Trimalchio, does not dominate the conversation at his own dinner by suggesting literary topics or by making comic errors of learning and mythology, the two guests, Sallust and Glaucus, from whose more cultured perspective we view events, condemn him as "a vulgar old fellow" (cf. the comments Encolpius and Ascyltos make about Trimalchio). Again the food has little importance, and the Petronian echoes focus on the luxurious surroundings and accountrements: the diners are entertained by acrobats (cf. §53.11), a slave drops a precious ornament (cf. §52.4), and the guests are presented with a series of riddling gifts (cf. §56.8–10).

W. Wilkie Collins, Antonina (1850)

In our second historical fiction, *Antonina* (1850), the little-known first novel by Wilkie Collins (subsequently author of the Victorian best-sellers *The Moonstone* and *The Woman in White*) and a work much influenced by Lytton (above), allusion to the *Cena Trimalchionis* appears again. *Antonina* is set in the years around the sack of Rome by Alaric in AD 410, and one of its themes is the degeneracy of the Roman aristocracy. In Chapter 7 the heroine is invited to the house of the Roman senator Vetranio, a villain who is about to attempt to seduce her. Vetranio, though an aristocrat, clearly resembles the upstart freedman Trimalchio in several more ways than the shape of his name. In his palace we find a grand notice:

> This public notice, […] intended for the special edification of all the inhabitants of Rome, was thus expressed:
> "ON THIS DAY, AND FOR TEN DAYS FOLLOWING, THE AFFAIRS OF OUR PATRON OBLIGE HIM TO BE ABSENT FROM ROME."
> Here the proclamation ended, without descending to particulars. It had been put forth, in accordance with the easy fashion of the age, to answer at once all applications at Vetranio's palace during the senator's absence.

This clearly recalls the notice in Trimalchio's house, similarly capitalized in Victorian editions, at §30.3: *hoc habebat inscriptum: III ET PRIDIE KALENDAS IANVARIAS C. NOSTER FORAS CENAT* ("this was the inscription on it: 'On the 30th and 31st December our master Gaius dines out.'") Both inscriptions advertise the prestige and wealth of the house's owner: Trimalchio is claiming to entertain at home almost every night of the year, while Vetranio assumes that his absence is a major matter of public interest.

More echoes of Petronius occur in the description of the sleeping Vetranio:

> Immediately above the sleeping senator hung his portrait, in which he was modestly represented as rising by the assistance of Minerva to the top of Parnassus, the nine Muses standing round him rejoicing. At his feet reposed a magnificent white cat, whose head rested in all the luxurious laziness of satiety on the edge of a golden saucer half filled with dormice stewed in milk. The most indubitable evidences of the night's debauch appeared in Vetranio's disordered dress and flushed countenance as the freedman regarded him. For some minutes the worthy Carrio stood uncertain whether to awaken his master or not, deciding finally, however, on obeying the commands he had received, and disturbing the slumbers of the wearied voluptuary before him. To effect this purpose, it was necessary to call in the aid of the singing-boy; for, by a refinement of luxury, Vetranio had forbidden his attendants to awaken him by any other method than the agency of musical sounds.

Several details here evoke Trimalchio in the *Satyrica*. The self-aggrandizing portrait of Vetranio being assisted by Minerva to climb Parnassus recalls the portrait of Trimalchio in the vestibule of his house, which shows him being led by Minerva into Rome (§29.3); the cat dining on dormice from a golden saucer cleverly recalls both the dormice eaten by humans at the *Cena* (§31.10) and Trimalchio's indiscriminate use of gold for domestic artifacts, including a golden cage for his pet magpie (§28.9); and the use of music as an alarm recalls Trimalchio's constant need to be accompanied by singing musicians (§32.1; see Rimell, LETTING THE PAGE RUN ON).

Finally, when Vetranio awakes to the sound of music, he questions one of the performers:

> "Of what rank of my musicians are you at present, Glyco?"
> "Of the fifth," replied the boy.
> "Were you bought, or born in my house?" asked Vetranio.
> "Neither; but bequeathed to you by Geta's testament," rejoined the gratified Glyco.

"I advance you," continued Vetranio, "to the privileges and the pay of the first rank of my musicians; and I give you, as a proof of my continued favour, this ring."

This scene echoes Trimalchio's dialogue with a cook at §47.12–13:

"Which company do you belong to?" The cook told him the fortieth.
"Were you purchased," asked the host, "or are you home-born?"
"Neither," said the cook. "I was bequeathed to you in the will of Pansa."
"Be sure, then," said Trimalchio, "to make a good job of serving this course, or I'll order you to be demoted to the company of messengers." (Trans. Walsh 1996, used throughout this chapter.)

Both grandees pointedly stress that they have very large numbers of slaves and cannot be expected to know them all; Vetranio offers an inducement (to keep a secret) and Trimalchio threatens punishment, both the acts and attitudes of powerful and domineering masters. Again, Wilkie Collins neatly varies his original, and also, in the name of Pansa, cleverly evokes a character from Lytton's novel (see above).

Three elements emerge from these two nineteenth-century imitations of Petronius's Trimalchio in Lytton and Wilkie Collins. As already noted, two aspects, the need to achieve Roman realism in historical scene-setting and consciousness that there was a literary tradition of fiction in Rome itself, both play a central role here, but with interesting cultural transformation. The upstart freedman Trimalchio is in both cases transformed into a decadent aristocrat, pointing to the standard Victorian, post-Gibbon view of the fatal decline of the Roman nobility which both authors follow, while the Petronian emphasis on food and its gross, overwhelming variety is suppressed in the interests of describing houses, surroundings, and other cultural practices, combining Victorian decorum about bodily matters with an anthropological and archaeological thrust. The point is made if we contrast these two nineteenth-century appropriations with the much more rumbustious use made of the same material by Smollett (above).

Edwin Shrake, *Peter Arbiter* (1973)

In this satirical novel, the Texan writer Edwin "Bud" Shrake attacks the gross luxury of contemporary, oil-rich Texas in what might be seen as a more scurrilous version of the legendary TV soap-opera *Dallas* (1978–91). The plot is well described by the work's dust-jacket as one in which "three social misfits, a runaway teenage boy, an old con-man poet, and a bisexual interior decorator, skip irreverently through the world of Texas's moneyed society, the politicos, ranchers and oilmen, in settings that range from a house with a golf course in the living room to a kinky sexual rejuvenation clinic". The same source confirms that Petronius is a model: the eponymous character of the title is the interior decorator and also the first-person narrator, clearly reflecting Petronius's role in Tacitus as *elegantiae arbiter* (Arbiter of Taste) as well as that of Encolpius.

In the third (unnumbered) chapter of the novel, the three adventurers are invited to dinner at the enormously grand house and estate of the millionaire Billy Roy Eanes, who is clearly set up as a Trimalchio figure. When the three first encounter Eanes himself they find him dressed as a quarterback, practicing football throws to children; he urinates publicly into a silver vase. This scene plainly recalls in several elements the scene at §27–8. In the vestibule of Billy Roy's personal gym we find more Petronian detail:

> A porter in white pants, white shirt and white sneakers counted us as we went out. Above the door was a golden cage from which a myna bird shrieked: "Billy Roy Eanes did it the hard way!"

This recalls the magpie in a golden cage at §28.9, but the ostentatious proclaiming of self-made origins also echoes the wall-paintings on Trimalchio's career at §29.3–6; a notice in the banquet-hall itself saying that "ON JUNE 19 / BILLY ROY EANES / DINES OUT" clearly recalls Trimalchio's notice (§30.3) that he dines out (only) on 30 and 31 December. The dinner is suitably gross and luxuriously served:

> Six blacks wheeled in a copper casting of Billy Roy's champion Clydesdale horse. Flanking the horse were platters, engraved BRE, bearing barbecued ribs, chicken, cole slaw, barbecue sauce, potato salad, pinto beans, jalapeño peppers, red chillis, sliced onions, scallions, pickles, garlic bread, hot sausages, beef tacos, boiled shrimps, fried quail and oysters on the half shell.

Later we find Petronian illusory food, eggs concealing figs, clearly alluding to the fig-pecker birds concealed in egg-yolk at §33.8, a joke course based on the 12 signs of the Zodiac, which recalls the famous original (§35.1), and a sow stuffed with live pigeons (cf. §49.1). Like Trimalchio (§32.1), Billy

Roy himself comes to the table late accompanied by music (this time country music), provides wine supposedly "100 Years Old" (cf. §34.6), and brings in a skeleton as a *memento mori* (a reminder of mortality) and stimulus for trite reflections (cf. §34.8–10). There are a number of further detailed echoes: for example, an apparently ungutted hog is revealed as stuffed with delicacies (cf. §49.10), a staff member drops a crystal goblet (cf. §52.4), and an acrobat lands on the host (cf. §54.1).

Just as in these specific parallels, Shrake's dinner sticks closely to the structure of the Petronian original. A regular guest informs the visitor about the host's wife, the host's business career, and selected further guests (cf. §37–8), and the host's exit to "make pee-pee" (cf. §41.9) is followed by conversation between those present, this time not freedmen but vulgar Texas dignitaries (a congressman, a millionaire businessman, a newspaper publisher, and an insurance broker). The Niceros werewolf story (§61–2) becomes a werewolf story from South America told by the old soldier General Enos Zachary; the late arrival is Calhoun the undertaker who again matches the stonemason Habinnas in the original (§65.5) as the recipient of the host's instructions about his monstrous tomb and inscription (§71.5–12); and the party is absurdly broken up by the host's own fire patrol who burst in responding to the terrible noise of the guests as they imagine they are at Billy Roy's funeral (§78.4–8).

Overall, Shrake successfully combines contemporary satirical subject matter with detailed Petronian allusion in his version of the *Cena Trimalchionis*, and his novel as a whole deserves more attention for the well-crafted turning of Petronian episodes into parallel modern comedies which similarly attack mindless materialism.

Tom Wolfe, *The Bonfire of the Vanities* (1987)

This novel (along with Oliver Stone's film *Wall Street* of the same year) is often thought of as the classic satire on 1980s New York greed and materialism. Petronian influence was not unknown previously in the American novel: F. Scott Fitzgerald's classic *The Great Gatsby* (1925) was originally entitled *Trimalchio* or *Trimalchio at West Egg*, and Jay Gatsby recalls Trimalchio as a parvenu extravagant host, a parallel explicitly made in Chapter 7, "his career as Trimalchio was over," as well as in the discarded title (see Briggs 1999 and 2000, Endres 2011, Slater 2011). This contact with Petronius is slight compared to that shown by Yale-educated Wolfe, who, like Edwin Shrake (see above), uses at least one episode which echoes the *Satyrica* in detail.

The Bonfire of the Vanities tells the story of Sherman McCoy, a million-aire Wall Street trader. In a central chapter of the book (Chapter 16, "The Masque of the Red Death") Sherman and his wife Judy go to a pretentious dinner-party given by a couple, the Bavardages, in their luxurious apart-ment on Fifth Avenue. This episode plainly draws on Petronius, and not just on the *Cena Trimalchionis*. The Bavardages (like Trimalchio) are presented as social and cultural upstarts from the point of view of Sherman himself (a WASP Yale graduate): his inner voice describes his hosts as "some over-bearingly vulgar people named Bavardage, a glorified traveling salesman and his wife." Like Trimalchio's house (§29.1–30.1), the Bavardages' apart-ment has a luxurious entrance-space ("the walls were covered in a brilliant Chinese-red silk"), and the dinner is compared in passing to "a feast of Lucullus," name-checking a famous Roman gourmet; the meal is suitably over-elaborate in Trimalchionic style, with a pseudo-naïve "simple, hearty American main course [...] insinuated between exotically contrived prologues and epilogues." The conversation and social intercourse is unbearably shallow and artificial.

These clear echoes of the *Cena Trimalchionis* are reinforced by an allusion to another part of the *Satyrica*. The guest of honor at the party, Aubrey Buffing, is an aged gay poet, who has more than a passing resemblance to old Eumolpus, Petronius's bad poet and erotic pursuer of young men. Though Buffing is a more elevated character than Eumolpus, being an English peer and apparently on the shortlist for the Nobel Prize for Literature, he is, like Eumolpus, apt to pronounce on literary subjects, and makes a substantial speech on the decadence of the contemporary literary scene:

> Poets are also not supposed to write epics any longer, despite the fact that the only poets who have endured are poets who have written epics. [...] No, we poets no longer even have the vitality to write epics. We don't even have the courage to make rhymes, and the American epic should have rhymes, rhyme on top of rhyme in a shameless cascade, rhymes of the sort that Edgar Allan Poe gave us [...].

The reference to Poe leads Buffing off into reflections about death, which put a damper on the party (the poet himself is dying of AIDS), but the observations on epic surely look back to Eumolpus's preface to his own poem on the civil war at §118:

> "Poetry, my young friends," said Eumolpus, "has beguiled many into believ-ing that they have set foot on Mount Helicon as soon as they have ordered

their lines into feet, and have woven their subtler thoughts into elaborate diction. […] But the others have either not identified the true path to poetry, or having identified it are afraid to tread it. For example, the person who tries his hand at the lofty theme of the Civil War must be steeped in literature, or he will sink under the burden of the subject. Historical events are not to be treated in verses, for historians handle such material far better. The free spirit of genius should plunge headlong into oracular utterances, the succour lent by the gods, and the Procrustean control of lapidary phrases."

Both critical reflections are made by fictional characters presented as older writers dealing with contemporary poets and the idea of epic; Eumolpus's remarks immediately precede his recitation of his own epic poem on the civil war of Caesar and Pompey; both poem and critical strictures can plausibly be seen as a comment on the contemporary epic of Lucan (Sullivan 1985a, 162–5); and Eumolpus, like Aubrey Buffing, argues that contemporary poets lack the spirit and courage to write a real epic. Tom Wolfe is thus splicing together two different Petronian scenes to produce a memorable episode of his own.

Robert Harris, *Pompeii* (2003)

The novel *Pompeii* (by the best-selling author of *Enigma* and *Imperium*, the latter on the career of Cicero) is a likely future film project at the time of writing (summer 2007) for Roman Polanski and would make a splendid screen thriller. Its plot concerns Marcus Attilius Primus, who, after the mysterious disappearance of his predecessor, takes over as water engineer for the aqueduct which serves Pompeii and its locality shortly before the eruption of Vesuvius in AD 79, from which he saves the girl Corelia through his knowledge of the city's water system. Corelia is the daughter of a self-made ex-slave millionaire Ampliatus, an obvious Trimalchio figure (if more sinister and powerful), who in the "Hora Septa" section of the book gives a dinner party which quite clearly recalls the *Cena Trimalchionis* in its elaborate fare, including the now familiar "mice rolled in honey and poppy-seeds" imitated by Smollett and Wilkie Collins (cf. §31.10), "sow's udder stuffed with kidneys" (cf. §36.1, §49.1), and "roast wild boar filled with live thrushes that flapped helplessly across the table" (cf. §40.3–5).

More interesting than these echoes, however, is the explicit evocation of the literary text of Petronius himself by the diners:

[Brittius] caught Popidius's eye and mouthed something at him. Popidius could not quite make it out. He cupped his ear and Brittius repeated it, shielding his mouth from Ampliatus with his napkin and emphasising every syllable: "Tri-mal-chi-o."

Popidius almost burst out laughing. Trimalchio! Very good! The freed slave of monstrous wealth in the satire by Titus Petronius, who subjects his guests to exactly such a meal and cannot see how vulgar and ridiculous he is showing himself. Ha ha! Trimalchio!

This is a splendidly self-reflexive moment in the novel: characters in AD 79 are made to invoke the Petronian text, available to them in historical time, which the writer is actually using as his literary source. The conspiratorial whispering of the two aristocrats Brittius and Popidius also recalls the way in which Encolpius and his friends comment adversely on Trimalchio's excesses in the *Cena*. This use of Roman fiction is perhaps part of Harris's careful research, which led him to read widely about Pompeii and aqueducts (Harris 2003: 339–40).

The Man and the Book: Petronius and the *Satyrica* as Fictional Subjects

The literary reception of the *Satyrica* has traditionally (and plausibly in my view) identified its author as Nero's *elegantiae arbiter*, memorably described by Tacitus (*Annals* 16.17–19; for the debate see INTRODUCTION, p. 5). Thus Petronius, the Tacitean character, and his work can appear together in later fiction.

Henryk Sienkiewicz, *Quo Vadis?* (1896)

The earliest example of this I have found is the novel *Quo Vadis?* (1896; cited here in the English translation of 1941), by the Polish writer Henryk Sienkiewicz (Nobel Laureate for Literature 1905), a book less well known than its homonymous 1951 film adaptation directed by Mervyn LeRoy in which Peter Ustinov won a best supporting actor Oscar as Nero. The hero of the book, Vinicius, is imagined as Petronius's nephew, and this allows Petronius to play a considerable role in the plot. Early in the novel Petronius purchases from a bookshop, and gives to Vinicius, a copy of a volume (Part 1 Chapter 2):

> "Here is a present for you," he said.
> "I thank you," replied Vinicius, looking at the title. "*The Satyricon*? A new work, then? And by whom?"
> "By myself. But since I do not wish to follow in the footsteps of Rufinus [...] I take care that no one shall know of it. Do not you either mention it to any one, I pray you."
> "You told me that you have never written verses," said Vinicius. "Yet here I see verses interlarding the prose."
> "When reading the work, turn your attention to the feast of Trimalchio [...]."

Vinicius immediately picks on a key literary feature of the work, its prosimetric form, and is told by Petronius to concentrate on the *Cena Trimalchionis* when he reads it. This perhaps points to the episode as the most substantial surviving section for the modern reader; it may also suggest that Sienkiewicz held that this part of the work has particular interest as a satire on Nero, as interpreters have sometimes argued (see Vout, THE SATYRICA AND NERONIAN CULTURE), since Petronius's contempt for the emperor who he is forced to serve is evident throughout the novel. But there is little further attempt to say much about the book or to use its material; indeed, the novel apparently published in Part 1 Chapter 2 appears again in Part 1 Chapter 12 as still being written ("Then he passed into his library, seated himself at a table of red marble, and set to work upon his 'Banquet of Trimalchio.'"). *Quo Vadis?* does have luxurious feasts, but none closely resembles the *Cena*, and Petronius's death scene, when he is forced to suicide by Nero (Part 2 Chapter 33), resists the temptation to include the novel among Petronius's last dispositions, though scholars have sometimes suggested that the written account of Nero's debaucheries, which Tacitus mentions as Petronius's last composition, is actually the *Satyrica* itself (see INTRODUCTION, p. 5).

Antony Burgess, *The Kingdom of the Wicked* (1985)

This typically exuberant late novel by the author of *A Clockwork Orange* (1963) tells the story of the first generations of Christianity against the backdrop of colorfully vicious Roman emperors (Tiberius, Gaius, and

Nero). The fourth chapter traces the last phase of St Paul's career in Neronian Rome with at least half an eye on the excesses of Nero's court. Here Petronius is presented in Tacitean mould as the chief adviser for all Nero's complex and contrived forms of debauchery and crime: Burgess reports (pp. 261–2) the contents of an (invented) literary work in which Petronius argues that the needs of art and beauty can override human rights and that the lives of others can be used as mere artistic fodder, and it is this absolutist aesthetic position which both Nero and Petronius pursue. Acquiescent in Nero's matricide, Petronius (though apparently attended professionally by the physician apostle Luke, and the first reader of the latter's *Acts of the Apostles*, pp. 317, 329) puts himself forward as the artificer of "fatal charades" (themed executions, cf. Coleman 1990) for the Christians blamed for the burning of Rome (p. 331):

> "Refine the taste of the people – has that not always been our aim? Confine the death of these fanatics to the arena but in no brutal manner. Let them be drawn into representations of Roman myth and history. Greek too. Will you leave it to your humble friend and coadjutor to sketch a programme?"

This talent for designing death is invoked again as Nero plans the end for Seneca (p. 340):

> Nero called: "Petronius!"
> "*Dear* Caesar?"
> "You know elegant ways to live. Do you also know elegant ways to die?"
> "Oh, suicide," Petronius said promptly. "In a hot bath preferably. A gentle slashing of the wrists. The water reddens to a delicate rose and deepens to a royal purple. One fades out as in a dream."

Ironically, this scenario generated for Seneca's death is largely repeated two pages later when Petronius himself is forced to suicide.

Here, then, we have the Tacitean *elegantiae arbiter*, but very much attuned to Nero's dark side: this Petronian concern with the aesthetic promotion of the deaths of others is Burgess's invention, though the staging of Petronius's own death scene is a recognizable version of Tacitus *Annales* 16.19. The amoral treatment of others as propounded and prosecuted by Burgess's Petronius seems to owe something to the plot and aesthetics of the *Satyrica*, but that work itself comes into the novel only briefly and by implication. During an imagined interview between Nero and St Paul, Petronius is said to be "writing on his estate ten miles down the Via Ostiensis" (p. 311). It seems very likely that this late Petronian work is intended as the *Satyrica,* but this is never confirmed. Burgess, like others, is clearly fascinated by the contradictions of Petronius's role as supreme aesthete and minion to a bloody tyrant, but does not explore deeply his role as novelist.

Jesse Browner, *The Uncertain Hour* (2007)

This recent novel, from a New York writer not previously known for classical subject matter, features Petronius as its chief character; it interestingly makes the young poet Martial his closest friend, and is set on the last day of his life in AD 66. The plot (picking up on elements of Tacitus *Annales* 16.19) presents Petronius as given some hours' notice of his impending forced suicide after losing the favor of Nero, and is largely devoted to the arrangements he makes for his own exit. These involve an elaborate and carefully planned dinner with courses plainly drawn from the *Cena:* "stuffed peahen, some nice plump figpeckers in peppered egg yolk [cf. §33.8] and Corycian saffron, turtle rumps, dormice in honey and poppy seeds [cf. §31.10], sow's vulva" (p. 25). Later on, Petronius himself gives an account of a supposedly real character, Vatia, an extravagant aristocrat who is clearly set up as a partial model for the fictional Trimalchio in the (yet unmentioned) *Satyrica* (pp. 74–5):

> "The caterer's guild of Naples named a dish after him. It was called "Vatia's Standard." It was a duck, stuffed with truffles, then stuffed inside a goose that was stuffed inside a peacock that was stuffed inside a heron that was stuffed inside a swan that was baked and gilded with egg yolk and gold leaf and carried in at the end of a long pike by a company of chefs dressed as legionaries and haruspices. He was fabulously wealthy – he'd been commander of the Praetorians at one point – but he acted like a vulgar freedman, boasting and counting his money at the dinner table and farting ostentatiously and being familiar with his slaves."

The ridiculously complex dish alludes to the massively over-elaborated cuisine of the *Cena,* and its fancy-dress presentation at the dinner perhaps picks up the moment where the arrival of Trimalchio's roast boar is heralded by the distribution of coverlets depicting hunters and their equipment

(§40.1) as well as Trimalchio's general taste for turning his dinner into a kind of dramatic performance with costumes and the like (Panayotakis 1995); the comparison with "a vulgar freedman" surely points to Trimalchio too. That a link with the *Satyrica*'s Trimalchio is certainly intended is shown a little later, when Petronius quotes Vatia as saying "Pretend I'm dead. Say something nice about me" (p. 75), picking up Trimalchio's final words to his guests at §78.5: *fingite me* [...] *mortuum esse. dicite aliquid belli* ("imagine I'm dead – say something pleasant").

The novel is set in Petronius's villa at Cumae on the bay of Naples, and this allows allusion to the mysterious passage of the *Satyrica* made famous as the epigraph to T. S. Eliot's *The Waste Land* (§48.8; see Schmeling and Rebmann 1975):

> *Nam Sibyllam quidem Cumis ego ipse oculis meis vidi in ampulla pendere, et cum illi pueri dicerent*: Σίβυλλα, τί θέλεις; *respondebat illa*: ἀποθανεῖν θέλω.

> For at Cumae I saw the Sibyl with my very own eyes hanging in a bottle, and when the boys said to her, "Sibyl, what do you want?" She replied "I want to die."

Near the end of the novel, Petronius visits the famous tunnel-like Cave of the Sibyl with Martial and they find it disappointingly unoccupied. Martial then quips (p. 200):

> Not exactly the *Aeneid*, is it? What did you expect? An old witch in a bottle, just waiting up for your millennial appearance?

And it is Martial who is involved in the novel's most original twist on the origin of the *Satyrica*. Just before his death, Petronius entrusts a sealed amphora to Martial to take back to Rome and open only after Nero too has died. The poet, not unnaturally, enquires about the nature of its contents (p. 205):

> "What the fuck is it?"
> "It's a book. A satire, I suppose you could call it. I've been working on it for the past couple of years."
> "A book! You? What's it about?"
> "It's about you, I think. Well, you and me, in a different world. I've called you Ascyltus."

The identification with the sexually supercharged Ascyltos (cf., for example, §92.9) suits Browner's Martial, obsessed with sex in life as well as in poetry ("I fuck like a lion," p. 139); Petronius seems to be casting himself as Encolpius ("you and me"), who has indeed sometimes been seen as presenting the author's point of view, and the sexual interest of Petronius and Martial in the same woman, Petronius's mistress Melissa (p. 139), seems to pick up the erotic triangle of the *Satyrica* between Encolpius, Ascyltos, and the boy Giton. This is the only overt reference to the *Satyrica* in the novel, but it provides an intriguing suggestion of its possible role as *roman à clef*, a variation on the old interpretation that it was identical with the catalogue of Nero's debaucheries composed by Petronius just before his death according to Tacitus (see INTRODUCTION, p. 5).

Conclusion

This rapid survey of nine novels in English (of which one is translated from Polish but widely known in the anglophone world) shows that an interest in Petronius's novel and the figure of its author is well diffused in fiction in English from an eighteenth-century picaresque novel by a Scot to a 2007 work by a New Yorker. The reasons for this lasting influence are numerous. Firstly, it seems clear that several of the later novelists pick up Petronius's fiction as an authentication for their own literary work through a model from the Greco-Roman world; especially before the later nineteenth century, the uncertain literary status of the novel could thus be bolstered by appeal to an antique predecessor in a period where classical texts held a central cultural importance. This return to, and claiming of, classical models for fiction is a significant and interesting development in the growing cultural strength of the novel, and shows that novelists since the nineteenth century (unlike some contemporary scholars) have had no problem in seeing the *Satyrica* as a narrative of novelistic character. Secondly, all except *Peregrine Pickle*, *Peter Arbiter*, and *The Bonfire of the Vanities* are historical novels which seek to reconstruct a detailed Roman story-world: the dense social detail of Petronius, and especially of the *Cena Trimalchionis*, is especially useful for this purpose and again serves an authenticating function as a classical source. In Smollett, Shrake, and Wolfe, on the other hand, the transhistorical value of Petronius's novel as social satire is clearly the most important element: in these cases, the luxuriant detail of the *Cena*

Trimalchionis is used to satirize hyperluxury, pretentiousness, and gastronomic excess in the writer's own day. Finally, the colorful and amoral figure of Petronius himself, as presented by Tacitus, his identification with the author of the *Satyrica*, and his complex relationship with Nero clearly exercise a fascination on his successors as novelists and provide a motivation to include him as a fictional character. The earliest (incompletely) preserved Latin novel still lives on in fiction, appropriated for their own purposes and times by a series of successor novelists.

Further Reading

The most useful general treatment of the topic of Petronius and the modern novel (covering all of Europe and necessarily eclectic) is Gagliardi (1993); a briefer survey can be found in Riikonen (1987), and a full list of recent scholarly articles on the topic (for 1975–2005) can be found in Vannini (2007: 444–64); see also the survey in Harrison and Sandy (2008). For a brief survey of Petronian influence in England see Schmeling and Rebmann (1975); Stuckey (1972) looks at Petronius's reputation in England in the Restoration period, also glanced at by Huber (1990); Harrison (2004) gives more on links with Lytton; Walsh (1970: 224–51) gives a helpful survey of the impact of Petronius on the picaresque novel in Europe, Fusillo 2011 another of Petronian elements in some contemporary fiction. Proposed small-scale links with particular modern novelists apart from those alluded to above maybe be found in the following treatments: Richardson (1979: P. G. Wodehouse), Baldwin (1990: Henry Miller), Wiseman (1992: Antony Powell), Kimball (1994: James Joyce). Modern fiction writers and translators have occasionally attempted to complete the *Satyrica*'s unfinished plot, most recently Dalby (2005): to those listed at http://en.wikipedia.org/wiki/Supplements_to_the_Satyricon (accessed May 3, 2012) add Gillette (1965), which adds a new ending to a conventional translation.

12

Fellini-Satyricon

Petronius and Film

Joanna Paul

When watching Fellini-Satyricon, *the audience must fight as never before … their preconception about movies having to tell them a story with a start, a development, an end; preconceptions about historical pictures; preconceptions about myself, personally, because they know that before, Fellini always tells them some story. This is not a historical picture, a Cecil B. DeMille picture. It is not even a Fellini picture, in the sense of* La Strada, *or* Nights of Cabiria, *or even* La Dolce Vita. *They ask me why I make it. How do I know? Because, as a little boy, in Rimini, my papa took me to my first film, and it had Roman gladiators in it? Because for thirty years I have enjoyed Petronius, and now the moment comes right? I cannot answer.* (Federico Fellini, quoted in Murray 1976: 178)

The desire for answers, and the powerful influence of our preconceptions – about antiquity, and about the cinema – combine to make the experience of watching *Fellini-Satyricon* (1969) alternately frustrating, provocative, and rewarding. The Italian director's vision of ancient Rome, adapted from Petronius's *Satyrica* and yet an intensely personal creation, is a challenging film. It challenges our ideas of conventional cinematic narratives, and of a conventional cinematic ancient Rome which, for today's audiences, is more familiar from movies such as *Gladiator* (2000) than the Hollywood spectacle of DeMille's *Cleopatra* (1934), though both are equally distant from the bizarre, even nightmarish image of the past in Fellini. As Fellini himself recognized, our ideas about the director himself may also affect our response to the film, though, for audiences accustomed to mainstream Hollywood produce, these preconceptions are as likely to be based on unfamiliarity with his work as they are on the familiar expectations assumed by Fellini in the above quotation.

The aim of this chapter, then, is to provide a companion for those watching *Fellini-Satyricon* that will help the viewer negotiate his or her way through its challenges (though without presuming to provide any easy answers or explanations). Much has already been written about this film, especially from a film studies perspective, and this discussion will pay attention to how *Fellini-Satyricon* works as a piece of cinema. But it will also examine the film as a reception of the ancient world – and of Petronius in particular – which might help us gain some insight into how Fellini interprets the modern world's relationship with our ancient past. The intention is not simply to list differences and similarities between Fellini and Petronius (or Fellini and other ancient sources), to applaud what the film gets "right" and to condemn its "mistakes." Such an approach, best represented by the classicist Gilbert Highet's enquiry "Whose Satyricon? Petronius's or Fellini's?" (Highet 1970), has its uses, and Jon Solomon also helpfully outlines continuities between text and film (2001a: 274–81) – but it is important to go beyond straightforward comparison. Much of Fellini's film is interesting and intriguing precisely because it departs so radically from the text of the *Satyrica*, and yet it is Petronius's text that remains the springboard for Fellini's cinematic flight of fantasy, the fertile source for what is undoubtedly "one of the cinema's most provocatively individual approaches to the ancient world" (Solomon 2001a: 274).

Fellini and the Birth of *Fellini-Satyricon*

Federico Fellini (1920–93) occupies a place in the pantheon of world cinema as one of the most revered directors of the twentieth century. Born in a northern Italian city, Rimini, he began his career as a writer, working with the leading figures of Italian filmmaking in the post-war period. At this time, Italy was a considerable force in world cinema, renowned for its confrontation of social problems in films such as Rossellini's *Roma, città aperta* (*Rome, Open City*, 1945), for which Fellini was a scriptwriter. In the 1950s, he began directing his own films, and would make over 20, including *La Strada* (1954) and *La Dolce Vita* (1960). Seen as a distinctively Italian filmmaker, preoccupied with his native Romagna and his adopted city, Rome, he soon moved away from the social concerns of neo-realism towards a more personal, subjective approach. Partly fed by his interest in psychoanalysis, his films from the sixties onwards were inspired by dreams, inner

Figure 12.1 Federico Fellini and Donyale Luna (Enotea) on the set of *Fellini-Satyricon*. (Photo: akg-images, London.)

life, and memory. With this came a desire for total control over his creations, such that often entire outdoor locations – such as Rome's Via Veneto in *La Dolce Vita* – would be recreated inside Cinecittà studios.

The idea of filming Petronius's *Satyrica* first came to mind in 1942, when Fellini was working for a satirical magazine and developing a project with the famous Italian actor Aldo Fabrizi, with whom he had become friendly. When the idea resurfaced in the sixties different cinematic styles were considered – perhaps even a musical, according to one account (Giacovelli 2002: 125–6). But once the project was underway, with Alberto Grimaldi as producer, it developed according to Fellini's own unique vision. Being a strong believer in the importance of original screenplays, it was perhaps surprising that he would now turn to literary adaptation; but it was the uniquely challenging nature of this literary source – as the next section will show – that appealed to Fellini, who was at that time experiencing something of a personal and creative crisis of confidence, and wanted a project that would revive his imaginative powers (Bondanella 1988) (fig. 12.1)

Slavery to ancient sources or to academic expertise was never a guiding principle in the making of *Fellini-Satyricon*. A certain amount of research occurred during pre-production (Fellini was said to have been reading scholars such as Carcopino, Vogt, and Marmorale, and he consulted the Italian classicists Ettore Paratore and Luca Canali), and, perhaps as a result, unexpected fragments of the ancient world do emerge in the film, as we shall see. But it was not Fellini's style to revere the academic authorities. In one account, his visit to Paratore is presented as paying mere lip-service to the Petronian authority, with Fellini and Bernardino Zapponi (his script collaborator) subdued and uneasy in his presence (Zapponi 1970: 35–6). Scholarly consultation had a role to play in shaping Fellini's methodology, but a mostly perverse one: "*voleva conoscere bene quel che si apprestava a deformare*" ("he wanted to know well that which he was getting ready to deform") (Giacovelli 2002: 126). This claim to know the past well may jar with some of the interpretations Fellini would later offer for the film – that it dramatizes the imperfect and incomplete state of our knowledge – but if so, it would be only the first of a number of contradictions surrounding Fellini's concept of the film.

Filming began in November 1968, mostly inside the great studio complex in Rome, Cinecittà (where it was apparently the biggest production since William Wyler directed *Ben-Hur* there 10 years before). The 26-week shoot was completed by July, having unfolded relatively smoothly but for one potentially catastrophic obstacle – a rival *Satyricon* which had been filmed in 1968, directed by Gian Luigi Polidoro. It was released in April 1969, but the filmmakers were soon hauled into court on charges of obscenity and corrupting minors. They received suspended sentences, and Fellini's distributors, United Artists, bought the rights to Polidoro's film for US$1 million, in order to keep it out of circulation. It was quickly apparent that the rival project would scarcely affect Fellini's chances of success, though it did have a permanent impact on the film's title. Since Polidoro's producer had secured the rights to the title *Satyricon* in 1962, Fellini had to come up with something different. A number of alternative titles were considered (Giacovelli 2002: 130), but the final (and, as we shall see, apt) choice was *Fellini-Satyricon*.

The film was released in Italy in September 1969, premiering on the last night of the Venice Film Festival (though not as part of the competition). The rest of the world greeted the film in 1970, with the New York premiere at Madison Square Garden directly after a rock concert occupying a hallowed place in *Fellini-Satyricon* history (or mythology). In 1983, Fellini recalled the audience as an orgy of 10,000 hippies, with whom he was so fascinated, and whose culture had certainly influenced the film: "many slept, others made love … Unforeseeably, mysteriously, in that most improbable setting, *Satyricon* seemed to have found its natural position" (quoted in Cordelli and Costantini 2004: 136). Fellini received an Academy Award nomination for Best Director, but initially *Fellini-Satyricon* met with some critical caution and relatively modest success on its wider release. The director himself had heralded the film as a journey into "unknowingness" (*sconosciutezza*), so it was no surprise that many audiences were baffled, entranced, and repulsed in equal measures by what they saw and heard. For Fellini, this was precisely the point.

The Narrative of *Fellini-Satyricon*

As Fellini acknowledged in our opening quotation, one of the biggest challenges of *Fellini-Satyricon* is its narrative – disjointed and incoherent, it is not easy to track what is happening (cf. Slater READING THE SATYRICA, p. 17). The following synopsis serves as an *aide-memoire*, and as an illustration of the narrative fragmentation, with an indication of where (if at all) the film episodes relate to Petronius – this is necessarily approximate, as the ensuing discussion will make clear (cf. INTRODUCTION, p. 10). (The names of the characters are given as they appear in the film – that is, Italian versions of the Latin; see Bondanella 1988: 195–7 for a longer synopsis.)

- Encolpio rages that Ascilto has stolen Gitone from him and sold him to an actor (cf. §9–10).
- Gitone appears on stage with Vernacchio, the comic actor; Encolpio forces Vernacchio to return him.
- Encolpio and Gitone walk through the seedy streets of the Suburra, a district of Rome.
- Ascilto arrives at the tenement block where Gitone and Encolpio are (cf. §11). Gitone leaves with Ascilto, and the tenement collapses.
- In an art gallery, the poet Eumolpo laments the state of society to Encolpio (cf. §83–8).
- The two men make their way to Trimalcione's dinner past a candle-lit bath.
- At the dinner, a succession of strange and marvelous dishes is brought in; there is dancing, poetry recital, and Trimalcione holds forth in front of his guests (cf. §26–70) (fig. 12.2).
- After dinner, Trimalcione conducts a mock funeral (cf. §71–8), before the story of the widow of Ephesus is staged (cf. §111–12).
- Encolpio finds himself in a barren landscape with Gitone and Encolpio; they are taken onto a ship in a chain gang.
- On board ship, Encolpio is made to fight, and then to "marry" its captain, Lica, before Lica is killed (cf. §100–10).
- In a villa, a noble couple free their slaves and children before committing suicide; Encolpio and Ascilto then arrive and cavort with the remaining slave-girl.
- In a desert landscape, a nymphomaniac is taken to the hermaphrodite oracle.
- The oracle is stolen from the temple by Encolpio and Ascilto, but dies.
- Encolpio is made to fight a minotaur at the "Festival of Mirth" in front of a crowd. When he encounters "Ariadne," he suffers from impotence (cf. §126–32).
- Now with Eumolpo again, a visit to a brothel cannot cure Encolpio's impotence and he is directed to see Enotea, a sorceress of shifting appearance. Encolpio begs for help and is cured (cf. §134–9).
- By the sea, and Ascilto and Eumolpo are dead. As Eumolpo's will is read, and his friends cannibalize his corpse, Encolpio leaves with a group of youths (cf. §140–1).

Figure 12.2 Dining at the "feast of Trimalchio", *Fellini-Satyricon*. (Photo: akg-images, London.)

Even from the synopsis, a sense of narrative fragmentation emerges. The episodes of the film are by no means entirely unconnected; Encolpio, of course, links them all, and, especially in the opening portion, the competition for Gitone's affections provides some motivation for the action. But any sense of narrative coherence quickly ebbs away, with sudden cuts between disparate settings jolting the viewer. The ending underscores the fragmentation, with Encolpio's voiceover ending mid-sentence: "… and on an island covered in sweet-smelling grass, a young Greek told me that in years …"

It is interesting and important to note that, by comparison, Fellini's lengthy treatment of the film – the narrative outline written prior to the screenplay (Zanelli 1970a: 43–90) – is relatively coherent. A good deal of explanatory narrative and dialogue help to orientate the reader, and the connections between episodes are often made more explicit. For example, in the finished film, the narrative rupture between the dinner at Trimalcione's and the voyage on Lica's ship is marked; in the treatment, though, Encolpius is introduced to Lichas and his wife Tryphaena (the English translation retains the Latin names) at the dinner and converses and cavorts with them, before, as the party ends at dawn the next day, Lichas stops his chariot to tell Encolpius, "I was looking for you … Our boat is ready to sail. Are you coming?" (Zanelli 1970a: 65) Since Lichas and Tryphaena play no part in Petronius's Trimalchio episode, it is possible to argue that the treatment, at least, seeks to *increase* the coherence and unity of the original text rather than emphasize its fragmentation. Why this should be so is hard to say with any certainty, but we should perhaps beware of setting too much store by the relative coherence of the treatment. This kind of prose narrative is just one part of the pre-production process, and since a treatment is often part of the "pitch" – the selling of a film to a studio or producer – it might be desirable for it to be accessible and comprehensible. Elsewhere, the emphasis remains firmly on fragmentation. The screenplay (included in Zanelli 1970a: 93–274, with the editor's notes making quite clear that this was the shooting script devised at the beginning of production, which would undergo some revisions in the final cut) outlines a thoroughly disjointed narrative, and even the treatment itself ends with "And here the story disintegrates; it splits into tiny fragments, which are however the best conclusion to this vast, incomplete mosaic; a mosaic of which we have reconstructed only a few small episodes." (Zanelli 1970a: 90)

Therefore, it seems fairly clear that fragmentation was a guiding principle from the outset, and even if it became more and more important as filming progressed, the fact that the coherency of the treatment would be "modified on a massive scale during the actual shooting of the film" (Bondanella 1988: 186) should not come as a surprise. The fragmentary narrative reflects both the fragmentary state of the extant *Satyrica* and, more profoundly, the fragmentary state of our knowledge of antiquity (Wyke 1997: 189). Our inability to orientate ourselves in the *Fellini-Satyricon* world is a conscious and important effect created by the film through its narrative and the visual disorientation that will be discussed in due course. We could almost wonder whether Fellini chose the *Satyrica* largely *because* of its incomplete survival. Doubtless there were other various and shifting reasons, but it does seem that the damaged state of the *Satyrica* was both attractive and a headache, and Zapponi, certainly, thought that the gaps should be widened, not bridged (1970: 34). Fellini, too, saw his relationship with Petronius as something quite different to the conventional idea of adaptation. Cinematic versions of literature are sometimes disregarded as secondary, inferior even, but Fellini was quite clear that his film was in no way to be seen as a slavish homage to a revered original. It is Petronius, but "a free adaptation of the Petronius classic," as the opening titles announce, and "a complete departure from the adjectives usually thrown around when talking about Petronius: picaresque, allusive, sarcastic, modern, spectacular" (Zapponi 1970: 34). It is also a whole lot more besides Petronius, much of it the product of Fellini's rich imagination. The director himself described the film as 80 percent Fellini and 20 percent Petronius – a rather crass statistical analysis which needs to be taken with a pinch of salt, especially given Fellini's own interest in downplaying any rival to his creative authority, but revealing, and not without some accuracy, nonetheless. The advertising tagline "Rome. Before Christ. After Fellini" also loudly declares Fellini's ownership of the film (and responsibility for creating its world) over Petronius's.

Given what has been said above, one might wonder why Fellini did not continue this declaration of ownership with the title *Fellini's Satyricon* (for anglophone release, at least; admittedly, it would never have looked this way in Italian, which does not denote possession using apostrophes). But though the origins of the title *Fellini-Satyricon* might have been rather prosaic, it still reflects interestingly on the relationship between film and text. Though the sense of the director's possession of the *Satyricon* seems less obvious, still, yoking the two together in this way may imply that this is a *Satyricon* authored by Fellini and no one else: he has in effect replaced Petronius. The running together and hyphenation of the two elements could be even more radical in its effects: it is not so much that Fellini owns the *Satyricon* now, but rather that the two are one and the same. The fantasy world on screen is not just *by* Fellini but is, somehow, a visceral expression of his psyche. Or, on yet another reading, as Bernard Dick argues, the hyphen could be read as not conjoining but separating the two elements as adversaries: this is "Fellini confronting the *Satyricon* […], the present confronting the past" (Dick 1981: 145), an argument that is strengthened when we note that the hyphen was not present in all releases of the film world-wide. Indeed, the original trailer intercuts images from the film with the words "Fellini" and "Satyricon" flying across the screen separately, only displaying them together at its very end. However we interpret the title, though, it is surely the complex and tangled linking of the director with his ancient source that we are meant to notice, whether the relationship is one of ownership, co-identification, antagonism, or all three.

Fellini's autonomy from Petronius is further illustrated by the range of other ancient texts he uses to feed his imagination – chosen arbitrarily, he says (Fellini 1970: 44). He mentions Apuleius's *The Golden Ass* (also known as the *Metamorphoses*), Horace's *Satires*, Ovid's *Metamorphoses*, and Suetonius's *The Twelve Caesars,* but offers no clue as to what role they actually played in the film. For that, Sullivan provides the necessary source criticism, identifying a range of intertexts from the significant (similarities between Encolpio and Apuleius's Lucius, who is also tricked during a "Festival of Mirth" and coerced into copulating in public), to the less obvious, such as Juvenal's description of Roman tenements collapsing (Juv. 3.193–6), which Sullivan observes as a possible influence early in the film (Sullivan 2001). What becomes clear, from Fellini's vague comments and Sullivan's more detailed investigation, is that Fellini's use of non-Petronian material is as shifting and elusive as his use of the *Satyrica*, with neither open to easy identification. This should not matter in the slightest, for it is but another illustration of the complexities of our relationship with the past. There is no easily discernible connection between ancient and modern but rather a mélange of ancient texts – and images, ideas, people, events – which "Fellini invents, blends, reworks, and borrows" (Dick 1981: 151). The recital of poetry at Trimalcione's feast neatly exemplifies this: even in Petronius, Trimalchio introduces his Homeric recital with a garbled account of the story (§59), and in the film, when Trimalcione declaims his poetry, Eumolpo accuses him of stealing it from Lucretius. Behind-the-scenes accounts also reveal that the poetry actually being recited is still further from what it seems: Trimalcione and Eumolpo are not reciting ancient poetry but, respectively, Pirandello (an Italian writer and poet) and the menu from the actor's restaurant!

On the level of narrative structure and detail, Petronius's impact is only partial. Thematically, though, it can be argued that *Fellini-Satyricon* is more "Petronian" than anything else. Of course, we might not agree on what being "Petronian" means, but it does seem that the director saw in Petronius's portrait of first-century AD Rome something that resonated with his own world-view, which he might try to bring to the screen – albeit with a healthy dose of his own perspective. The question of moralizing is central here. Critics have long debated the extent to which Petronius offers a moral critique of his world in the *Satyrica* – and it should not go unnoticed that these debates sometimes emerge from the context of Petronian receptions themselves. Walsh argued that readings of Petronius as a "serious analysis of the sicknesses of Roman society" (Walsh 1996: xx) were influenced by T. S. Eliot's use of the *Satyrica* in *The Waste Land*, and that the arguments of scholars such as Bacon, Highet, and Arrowsmith were formed "under the impulse of urban discontents," their experience of squalid (mainly American) cities encouraging them "to see in the *Satyricon* a descriptive analysis of a society choking with its own vices" (Walsh 1974: 189). It is interesting that Walsh was moved to pose the question "Was Petronius a Moralist?" in 1974, soon after the film's release. Had Fellini brought the issue of Petronius's moral stance to the fore again, and was he also reading and recreating the novel as a moral indictment of society's vices (in much the same way that modern novelists sometimes do, according to Stephen Harrison's contribution to this collection)? The evident pleasure Fellini took in recreating this vice and depravity might suggest not. Even closer to the film's release, in 1971, Zeitlin had argued that the *Satyrica* "sees only a disordered world unsupported by the rational guidance of the gods or their substitutes" (Zeitlin 1971: 677) rather than a wicked, sinful world. The Petronian world of anarchy and confusion outlined by Zeitlin, and then Walsh, seems to fit well with the amoral, rather than immoral, world of *Fellini-Satyricon*, in which irrationality and illusion are also king. Fellini himself noted the similarities between Petronius's world-view, as he understood it, and his own, seeing analogies between the novel's depiction "of a society at the height of its splendor but revealing already the signs of a progressive dissolution" and the modern world (Fellini 1970: 43). He called these analogies "disconcerting," which suggests a morally-fearful standpoint, but *Fellini-Satyricon* is not an out-and-out moralizing film. Though Fellini expressed dissatisfaction with the world around him, he was also fascinated with hippy counterculture, the "natural innocence and splendid vitality" that he saw in "Encolpius and Ascyltos, two hippy students, like any of those hanging around today" (Fellini 1970: 44). Their amoral, "free love" antics, were not coming in for criticism; if anything, disapproval is reserved for the greedy and vulgar older generation represented by Trimalcione and Eumolpo's friends who, at the end of the film, are literally cannibalizing the dead poet. Encolpio and his new companions are celebrated for sailing away, leaving such rapacious behavior behind.

Discussion over whether the *Satyrica* was intended to be comic and light-hearted or not also shaped responses to Fellini's take on it. Though Zeitlin took a fairly serious view of the *Satyrica* and its purpose, Walsh and others see the text as essentially humorous. The classicist Erich Segal thus criticized Fellini for taking Petronius's "lusty, amoral, life-oriented" novel and making "a film that croaked *memento mori*" (remember your mortality) (Segal 1971: 56). Certainly, reviewers found the mood of the film downcast rather than uplifting: the *Corriere della Sera* called Fellini's Romans "an unhappy race searching desperately to exorcise their fear of death" (September 5, 1969), and for *Panorama*, "The atmosphere is almost always morbid, claustrophobic, and nocturnal" (September 18, 1969). Yet one of the reasons why Walsh was keen to see Petronius as comic – the emphasis on performance – persists in Fellini. The *Satyrica*'s engagement with notions of theatrical performance, particularly mime, has been discussed elsewhere in this volume (by Shelley Hales, FREEDMEN'S CRIBS, p. 174, and Richlin, SEX IN THE SATYRICA, p. 96; see also Panayotakis 1995), and Fellini too embraces this theme wholeheartedly. Important episodes are presented as staged performances, whether literally so – the opening scene in the theatre, or Encolpio's (lack of) "performance" at the Festival of Mirth – or more subtly, as with "The Widow of Ephesus." This episode appears simply to be narrated by a character (as it is narrated by Eumolpus at §111–12), its visualization presented purely for the benefit of us, the cinematic audience; but at its end, it is revealed that it has also been playing out in front of Trimalcione's dinner guests (who have enjoyed a banquet-as-performance in Fellini as much as they do in Petronius, as Shelley Hales shows elsewhere in this volume, p. 174). The theme of performance pervades the whole film, in fact. The characters continually watch each other (and us), and (are sometimes forced to) pretend to be what they are not (Encolpio as Lica's "bride," for example, or as "Theseus" fighting the Minotaur), blurring the boundaries between real and illusory (Dick 1981: 154–5; Wyke 1997: 189). For the most part, though, the effect is not so much comic as another way in which the film unnerves and destabilizes an audience.

The Sights and Sounds of *Fellini-Satyricon*

When discussing cinematic adaptations of literary texts, it is easy to concentrate on the "literary" aspects of the film – narrative, dialogue, and so on – and to forget that cinema is also a visual (and aural) medium; and perhaps, in the case of *Fellini-Satyricon, primarily* a visual (and aural) medium. The visual dimension is absolutely key to communicating Fellini's intentions. Though no more coherent or readily intelligible than the narrative, the images have an immediate and sometimes shocking impact, compounding the destabilizing effects of the disjointed narrative. For the film's *mise en scène* – the overall appearance of what we see – Fellini wanted:

> Lots of corridors, rooms, courtyards, alleys, stairways, and other such narrow, frightening passages. Nothing luminous, white, or shining. The clothes all of dingy, opaque colors, suggesting stone, dust, mud. Colors like black, yellow, or red, but all clouded as if by a constant rain of ashes. In the figurative sense, I shall try to effect a conglomeration of the Pompeian with the psychedelic, of Byzantine art with Pop art, of Mondrian and Klee with barbaric art. (Moravia 1970: 28)

The claustrophobia of the interior spaces and the unreality of even many exterior ones was achieved by confining much of the filming to the studios at Cinecittà. Nor is it a recognizably Roman scene – at least, it is not the "luminous, white, or shining" Rome recognizable from mainstream cinema. The mention of Pompeii also marks Fellini's antiquity as distinct from the popular vision, which usually fixates on Rome. In one way, it indicates alignment with Petronius, whose action is assumed to play out, in part at least, on the Bay of Naples; but the narrative location is not the only reason why Fellini includes Pompeii in his eclectic vision of the past. Though a number of features of *Fellini-Satyricon* have been identified as "Pompeian" – Trimalcione's dining-room as Pompeian *triclinium*, the baths as Pompeian *thermae*, and the graffitied walls as Pompeian city walls, to name a few examples (Dick 1981: 154 n. 7) – this is of limited usefulness for understanding Fellini. If we attempt to find sources for such features, Pompeii is bound to come to mind first, since there is nothing else that provides evidence for ancient domestic and everyday urban life quite so vividly. Moreover, Fellini himself was somewhat flippant about the site: "I never knew exactly how much my fascination and enthusiasm were owing to the frescoes and how much to a magnificent Swedish woman who was walking in front of me" (quoted in Baxter 1993: 241). It is, rather, the imaginative importance of Pompeii that Fellini exploits when he mentions it as inspiration. Its obvious associations with death and destruction contribute to the film's morbid atmosphere, encapsulated in one shot (in the Suburra sequence) of a still body looking simultaneously like a corpse covered in a "rain of ashes" and one of the famous plaster casts of Vesuvius's victims. In addition, Pompeii's status as a piece of antiquity which simultaneously seduces us with its apparent completeness, intelligibility, and immediacy, and yet requires excavation and imagination to make any sense of it, makes it an ideal reference point for Fellini's exploration of our route to the past.

Deciding which actors should embody Petronius's characters also became an important visual strategy for Fellini. When production began, the most unlikely names were tossed around, including "[Elizabeth] Taylor, [Richard] Burton, [Brigitte] Bardot, [Peter] O'Toole, [French actor Louis] de Funés, Jerry Lewis, [Marlon] Brando, Lee Marvin, the Beatles, the Maharishi, Lyndon Johnson and de Gaulle" (quoted in Baxter 1993: 240). Though most of this was clearly a flight of fantasy and free association, some grand names were in fact approached, including Groucho Marx and Boris Karloff (both declining). Such well-known faces – whether part of a realistic wish list or not – were appropriated as yet another destabilizing ploy: recognizable celebrity faces would offer the appearance of familiarity and accessibility, while also appearing jarringly out of place in Fellini's bizarre ancient world. Accordingly, the alternative to this starry cast was "no one, not a known face, to increase the sense of foreignness" (quoted in Baxter 1993: 240), obscure actors who would provide "abstract and unnerving masks" (Zanelli 1970b: 11). Although some of the eventual cast were well known (for example, Alain Cuny, playing the ship's captain, Lica), the main actors were not at all prominent in film and, in the case of Max Born (Gitone), plucked from a street corner in London.

Though the main protagonists' appearance is relatively normal, allowing some audience identification with them, the extensive cast of supporting characters sport deliberately peculiar and unsettling appearances, so as to disorientate and bemuse the audience (fig. 12.3). In the walk through the Suburra, Encolpio and Gitone pass an array of bizarre characters encompassing every kind of human appearance and behavior: old, young, obese, crippled, dwarves, all confronting the audience (internal and external) with odd gestures and mannerisms, such as the flickering tongues of the female

Figure 12.3 Guests at the "feast of Trimalchio", *Fellini-Satyricon*. (Photo: akg-images, London.)

characters, or the man squatting to defecate in a corner. Added to this are the characters around which later episodes pivot, many marked out by extremity or perversity: the nymphomaniac encountered in a desert whose lust has turned her into a slavering, snarling woman chained to a cart; or the sacred hermaphrodite Sibyl, a fragile albino killed by the heat of the sun. Such use of grotesque characters or "freaks" is a recognized hallmark of a Fellini film, a way of illustrating his belief that life is "mysterious and ineffable" by "defamiliarizing the material presented and [...] exceeding boundaries" (Stubbs 1993: 62). But it gains especial force in this film, suggesting that our ancient past is even more mysterious and ineffable than the present. In fact, ineffability produces a cinematic device of its own here, since the dialogue throughout the film, though in Italian, is made strange by deliberately out-of-sync dubbing. The profound feeling of dislocation that this induces is one of the most direct ways in which *Fellini-Satyricon* explores the impossibility of the past speaking directly to us. (One can only imagine how much more pronounced this effect would have been if Fellini had stuck with his original plan of using a harsh Latin for the dialogue.) In addition, the disturbing soundscape is enhanced by the film's score, which uses a variety of discordant sounds and musical styles – mixing synthesized music with, among others, fragments of Balinese and African music, and is far removed from the conventional grand score of the Hollywood ancient world (Solomon 2001b; cf. Rimell, LETTING THE PAGE RUN ON, on the use of sound in the *Satyrica*).

Among the curious, sometimes overtly hallucinatory qualities of *Fellini-Satyricon*'s visuals, one particular motif takes center-stage in determining audience response to the film. The image of the fragment is readily understood as an effective way of representing the loss and inaccessibility of the past, and we have already seen how the film's narrative uses the fragment as an organizing principle to just that effect. Visually, too, the recurrence of fragments – in the fabric of the city and its people – depicts Fellini's ancient world as one that is as broken, disjointed, and as ruined as its narrative. A piece of a giant sculptural head is drawn along by horses and the gallery scene shows its art in pieces. The towering tenement block in the Suburra crumbles into a ruin, and the protagonists, on the way to Trimalcione's, pass by broken blocks of monumental masonry that spell out "Trimalchio".

Most striking is Fellini's use of the fresco, perhaps today's most fragile remnant of ancient visual culture, so quickly does it fragment and fade. Besides the presentation of fragmented paintings in the art gallery, the film itself is conceived of as a series of frescoes. The use of Cinemascope (a filming method with a flattened, elongated frame and a relatively shallow depth of field) and sequences of long tracking shots help to achieve this effect. The Suburra scene is by far the best example, as the camera tracks Encolpio and Gitone walking along, rather than through, the city, passing a series of weird and wonderful sights that it allows us to look at but never to enter into the scene. Fellini's characters themselves can become part of the fresco, though. A number of the extras have make-up resembling paint peeling from a wall (wonderfully evoking Petronius's description of the *cinaedus* – "a man who likes to be sexually penetrated" – with flaking make-up, so "that you would have thought that a wall was flaking after being damaged by rain," §23.5, trans. Walsh 1996), and the characters often appear against blank expanses of sky or wall (Dick 1981: 146). The metaphor is strikingly concluded at the end of the film, where the main characters are depicted as painted images on a crumbling wall on a seashore. "The solid wall which opened the film has become fissured and, with it, unity and wholeness on every level – from the narrative to the historical to the individual" (Burke 1989: 44).

"The Meaning should Become Apparent
Only at the End" (Fellini)

Since Fellini uses the fragment so effectively as a visual and narrative symbol of antiquity's condition today, it is fitting that he should also use archaeology as a metaphor to help explain how, through film, we might encounter that fragmentary past and attempt to reconstruct it. Fellini described his adaptation of Petronius as having been achieved:

> [...] not through the fruit of a bookish, scholastic documentation, a literal fidelity to the text, but rather in the way an archaeologist reconstructs something alluding to the form of an amphora or a statue from a few potsherds. Our film, through the fragmentary recurrence of its episodes, should restore the image of a vanished world without completing it [...]. The film should suggest the idea of something disinterred: the images should evoke the texture of ashes, earth and dust. (Fellini 1970: 45)

Fellini-Satyricon, the director claims, sets out to gather pieces of our knowledge of the past and present them in an approximately coherent way, but it does not claim that their original coherence can ever be regained, just as archaeology cannot recover complete and pristine artifacts. Moreover, these pieces are invested with new "meanings and resonances" because of their fragmentary state: "Are not the ruins of a temple more fascinating than the temple itself?" asks Fellini (Zanelli 1970b: 4). This is one way of explaining the film's strategy, but it is perhaps not as effective as it might be – certainly, most archaeologists would not settle for seeing their work as allusive (or illusory) – and so Fellini turned to additional frames of reference. The film was once memorably described as "science-fiction of the past," in order to suggest that the Romans are as alien and distant as Martians. Another recurring image was that of the dream. Fellini "tried first of all," he said, "to eliminate what is generally called history [...], the idea that the ancient world "actually" existed [...], the ancient world perhaps never existed; but there's no doubt that we have dreamt it" (Moravia 1970: 26). Antiquity is like a dream that, upon waking, we half remember, that remains faintly present throughout the day but slips our grasp whenever we try to confront it directly; or even a dream that is remembered clearly, but whose meaning escapes us. Without being able to fully remember or understand it, we cannot completely recognize or engage with antiquity either (Moravia 1978: 163).

It can be helpful to see these metaphors as, in a sense, "keys" to the film, providing some insight into why Fellini consciously made it so impenetrable. But it is also worth noting the doubtful responses of some film critics who decided that *Fellini-Satyricon* was still an unsuccessful presentation of the past and our relationship with it, despite – or perhaps because of – Fellini's attempts to explain what he was doing. The director claimed that "the film demands a detached, cold and impassive approach" (quoted in Murray 1976: 182; see also Fellini 1970: 46), that he wanted to observe the Roman world in the same way that one might dispassionately observe the "habitat of trout" (Zanelli 1970b: 9), once again emphasizing antiquity's distance. But he admitted that this attempted objectivity was "extremely difficult" for him, and many critics ultimately judged it a failed attempt, since an aloof, remote standpoint was so at odds with Fellini's usual personal approach (Zanelli 1970b: 10; Murray 1976: 182–4). The film's tagline has renewed importance for this argument: "Rome. Before Christ. After Fellini" discredits the idea of objective observation, and significantly introduces Christianity as a force to be reckoned with. Though Petronius's temporal setting is, of course, not "BC," it is a world in which (apparently) Christianity does not figure, and Fellini tries to reflect this on film, to "forget (*dimenticare*) 2000 years of Catholicism" (Cordelli and Costantini 2004: 141). But Segal was just one critic who thought Fellini unable to forget: "Fellini seeks Rome in Rome and cannot find it, for his emotional archaeology dares not dig below the floor of Vatican City" (Segal 1971: 57). Further problems were raised with Fellini's repeated claims that analogies could be found between ancient and modern, apparently contradicting his assertions of the incomprehensible nature of that past. It is fair to ask how we are meant to "recognise all the principal characters in the drama," as Fellini claimed we can (1970: 44), if we are not meant to understand that past: without comprehension, is recognition not impossible? But while some found fault with the director for this, others praised him for communicating the "supreme paradox" of antiquity as simultaneously alien *and* timeless (Dick 1981: 148).

In the final reckoning, then, Fellini's attempts to make sense of his film can seem as confusing as the film itself. But this in itself is a useful illustration of how *Fellini-Satyricon* works as a reception of Petronius and of the ancient world more generally. Fellini hoped (or at least appeared to hope) that by assuming an objective stance, turning his lens onto a distant and incomprehensible ancient world, he would be able to "deconsecrate the myth of antiquity which has hitherto prevailed and still prevails in Western

Figure 12.4   Martin Potter (Encolpio) and Fanfulla (Vernacchio), *Fellini-Satyricon*.
(Photo: P.E.A./Artistes Associés/The Kobal Collection.)

culture" (Moravia 1970: 27; see also Wyke 1997: 191; Solomon 2001a: 280).
As he remarked to Zanelli, "Our vision of the Roman world has been
distorted by text books – we are the victims of aesthetic judgments" (Zanelli
1970b: 8), and so the film radically departed from the conventions of representing ancient Rome enshrined in the Hollywood epics of the fifties and
sixties. But while *Fellini-Satyricon* might swerve away from the conventions
of "the classical tradition," it is at the same time adding another, provocative
layer to the mass of Petronian receptions. As Dick suggests, "Petronius's
Satyricon is like the graffiti-covered wall that opens the film; the work is so
overlaid with conjecture […] and so obscured by critical debate […] that
its visual equivalent would be a marked-up wall" (1981: 146). Though
Fellini-Satyricon strives, on one level, to remove that graffiti, to offer us a
startling new vision of Petronius – and the ancient past – it is also, inescapably,
itself another mark on that wall.

Further Reading

A good deal of scholarship in recent years has concerned itself with the ancient world on film: though the focus has tended to be on Hollywood films, Solomon (2001a) and Wyke (1997) each provide brief but helpful overviews of *Fellini-Satyricon*; Sullivan's contribution (2001) to *Classical Myth and Culture in the Cinema* is also recommended reading. For detailed accounts of Fellini and his films one must look to the work of film scholars such as Bondanella (1988 and 1992); Baxter (1993) and Kezich (2006) are both useful scholarly biographies of the director.

It is unfortunate that the most useful contemporary account of the film (Zanelli 1970a) is out of print and not easy to come by, but the voices of Fellini and others who were closely involved in the making of film are preserved in the works mentioned above; his interview with Alberto Moravia (1970) is thought-provoking, and inspires some interesting ideas in Moravia's later discussion of the film (1978). Cordelli and Costantini's Italian anthology of interviews with Fellini (2004) also contains much of interest; Costantini (1997) is an English version.

Newcomers to the field of classical receptions who may wish to explore further the ways in which the modern world confronts and responds to antiquity should consult Hardwick (2003). Finally, for further viewing, *Fellini's Roma* (1972) is a fascinating counterpart to *Fellini-Satyricon*, a cinematic portrait of Fellini's city which draws on *Fellini-Satyricon*'s themes, but which finds still new ways to explore and represent the presence – or absence – of the ancient world.

Bibliography

All items of modern literature cited in the main text are listed here. Where possible, we have noted the existence of translations and reprints which may be more easily accessible.

Andreau, J. 1993. The Freedman. In A. Giardina (ed.), *The Romans*. Trans. L. G. Cochrane. Chicago and London. 175–97.

Andreau, J. 1999. *Banking and Business in the Roman World*. Cambridge.

[Anon.] (trans.). 1933. *The Satyricon of Petronius; the only complete translation into English […] Drawings by Jean de Bosschère*. London.

Arrowsmith, W. (trans.) 1959. *The Satyricon of Petronius*. Ann Arbor, MI.

Arrowsmith, W. 1966. Luxury and Death in the *Satyricon*. *Arion* 5: 304–31.

Astbury, R. 1977. Petronius, P.Oxy. 3010, and Menippean Satire. *Classical Philology* 72: 22–31. (Reprinted in Harrison 1999: 74–84.)

Ausbüttel, F. M. 1982. *Untersuchungen zu den Vereinen im Westen des römischen Reiches*. Kallmünz.

Bagnani, G. 1954. The House of Trimalchio. *American Journal of Philology* 75: 16–39.

Bakhtin, M. 1968. *Rabelais and His World*. Trans. H. Iswolsky. Bloomington, IN.

Bakhtin, M. 1981. *The Dialogic Imagination*. Trans. C. Emerson and M. Holquist. Austin, TX.

Baldwin, B. 1990. Henry Miller and Petronius. *Petronian Society Newsletter* 20: 8–9.

Bang, P. 2006. Imperial Bazaar: Towards a Comparative Understanding of Markets in the Roman Empire. In Bang, Ikeguchi and Ziche (eds) 2006: 52–88.

Bang, P., Ikeguchi, M., and Ziche, M. (eds) 2006. *Ancient Economies Modern Methodologies. Archaeology, Comparative History, Models and Institutions*. Bari.

Barton, I. M. 1996. *Roman Domestic Buildings*. Exeter.

Bartsch, S. 1989. *Decoding the Ancient Novel: The Reader and the Role of Description in Heliodorus and Achilles Tatius*. Princeton, NJ.

Bartsch, S. 1994. *Actors and the Audience: Theatricality and Doublespeak from Nero to Hadrian*. Cambridge, MA and London.

Baxter, J. 1993. *Fellini*. London.

Beard, M. 1998. *Vita inscripta*. In W. W. Ehlers (ed.), *La Biographie antique: Huit exposés suivis de discussions* (*Entretiens sur l'Antiquité classique* 44). Geneva. 83–113.

Beard, M. 2007. *The Roman Triumph*. Cambridge, MA and London.

Beck, R. 1973. Some Observations on the Narrative Technique of Petronius. *Phoenix* 27: 42–61. (Reprinted in Harrison 1999: 50–73.)

Biville, F. 1996. *Et tu cum esses capo, coco coco* (Petr. 59.2). Metaphores et onomatopées animalières dans *Sat.* 57–9. *Latomus* 55: 855–62.

Biville, F. 2003. *Familia vero – babae babae!* (*Satyricon* 37.9). Exclamations et interjections chez Pétrone. In J. Herman and H. Rosén (eds), *Petroniana: Gedenkschrift für Hubert Petersman*. Heidelberg. 37–57.

Blanchard, C. (trans.) 1866. *The Satyricon; or, Trebly Voluptuous*. New York.

Bodel, J. 1984. *The Freedmen in the Satyricon of Petronius*. Unpublished PhD Dissertation. Ann Arbor, MI.

Bodel, J. 1989. Trimalchio and the Candelabrum. *Classical Philology* 84: 224–31.

Bodel, J. 1994. Trimalchio's Underworld. In Tatum 1994: 237–59.

Bodel, J. 1997. Monumental Villas and Villa Monuments. *Journal of Roman Archaeology* 10: 5–35.

Bodel, J. 1999a. The *Cena Trimalchionis*. In Hofmann 1999: 38–51.

Bodel, J. 1999b. Death on Display: Looking at Roman Funerals. In B. Bergmann and C. Kondoleon (eds), *The Art of Ancient Spectacle*. New Haven, CT and London. 259–81.

Bondanella, P. 1988. Literature as Therapy: Fellini and Petronius. *Annali d'Italianistica* 6: 179–98.

Bondanella, P. 1992. *The Cinema of Federico Fellini*. Princeton, NJ.

Bonner, S. F. 1977. *Education in Ancient Rome: From the Elder Cato to the Younger Pliny*. Berkeley, CA.

Booth, A. D. 1979. The Schooling of Slaves in First-Century Rome. *Transactions of the American Philological Association* 109: 11–19.

Boyce, B. 1991. *The Language of the Freedmen in Petronius' Cena Trimalchionis*. Leiden.

Bradley, K. 1987. *Slaves and Masters in the Roman Empire: A Study in Social Control*. New York and Oxford.

Bradley, K. 1994. *Slavery and Society at Rome*. Cambridge.

Branham, R. B. and Kinney, D. (trans.) 1996. *Satyrica: Petronius*. Berkeley, CA.

Briggs, W. W. 1999. Petronius and Virgil in *The Great Gatsby*. *International Journal of the Classical Tradition* 6: 226–35.

Briggs, W. W. 2000. The Ur-*Gatsby*. *International Journal of the Classical Tradition* 6: 577–84.

Browner, J. 2007. *The Uncertain Hour*. New York.

Bryson, N. 1990. *Looking at the Overlooked*. London.

Bücheler, F. 1862. *Petronii Arbitri Satirarum Reliquiae*. Berlin.

Buckland, W. W. 1908. *The Roman Law of Slavery*. Cambridge.

Burgess, A. 1985. *The Kingdom of the Wicked*. London.

Burke, F. 1989. Fellini: Changing the Subject. *Film Quarterly* 43(1): 36–48.

Burnaby, W. 1694. *The Satyr of Titus Petronius Arbiter, a Roman Knight. With its Fragments, recover'd at Belgrade. Made English by Mr. Burnaby of the Middle-Temple, and another Hand*. London.

Callebat, L. 1998. Langages des *Satyrica* de Pétrone. *Biblos* 68: 1–11.

Cameron, A. 1969. Petronius and Plato. *Classical Quarterly* 19: 367–70.

Cameron, A. 1970. Myth and Meaning in Petronius: Some Modern Comparisons. *Latomus* 29: 397–425.

Cameron, H. D. 1970. The Sibyl in the *Satyricon*. *Classical Journal* 65: 337–8.

Camodeca, G. 1999. *Tabulae Pompeianae Sulpiciorum (TPSulp.). Edizione critica dell'archivio puteolano dei Sulpicii*. Rome.

Campanile, E. 1957. Osservazioni sulla lingua di Petronio. *Annali della Scuola Normale Superiore di Pisa: Classe di lettere e filosofia*, ser. 2, vol. 26: 54–69.

Canali, L. 1987. Servi e padroni nel *Satyricon* di Petronio. In L. Canali, *Vita, sesso, morte nella letteratura latina*. Milan. 47–67.

Carey, S. 2002. A Tradition of Adventures in the Imperial Grotto. *Greece & Rome* 49(1): 44–61.

Carroll, M. 2006. *Spirits of the Dead: Roman Funerary Commemoration in Western Europe*. Oxford.

Casson, L. 2001. *Libraries in the Ancient World*. New Haven, CT.

Castrén, P. 1975. *Ordo Populusque Pompeianus: Polity and Society in Roman Pompeii*. Rome.

Champlin, E. 1991. *Final Judgments: Duty and Emotion in Roman Wills, 200 BC–AD 250*. Berkeley, CA.

Champlin, E. 2003. *Nero*. Cambridge, MA.

Cizek, E. 1975a. À propos des premiers chapitres du *Satyricon*. *Latomus* 34: 197–202.

Cizek, E. 1975b. Face à face éloquent: Encolpe et Agamemnon. *La Parola del Passato* 30: 91–101.

Clarke, J. R. 1998. *Looking at Lovemaking: Constructions of Sexuality in Roman Art 100 B.C. – A.D. 250*. Berkeley, CA.

Cleto, F. (ed.) 1999. *Camp: Queer Aesthetics and the Performing Subject*. Ann Arbor, MI.

Cloud, D. 1989. The Client–Patron Relationship: Emblem and Reality in Juvenal's First Book. In A. Wallace-Hadrill (ed.), *Patronage in Ancient Society*. London and New York. 206–18.

Coleman, K. M. 1990. Fatal Charades: Roman Executions Staged as Mythological Enactments. *Journal of Roman Studies* 80: 44–73.

Collignon, A. 1892. *Étude sur Pétrone: La critique littéraire, l'imitation et la parodie dans le Satiricon.* Paris.

Collins, W. Wilkie. 1850. *Antonina.* London. [Cited from the 2005 reprint, Cirencester.]

Connors, C. M. 1998. *Petronius the Poet: Verse and Literary Tradition in the Satyricon.* Cambridge.

Conte, G. B. 1994. *Latin Literature: A History.* Baltimore, MD.

Conte, G. B. 1996a. *The Hidden Author: An Interpretation of Petronius's Satyricon.* Trans. E. Fantham. Berkeley, CA.

Conte, G. B. 1996b. *The Rhetoric of Imitation.* New York.

Cooley, A. and Cooley, M. G. L. 2004. *Pompeii: A Sourcebook.* London.

Cordelli, V. and Costantini, R. 2004. *Le invenzioni della memoria: Il cinema di Federico Fellini.* Udine.

Costantini, C. 1997. *Conversations with Fellini.* San Diego, CA.

Courtney, E. 1962. Parody and Literary Allusion in Menippean Satire. *Philologus* 106: 86–100.

Courtney, E. 1987. Petronius and the Underworld. *American Journal of Philology* 108: 408–10.

Courtney, E. 1991. *The Poems of Petronius.* Atlanta, GA.

Courtney, E. 2001. *A Companion to Petronius.* Oxford.

Crompton, L. 1985. *Byron and Greek Love: Homophobia in 19th-Century England.* London.

Currie, H. MacL. 1989. Petronius and Ovid. In C. Deroux (ed.), *Studies in Latin Literature and Roman History* 5. Brussels. 317–35.

D'Arms, J. H. 1981. *Commerce and Social Standing in Ancient Rome.* Cambridge, MA and London.

D'Arms, J. H. 1999. Performing Culture: Roman Spectacle and the Banquets of the Powerful. In B. Bergmann and C. Kondoleon (eds), *The Art of Ancient Spectacle.* New Haven, CT and London. 301–19.

D'Arms, J. H. and Kopff, E. C. (eds) 1980. *The Seaborne Commerce of Ancient Rome: Studies in Archaeology and History.* Memoirs of the American Academy at Rome 36. Rome.

Dalby, A. 2005. The *Satyrica* Concluded. *Gastronomica* 5: 65–72.

De Ligt, L. 1993. *Fairs and Markets in the Roman Empire: Economic and Social Aspects of Periodic Trade in Pre-Industrial Society.* Amsterdam.

Dell'Era, E. 1970. *Problemi di lingua e stile in Petronio.* Rome.

Di Capua, F. 1948. Il ritmo prosaico di Petronio. *Giornale Italiano di Filologia* 1: 37–55.

Dick, B. F. 1981. Adaptation as Archaeology: *Fellini-Satyricon* 1969, from the 'novel' by Petronius. In A. S. Horton and J. Magretta (eds), *Modern European Filmmakers and the Art of Adaptation.* New York. 145–67.

Donahue, J. F. 1999. Euergetic Self-Representation and the Inscription at *Satyricon* 71.10. *Classical Philology* 94(1): 69–74.

Doody, M. A. 1996. *The True Story of the Novel*. London.

Dronke, P. 1994. *Verse with Prose from Petronius to Dante*. Cambridge, MA and London.

Duff, A. M. 1928. *Freedmen in the Early Roman Empire*. Oxford. (Reissued Cambridge 1958.)

Dunbabin, K. M. D. 1986. *Sic erimus cuncti* … The Skeleton in Graeco-Roman Art. *Jahrbuch des Deutschen Archäologischen Instituts* 101: 185–255.

Dunbabin, K. M. D. 2003. *The Roman Banquet: Images of Conviviality*. Cambridge.

Duncan Jones, R. P. 1997. Numerical Distortion in Roman Writers. In J. Andreau, P. Briant, and R. Descat (eds), *Économie Antique: Prix et formation des prix dans les économies antiques*. Saint-Bertrand-de-Comminges. 147–59.

Dupont, F. 1977. *Le plaisir et la loi: Du banquet de Platon au Satiricon*. Paris.

Eck, W. 1984. Senatorial Self-Representation: Developments in the Augustan Period. In F. Millar and C. Segal (eds), *Caesar Augustus: Seven Aspects*. Oxford. 129–67.

Edwards, C. 1993. *The Politics of Immorality in Ancient Rome*. Cambridge.

Edwards, C. 2000. *Suetonius: Lives of the Caesars*. Oxford.

Edwards, C. 2007. *Death in Ancient Rome*. New Haven, CT and London.

Elsner, J. 1993. Seductions of Art: Encolpius and Eumolpus in a Neronian Picture Gallery. *Proceedings of the Cambridge Philological Society* 39: 30–47.

Elsner, J. 1995. *Art and the Roman Viewer: The Transformation of Art from the Pagan World to Christianity*. Cambridge.

Elsner, J. 1998. *Imperial Rome and Christian Triumph: The Art of the Roman Empire AD 100–450*. Oxford.

Elsner, J. and Masters, J. (eds) 1994. *Reflections of Nero: Culture, History and Representation*. London.

Endres, N. 2011. Petronius in West Egg: *The Satyricon* and *The Great Gatsby*. In M. Futre Pinheiro and S. J. Harrison (eds), *Fictional Traces: Receptions of the Ancient Novel*. Groningen. 2: 111–24.

Erdkamp, P. 2005. *The Grain Market in the Roman Empire: A Social, Political and Economic Study*. Cambridge.

Fellini, F. 1970. Preface. In Zanelli 1970a: 43–6.

Finkelpearl, E. D. 1998. *Metamorphosis of Language in Apuleius: A Study of Allusion in the Novel*. Ann Arbor, MI.

Finley, M. I. 1999 (updated edn). *The Ancient Economy*. Updated with a new foreward by Ian Morris. Berkeley, CA. (1st edn London 1973.)

Forbes, C. A. 1955. The Education and Training of Slaves in Antiquity. *Transactions of the American Philological Association* 86: 321–60.

Fowler, D. P. 1991. Narrate and Describe: The Problem of Ekphrasis. *Journal of Roman Studies* 81: 25–35.

Freud, S. 1960. *Jokes and Their Relation to the Unconscious*. Trans. J. Strachey. New York.

Frier, B. W. and Kehoe, D. P. 2007. Law and Economic Institutions. In Scheidel, Morris, and Saller 2007: 113–43.

Fusillo, M. 2011. Petronius and the Contemporary Novel: Between New Picaresque and Queer Aesthetics'. In M. Futre Pinheiro and S. J. Harrison (eds), *Fictional Traces: Receptions of the Ancient Novel.* Groningen. 2: 135–43.

Gagliardi, D. 1984. Il corteo di Trimalchione: Nota a Petron. 28.4–5. *Rivista di Filologia e di Istruzione Classica* 112: 285–7.

Gagliardi, D. 1993. *Petronio e il romanzo moderno.* Florence.

Galli, L. 1996. Meeting Again: Some Observations about Petronius *Satyricon* 100 and the Greek Novels. *Groningen Colloquia on the Novel* 7: 33–45.

Garnsey, P. 1970. *Social Status and Legal Privilege in the Roman Empire.* Oxford.

Garnsey, P. 1981. Independent Freedmen and the Economy of Roman Italy under the Principate. *Klio* 63: 359–71.

Garnsey, P. 1988. *Famine and Food Supply in the Graeco-Roman World: Responses to Risk and Crisis.* Cambridge.

Garnsey, P. and Saller, R. P. 1987. *The Roman Empire: Economy, Society and Culture.* Berkeley and Los Angeles, CA.

Gaselee, S. 1910. *The Bibliography of Petronius.* London.

Giacovelli, E. 2002. *Tutti i film di Federico Fellini.* Turin.

Gillette, P. 1965. *Petronius: Satyricon.* Los Angeles.

Gleason, M. 1995. *Making Men: Sophists and Self-Presentation in Ancient Rome.* Princeton, NJ.

Gonzales, J. 1986. The Lex Irnitana: A New Copy of the Flavian Municipal Law. *Journal of Roman Studies* 76: 147–243.

Gowers, E. 1993. *The Loaded Table: Representations of Food in Roman Literature.* Oxford.

Grafton, A. 1990. Petronius and Neo-Latin Satire: The Reception of the *Cena Trimalchionis. Journal of the Warburg and Courtauld Institutes* 53: 237–49.

Gratwick, A. S. (ed.) 1993. *Plautus: Menaechmi.* Cambridge.

Gratwick, A. S. (ed.) 1999 (2nd edn). *Terence: The Brothers.* Warminster.

Griffin, M. T. 1984. *Nero: The End of a Dynasty.* New Haven, CT.

Grossvogel, D. I. 1971. Fellini's *Satyricon. Diacritics* 1(1): 51–4.

Gunderson, E. 2003. *Declamation, Paternity, and Roman Identity: Authority and the Rhetorical Self.* Cambridge.

Habermehl, P. 2006. *Petronius: Satyrica 79–141: Ein philologisch-literarischer Kommentar. Bd. 1: Sat. 79–110.* Berlin.

Habermehl, P. Forthcoming. *Petronius: Satyrica 79–141: Ein philologisch-literarischer Kommentar. Bd. 2: Sat. 111–141.* Berlin.

Hägg, T. 1983. *The Novel in Antiquity.* Oxford.

Hales, S. 2003. *The Roman House and Social Identity.* Cambridge.

Hallett, J. P. 2003. Resistant (and Enabling) Reading: Petronius' *Satyricon* and Latin Love Elegy. In Panayotakis, Zimmerman, and Keulen 2003: 329–43.

Halporn, J. W., Ostwald, M., and Rosenmeyer, T. G. 1963. *The Meters of Greek and Latin Poetry*. London.

Hardwick, L. 2003. *Reception Study*. Greece and Rome New Surveys in the Classics 33. Oxford.

Harris, R. 2003. *Pompeii*. London.

Harrison, S. J. 1998. The Milesian Tales and the Roman Novel. *Groningen Colloquia on the Novel* 9: 61–73.

Harrison, S. J. (ed.) 1999. *Oxford Readings in the Roman Novel*. Oxford.

Harrison, S. J. 2004. Two Victorian Versions of the Roman Novel. In M. Zimmerman and R. T. van der Paardt (eds), *Metamorphic Reflections: Essays Presented to Ben Hijmans at His 75th Birthday*. Leuven and Paris. 265–78.

Harrison, S. J. and Sandy, G. 2008. Novels Ancient and Modern. In T. Whitmarsh (ed.), *The Cambridge Companion to the Ancient Novel*. Cambridge. 300–20.

Haslam, M. 1981. Narrative about Tinouphis in Prosimetrum. In *Papyri Greek and Egyptian, Edited by Various Hands in Honour of Eric Gardner Turner on the Occasion of His Seventieth Birthday*. Graeco-Roman Memoirs 68. London. 35–45.

Heinze, R. 1899. Petron und der griechische Roman. *Hermes* 34: 494–519. (Reprinted in H. Gärtner (ed.) 1984, *Beiträge zum griechischen Liebesroman*. Hildesheim: 15–40.)

Henderson, J. 1989. Tacitus/the World in Pieces. *Ramus* 18: 167–210. (Revised in Henderson 1998: 257–300.)

Henderson, J. 1998. *Fighting for Rome: Poets and Caesars, History and Civil War*. Cambridge.

Heseltine, M. (trans.) [1913]. 1969 (revised edn). *Petronius*. Revised by E. H. Warmington. Loeb Classical Library 15. Cambridge, MA. (1st edn 1913.)

Highet, G. 1970. Whose *Satyricon*? Petronius's or Fellini's? *Horizon* 12: 42–7.

Highet, G. 1998. *The Unpublished Lectures of Gilbert Highet*. Edited by R. J. Ball. New York.

Hill, T. D. 2004. *Ambitiosa Mors: Suicide and Self in Roman Thought and Literature*. New York and London.

Hinds, S. 1998. *Allusion and Intertext. Dynamics of Appropriation in Roman Poetry*. Cambridge.

Hofman, J. B. 1951. *Lateinische Umgangssprache*. Heidelberg.

Hofmann, H. (ed.) 1999. *Latin Fiction: The Latin Novel in Context*. London and New York.

Hölscher, T. 2006. The Transformation of Victory into Power: From Event to Structure. In S. Dillon and K. Welch (eds), *Representations of War in Ancient Rome*. Cambridge. 27–48.

Holzberg, N. 1995. *The Ancient Novel: An Introduction*. Trans. C. Jackson-Holzberg. London.

Hook, B. S. 2005. Oedipus and Thyestes among the Philosophers: Incest and Cannibalism in Plato, Diogenes and Zeno. *Classical Philology* 100(1): 17–40.

Hooper, R. W. (trans.) 1999. *The Priapus Poems: Erotic Epigrams from Ancient Rome.* Urbana, IL.

Hope, V. M. 2007. *Death in Ancient Rome: A Sourcebook.* London.

Hopkins, K. 1974. Elite Mobility in the Roman Empire. In M. I. Finley (ed.), *Studies in Ancient Society.* London. 103–20.

Hubbard, T. K. (ed.) 2003. *Homosexuality in Greece and Rome.* Berkeley, CA.

Huber, G. 1990. Walter Charleton's 'Ephesian Matron': Ein Zeugnis der Petron-Rezeption im England der Restauration. *Groningen Colloquia on the Novel* 3: 139–57.

Huskinson, J. 2002–3. Theatre, Performance and Theatricality in Some Mosaic Pavements from Antioch. *Bulletin of the Institute of Classical Studies* 46: 131–65.

Iser, W. 1978. *The Act of Reading: A Theory of Aesthetic Response.* Baltimore, MD.

Isherwood, C. 1954. *The World in the Evening.* New York.

Jashemski, W. F. 1979. *The Gardens of Pompeii, Herculaneum and the Villas Destroyed by Vesuvius.* New Rochelle, NY and New York.

Jensson, G. 2004. *The Recollections of Encolpius: The Satyrica of Petronius as Milesian Fiction.* Ancient Narrative Supplementum 2. Groningen.

Johns, C. 1982. *Sex or Symbol? Erotic Images of Greece and Rome.* Austin, TX.

Johnston, D. 1999. *Roman Law in Context.* Cambridge.

Jones, C. 1991. Dinner Theater. In W. Slater (ed.), *Dining in a Classical Context.* Ann Arbor, MI. 185–98.

Jones, D. 2006. *The Bankers of Puteoli: Finance, Trade and Industry in the Roman World.* Stroud.

Joshel, S. R. 1992. *Work, Identity and Legal Status at Rome: A Study of the Occupational Inscriptions.* London.

Kahane, A. and Laird, A. (eds) 2001. *A Companion to the Prologue of Apuleius' Metamorphoses.* Oxford.

Kampen, N. B. (ed.) 1996. *Sexuality in Ancient Art.* Cambridge.

Kehoe, D. 1997. *Investment, Profit and Tenancy: The Jurists and the Roman Agrarian Economy.* Ann Arbor, MI.

Kehoe, D. 2007. The Early Roman Empire: Production. In Scheidel, Morris, and Saller 2007: 543–69.

Kennedy, G. 1978. Encolpius and Agamemnon in Petronius. *American Journal of Philology* 99: 171–8.

Kezich, T. 2006. *Federico Fellini: His Life and Work.* Trans. Minna Proctor with Viviana Mazza. London.

Kimball, J. 1994. An Ambiguous Faithfulness: Molly Bloom and the Widow of Ephesus. *James Joyce Quarterly* 31: 455–72.

Kinney, A. F. 1986. *Humanist Poetics: Thought, Rhetoric and Fiction in Sixteenth-Century England.* Amherst.

Klebs, E. 1889. Zur Composition von Petronius *Satirae. Philologus* 47: 623–35.

Kleijwegt, M. 1998. The Social Dimensions of Gladiatorial Combat in Petronius' *Cena Trimalchionis. Groningen Colloquia on the Novel* 9: 75–96.

Kleiner, D. E. E. 1977. *Roman Group Portraiture: The Funerary Reliefs of the Late Republic and Early Empire.* New York.

Kleiner, D. E. E. 1992. *Roman Sculpture.* New Haven, CT and London.

Kloft, H. 1994. Trimalchio als Ökonom: Bemerkungen zur Rolle der Wirtschaft in Petrons *Satyricon.* In R. Günther and S. Rebenich (eds), *E fontibus haurire: Beiträge zur römischen Geschichte und zu ihren Hilfswissenschaften (Festschrift H. Chantraine).* Paderborn. 117–31.

Kockel, V. 1983. *Die Grabbauten vor dem Herkulaner Tor in Pompeji.* Mainz.

Kockel, V. 1993. *Porträtreliefs stadtrömischer Grabbauten.* Mainz.

Konstan, D. 1994. *Sexual Symmetry: Love in the Ancient Novel and Related Genres.* Princeton, NJ.

Koortbojian, M. 1996. *In commemorationem mortuorum*: Text and Image along the 'Street of Tombs'. In J. Elsner (ed.), *Art and Text in Roman Culture.* Cambridge. 210–33.

Labate, M. 1995a. Eumolpo e gli altri, ovvero lo spazio della poesia. *Materiali e discussioni per l'analisi dei testi classici* 34: 153–75.

Labate, M. 1995b. Petronio, *Satyricon*, 80–81. *Materiali e discussioni per l'analisi dei testi classici* 35: 165–75.

Lafon, X. 2001. *Villa maritima: Recherches sur les villas littorales de l'Italie romaine (IIIe siècle av. J.C.-IIIe siècle ap. J.-C.).* Rome.

Leach, E. 2004. *The Social Life of Painting in Ancient Rome and on the Bay of Naples.* Cambridge.

Lefèvre, E. 1997. *Studien zur Struktur der 'Milesischen' Novelle bei Petron und Apuleius.* Stuttgart.

Lefkowitz, M. R. and Fant, M. B. (eds) 2005 (3rd edn). *Women's Life in Greece and Rome.* Baltimore, MD.

Lehmann, P. 1953. *Roman Wall Paintings from Boscoreale in the Metropolitan Museum of Art.* Cambridge, MA.

Lindsay, J. (trans.) 1944. *The Complete Works of Gaius Petronius* […] *with one hundred illustrations by Norman Lindsay.* New York. (Reprint of the [1927] Fanfrolico Press limited edition.)

Little, A. 1971. *Roman Perspective Painting and the Ancient Stage.* London.

Lo Cascio, E. 2007. The Early Roman Empire: The State and the Economy. In Scheidel, Morris, and Saller 2007: 619–47.

López Barja de Quiroga, P. 1995. Freedmen Social Mobility in Roman Italy. *Historia* 44: 326–48.

Love, J. 1991. *Antiquity and Capitalism: Max Weber and the Sociological Foundations of Roman Civilization.* London and New York.

Lytton, E. 1834. *The Last Days of Pompeii.* London.

McGlathery, D. B. 1998. Reversals of Platonic Love in Petronius' *Satyricon.* In D. H. J. Larmour, P. A. Miller, and C. Platter (eds), *Rethinking Sexuality: Foucault and Classical Antiquity.* Princeton, NJ. 204–27.

McKeon, M. 1987. *The Origins of the English Novel, 1600–1740*. Baltimore, MD.

McMahon, J. M. 1998. *Paralysin Cave: Impotence, Perception, and Text in the Satyrica of Petronius*. Leiden.

MacMullen, R. 1974. *Roman Social Relations, 50 B.C. to A.D. 284*. New Haven, CT and London.

Marmorale, E. V. 1948. *La questione petroniana*. Bari.

Martin, R. 1975. Quelques remarques concernant la date du *Satiricon*. *Revue des Études Latines* 53: 182–224.

Mayer, R. 1982. Neronian Classicism. *American Journal of Philology* 103(3): 305–18.

Meickle, S. 2002. Modernism, Economics and the Ancient Economy. In Scheidel and von Reden 2002: 233–50.

Melmoth, S. (trans.) 1902. *The Satyricon of Petronius*. Paris.

Millar, F. 1981. The World of the *Golden Ass*. *Journal of Roman Studies* 71: 63–75.

Morandini, M. 1996. Federico Fellini. In G. Nowell-Smith (ed.), *The Oxford History of World Cinema*. Oxford. 587.

Moravia, A. 1970. Documentary of a Dream: A Dialogue between Alberto Moravia and Federico Fellini. In Zanelli 1970a: 23–30.

Moravia, A. 1978. Dreaming up Petronius. In P. Bondanella (ed.), *Federico Fellini: Essays in Criticism*. Oxford. 161–8.

Morgan, J. R. 1998. On the Fringes of the Canon: Work on the Fragments of Ancient Greek Fiction 1936–1994. *Aufstieg und Niedergang der römischen Welt* 2.34.4: 3293–390.

Morgan, J. R. 2007. Kleitophon and Encolpius: Achilleus Tatius as Hidden Author. In M. Paschalis, S. Frangoulidis, S. Harrison, and M. Zimmerman (eds), *The Greek and the Roman Novel: Parallel Readings*. Ancient Narrative Supplementum 8. Groningen. 105–20.

Morley, N. 2007a. *Trade in Classical Antiquity*. Cambridge.

Morley, N. 2007b. The Early Roman Empire: Distribution. In Scheidel, Morris, and Saller 2007: 570–91.

Most, G. 1992. *Disiecti membra poetae*: The Rhetoric of Dismemberment in Neronian Poetry. In R. Hexter and D. Selden (eds), *Innovations of Antiquity*. London. 391–419.

Most, G. (ed.) 1997. *Collecting Fragments = Fragmente Sammeln*. Göttingen.

Mouritsen, H. 2005. Freedmen and Decurions: Epitaphs and Social History in Imperial Italy. *Journal of Roman Studies* 95: 38–63.

Müller, K. 2003 (4th edn revised). *Petronius: Satyricon reliquiae*. Munich.

Mulvey, L. 1975. Visual Pleasure and Narrative Cinema. *Screen* 16(3): 6–18. (Reprinted in Mulvey 1989.)

Mulvey, L. 1989. *Visual and Other Pleasures*. Bloomington, IN.

Murray, E. 1976. *Fellini the Artist*. Bembridge.

Nethercut, W. R. 1971. Fellini and the Colosseum: Philosophy, Morality and the *Satyricon*. *Classical Bulletin* 47(4): 53–9.

Newton, R. M. 1982. Trimalchio's Hellish Bath. *Classical Journal* 77: 315–19.

Newton, R. M. 1991. Petronian Urbanity in the 'Carpe, Carpe' Joke (Petr. *Sat.* 35. 7–36.8). *Syllecta Classica* 3: 67–9.

O'Neal, W. J. 1976. Vergil and Petronius: The Underworld. *Classical Bulletin* 52: 33–4.

Oniga, R. 2000. La création lexicale chez Pétrone. In M. Fruyt and C. Nicolas (eds), *La création lexicale en Latin: Actes de la table ronde du IXème Colloque international de linguistique latine (organiseé par Michèle Fruyt à Madrid le 16 avril 1997)*. Paris. 155–66.

Panayotakis, C. 1995. *Theatrum Arbitri: Theatrical Elements in the Satyrica of Petronius*. Leiden.

Panayotakis, C. 2006. Eumolpus' *Pro Encolpio* and Lichas' *In Encolpium*: Petr. *Sat.* 107. In S. N. Byrne, E. P. Cueva, and J. Alvares (eds), *Authors, Authority, and Interpreters in the Ancient Novel*. Ancient Narrative Supplementum 5. Groningen. 196–210.

Panayotakis, S., Zimmerman, M., and Keulen, W. (eds) 2003. *The Ancient Novel and Beyond*. Leiden.

Parsons, P. J. 1971. A Greek *Satyricon*? *Bulletin of the Institute of Classical Studies* 18: 53–68.

Paterson, J. 1998. Trade and Traders in the Roman World: Scale, Structure and Organisation. In H. Parkins and C. Smith (eds), *Trade, Traders and the Ancient City*. London and New York. 149–67.

Petersen, L. H. 2006. *The Freedman in Roman Art and Art History*. Cambridge.

Petersmann, H. 1977. *Petrons urbane Prosa: Untersuchungen zu Sprache und Text (Syntax)*. Österreichische Akademie der Wissenschaften, philosophisch-historische Klasse, Sitzungsberichte 323. Vienna.

Petersmann, H. 1999. Environment, Linguistic Situation, and Levels of Style in Petronius' *Satyrica*. Trans. M. Revermann. In Harrison 1999: 105–23. (Revised version of: Petersmann, H. 1985. Umwelt, Sprachsituation und Stilschichten in Petrons 'Satyrica'. *Aufstieg und Niedergang der römischen Welt* 2.32.3: 1687–705.)

Pleket, H. W. 1983. Urban Elites and Business. In P. Garnsey, K. Hopkins, and C. R. Whittaker (eds), *Trade in the Ancient Economy*. London. 131–44.

Pleket, H. W. 1993. Agriculture in the Roman Empire in Comparative Perspective. In H. Sancisi-Weerdenburg and H. C. Teitler (eds), *De Agricultura: In Memoriam Pieter Willem De Neeve (1945–1990)*. Amsterdam. 317–42.

Pomeroy, A. J. 1992. Trimalchio as *Deliciae*. *Phoenix* 46(1): 45–53.

Potter, D. S. (ed.) 2006. *A Companion to the Roman Empire*. Blackwell Companions to the Ancient World. Oxford.

Prag, J. R. W. 2006. *Cave Navem*: Petronius, *Satyricon* 30.1. *Classical Quarterly* 56(2): 538–47.

Purcell, N. 1987. Tomb and Suburb. In H. von Hesberg and P. Zanker (eds), *Römische Gräberstrassen: Selbstdarstellung, Status, Standard*. Munich. 25–42.

Raven, D. S. 1967. *Latin Metre*. London.

Reardon, B. P. (ed.) 2008 (revised). *Collected Ancient Greek Novels*. Berkeley, CA. (1st edn 1989.)

Reeve, M. D. 1983. Petronius. In L. D. Reynolds (ed.), *Texts and Transmission: A Survey of the Latin Classics*. Oxford. 295–300.

Rehm, R. 2002. *The Play of Space: Spatial Transformation in Greek Tragedy*. Princeton, NJ.

Relihan, J. C. 1993. *Ancient Menippean Satire*. Baltimore, MD.

Repath, I. D. 2005. Achilles Tatius' *Leucippe and Cleitophon*: What Happened Next? *Classical Quarterly* 55: 250–65.

Repath, I. D. 2010. Plato in Petronius: Petronius *in platanona*. *Classical Quarterly* 60(2): 577–95.

Révay, J. 1922. Horaz und Petron. *Classical Philology* 17: 202–12.

Reynolds, L. D. and Wilson, N. G. 1991 (3rd edn). *Scribes and Scholars: A Guide to the Transmission of Greek and Latin Literature*. Oxford.

Richardson, T.W. 1979. Some Shared Comic Features in Petronius and P. G. Wodehouse. *Echos du Monde Classique* 23: 64–9.

Richlin, A. 1992a (2nd edn). *The Garden of Priapus: Sexuality and Aggression in Roman Humor*. New York.

Richlin, A. (ed.) 1992b. *Pornography and Representation in Greece and Rome*. New York.

Richlin, A. 1993. Not before Homosexuality: The Materiality of the *Cinaedus* and the Roman Law against Love between Men. *Journal of the History of Sexuality* 3(4): 523–73.

Richlin, A. 1997. Gender and Rhetoric: Producing Manhood in the Schools. In W. J. Dominik (ed.), *Roman Eloquence*. London. 90–110.

Rickman, G. 1980. *The Corn Supply of the City of Rome*. Oxford.

Riikonen, H. K. 1987. Petronius and Modern Fiction: Some Comparative Notes. *Arctos* 21: 87–103.

Rimell, V. 2002. *Petronius and the Anatomy of Fiction*. Cambridge.

Rimell, V. 2005. The Satiric Maze: Petronius, Satire, and Novel. In K. Freudenberg (ed.), *The Cambridge Companion to Roman Satire*. Cambridge. 160–73.

Rimell, V. 2007. The Inward Turn: Writing, Voice and the Imperial Author in Petronius. In V. Rimell (ed.), *Seeing Tongues, Hearing Scripts: Orality and Representation in the Ancient Novel*. Ancient Narrative Supplementum 7. Groningen. 61–85.

Roberts, D. 2006. Petronius and the Vulgar Tongue: Colloquialism, Obscenity, Translation. *Classical and Modern Literature* 26(1): 33–55.

Robinson, O. F. 1997. *The Sources of Roman Law: Problems and Methods for Ancient Historians*. London and New York.

Rodger, A. 1990. The Jurisdiction of Local Magistrates: Chapter 84 of the *Lex Irnitana*. *Zeitschrift für Papyrologie und Epigraphik* 84: 147–61.

Rosati, G. 1983. Trimalchione in scena. *Maia* 35: 213–27. (Trans. into English by B. Graziosi as: Trimalchio on Stage. In Harrison 1999: 85–104.)

Rose, K. F. C. 1971. *The Date and Author of the Satyricon*. Leiden.

Rosenthal, S. 1976. *The Cinema of Federico Fellini*. London.

Rostovtzeff, M. I. 1957 (2nd edn). *The Social and Economic History of the Roman Empire*. Oxford.

Ruden, S. (trans.) 2000. *Satyricon*. Indianapolis, IN and Cambridge.

Rudich, V. 1993. *Political Dissidence under Nero: The Price of Dissimulation*. New York.

Russell, D. A. 1979. *De imitatione*. In D. West and A. J. Woodman (eds), *Creative Imitation and Latin Literature*. Cambridge. 1–16.

Sage, E. T. and Gilleland, B. B. 1969 (2nd edn). *Petronius: The Satiricon*. New York.

Saller, R. P. 1982. *Personal Patronage in the Roman Empire*. Cambridge.

Saller, R. P. 1983. Martial on Patronage and Literature. *Classical Quarterly* 33: 246–57.

Saller, R. P. 2002. Framing the Debate over Growth in the Ancient Economy. In Scheidel and von Reden 2002: 251–69.

Samatav, E. 1975. Una forma particolare di alliterazione nel *Satyricon* di Petronio. *Bollettino di Studi Latini* 5: 27–9.

Sandy, G. N. 1969. Satire in the *Satyricon*. *American Journal of Philology* 90: 293–303.

Sandy, G. N. 1974. *Scaenica Petroniana*. *Transactions of the American Philological Association* 104: 329–46.

Saylor, C. 1987. Funeral Games: The Significance of Games in the *Cena Trimalchionis*. *Latomus* 46: 593–602.

Scheidel, W. 1996. Finances, Figures and Fiction. *Classical Quarterly* 46: 222–38.

Scheidel, W. and von Reden, S. (eds) 2002. *The Ancient Economy*. Edinburgh.

Scheidel, W., Morris, I., and Saller, R. (eds) 2007. *The Cambridge Economic History of the Greco-Roman World*. Cambridge.

Schmeling, G. 2011. *A Commentary on the Satyrica of Petronius*. Oxford.

Schmeling, G. L. 1971. The *Exclusus Amator* Motif in Petronius. In *Fons Perennis: Saggi critici di filologia classica in onore del prof. Vittorio d'Agostino*. Turin. 333–57.

Schmeling, G. L. (ed.) 2003 (revised edn). *The Novel in the Ancient World*. Leiden.

Schmeling, G. L. and Rebmann, D. R. 1975. T. S. Eliot and Petronius. *Comparative Literature Studies* 12: 393–410.

Schmeling, G. L. and Stuckey, J. H. 1977. *A Bibliography of Petronius*. Leiden.

Schnur, H. C. 1959. The Economic Background of the *Satyricon*. *Latomus* 18: 790–9.

Segal, E. 1971. Arbitrary *Satyricon*: Petronius and Fellini. *Diacritics* 1(1): 54–7.

Selden, D. 1994. Genre of Genre. In Tatum 1994: 39–64.

Shero, L. R. 1923. The *Cena* in Roman Satire. *Classical Philology* 18: 126–43.

Shrake, E. 1973. *Peter Arbiter*. Austin, TX.

Sienkiewicz, H. 1941. *Quo Vadis?* Trans. C. L. Hogarth. London. (Polish original, Warsaw 1896.)

Slater, N. W. 1990. *Reading Petronius*. Baltimore, MD.

Slater, N. 2011. 'His Career as Trimalchio': Petronian Character and Narrative in Fitzgerald's Great American Novel'. In M. Futre Pinheiro and S. J. Harrison (eds), *Fictional Traces: Receptions of the Ancient Novel*. Groningen. 2: 125–34.

Smith, M. S. 1975. *Petronii Arbitri Cena Trimalchionis*. Oxford.

Smith, M. S. 1985. A Bibliography of Petronius (1945–1982). *Aufstieg und Niedergang der römischen Welt* 2.32.3: 1624–65.

Solin, H. 1971. *Beiträge zur Kenntnis der griechischen Personennamen in Rom*, I. Helsinki.

Solomon, J. 2001a. *The Ancient World in the Cinema*. New Haven, CT and London.

Solomon, J. 2001b. The Sounds of Cinematic Antiquity. In Winkler 2001: 319–39.

Soverini, P. 1985. Il problema delle teorie retoriche e poetiche di Petronio. *Aufstieg und Niedergang der römischen Welt* 2.32.3: 1706–79.

Stallybrass, P. and White, A. 1986. *The Politics and Poetics of Transgression*. Ithaca, NY.

Stefenelli, A. 1962. *Die Volkssprache im Werk des Petron im Hinblick auf die romanischen Sprachen*. Vienna.

Stephens, S. A. and Winkler, J. J. 1995. *Ancient Greek Novels: The Fragments*. Princeton, NJ.

Stubbs, J. C. 1993. The Fellini Manner: Open Form and Visual Excess. *Cinema Journal* 32(4): 49–64.

Stuckey, J. H. 1972. Petronius the 'Ancient': His Reputation and Influence in Seventeenth-Century England. *Rivista di Studi Classici* 21: 145–53.

Sullivan, J. P. (trans.) 1965. *Petronius: The Satyricon and the Fragments*. Harmondsworth.

Sullivan, J. P. 1968a. *The Satyricon of Petronius: A Literary Study*. London.

Sullivan, J. P. 1968b. Petronius, Seneca and Lucan: A Neronian Literary Feud? *Transactions of the American Philological Association* 99: 453–67.

Sullivan, J. P. 1985a. *Literature and Politics in the Age of Nero*. Ithaca, NY.

Sullivan, J. P. 1985b. Petronius' *Satyricon* and its Neronian context. *Aufstieg und Niedergang der römischen Welt* 2.32.3: 1666–86.

Sullivan, J. P. (trans.) 1986 (revised edn). *Petronius: The Satyricon, and Seneca: The Apocolocyntosis*. Harmondsworth.

Sullivan, J. P. 2001. The Social Ambience of Petronius' *Satyricon* and *Fellini Satyricon*. In Winkler 2001: 258–71.

Swanson, D. C. 1963. *A Formal Analysis of Petronius' Vocabulary*. Minneapolis, MN.

Tanner, T. 1979. *Adultery in the Novel: Contract and Transgression*. Baltimore, MD.

Tatum, J. (ed.) 1994. *The Search for the Ancient Novel*. Baltimore, MD and London.

Taylor, L. R. 1961. Freedmen and Freeborn in the Epitaphs of Imperial Rome. *American Journal of Philology* 82: 127–49.

Thébert, Y. 1993. The Slave. In A. Giardina (ed.), *The Romans*. Trans. L. G. Cochrane. Chicago, IL and London. 138–74.

Toynbee, J. M. C. 1971. *Death and Burial in the Roman World*. London.

Tran, N. 2006. *Les membres des associations romaines. Le rang social des collegiati en Italie et en Gaules sous le Haut-Empire*. Rome.

Treggiari, S. 1969. *Roman Freedmen during the Late Republic*. Oxford.

Van der Paardt, R. T. 1996. The Market-Scene in Petronius 12–15. *Groningen Colloquia on the Novel* 7: 63–73.

Van Mal-Maeder, D. 2003. La mise en scène déclamatoire chez les romanciers latins. In Panayotakis, Zimmerman, and Keulen 2003: 345–55.

Van Nijf, O. 1997. *The Civic World of Professional Associations in the Roman East*. Amsterdam.

Vannini, G. 2007. Petronius 1975–2005: bilancio critico e nuove proposte. *Lustrum* 49: 7–512.

Verboven, K. 2002. *The Economy of Friends: Economic Aspects of Amicitia and Patronage in the Late Republic*. Brussels.

Verboven, K. 2007. The Associative Order: Status and Ethos among Roman Businessmen. *Athenaeum* 95: 859–91

Veyne, P. 1961. Vie de Trimalchion. *Annales, économies, sociétés, civilisations* 16: 213–47. (Re-edited in Veyne, P. 1991. *La société romaine*. Paris. 13–56.)

Veyne, P. 1963. *Cave Canem*. *Mélanges d'archéologie et d'histoire de l'école française de Rome* 75: 59–66.

Veyne, P. 1979. Mythe et réalité de l'autarcie à Rome. *Revue des Études Anciennes* 81: 261–80.

Völker, T. and Rohmann, D. 2011. *Praenomen Petronii*: The Date and Author of the *Satyricon* Reconsidered. *Classical Quarterly* 61(2): 660–76.

von Hesberg, H. 1992. *Römische Grabbauten*. Darmstadt.

Vout, C. 2009. Representing the Roman Emperor. In A. Feldherr (ed.), *The Cambridge Companion to Roman Historiography*. Cambridge.

Wallace-Hadrill, A. 1983. *Suetonius: The Scholar and His Caesars*. London.

Wallace-Hadrill, A. 1990. Pliny the Elder and Man's Unnatural History. *Greece & Rome* 37: 80–96.

Wallace-Hadrill, A. 1994. *Houses and Society in Pompeii and Herculaneum*. Princeton, NJ.

Walsh, P. G. 1970. *The Roman Novel: The 'Satyricon' of Petronius and the 'Metamorphoses' of Apuleius*. Cambridge. (Reprint: Bristol Classical Press. 1995.)

Walsh, P. G. 1974. Was Petronius a Moralist? *Greece & Rome* 21(2): 181–90.

Walsh, P. G. (trans.) 1996. *The Satyricon*. Oxford.

Ward-Perkins, B. 2005. *The Fall of Rome and the End of Civilization*. Oxford.

Warmington, B. H. 1999. *Suetonius: Nero*. London.

Weaver, P. R. C. 1972. *Familia Caesaris: A Social Study of the Emperor's Freedmen and Slaves*. Cambridge.

Wells, C. M. 1992 (2nd edn). *The Roman Empire*. London.

Whitehead, J. 1993. The *Cena Trimalchionis* and Biographical Tradition in Roman Middle Class Art. In P. Holliday (ed.), *Narrative and Event in Ancient Art*. Cambridge. 299–325.

Whitmarsh, T. 2005. The Greek Novel: Titles and Genre. *American Journal of Philology* 126: 587–611.

Whittaker, C. R. 1985. Trade and the Aristocracy in the Roman Empire. *Opus* 4: 49–75.

Wilson, A. 2008. Large-scale Manufacturing, Standardization and Trade. In J. P. Oleson (ed.), *The Oxford Handbook of Engineering and Technology in the Classical World*. Oxford. 393–417.

Wilson et al. (trans.) 1708. *The Satyrical Works of Titus Petronius Arbiter* [...] *in Three Parts. Together with* [...] *a Key to the Satyr, by a Person of Quality*. London.

Winkler, M. (ed.) 2001. *Classical Myth and Culture in the Cinema*. Oxford.

Wiseman, T. P. 1987. *Conspicui postes tectaque digna deo*: The Public Image of Aristocratic and Imperial Houses in the Late Republic and Early Empire. In *L'Urbs: Espace urbain et histoire (Ier siècle av. J.-C. – IIIe siècle ap. J.-C.)*. CEFR 98. Rome and Paris. 393–413.

Wiseman, T. P. 1992. The Centaur's Hoof. In T. P. Wiseman. *Talking to Virgil*. Exeter. 51–70.

Wolfe, T. 1987. *The Bonfire of the Vanities*. London.

Woolf, G. 1996. Monumental Writing and the Expansion of Roman Society in the Early Roman Empire. *Journal of Roman Studies* 86: 22–39.

Woolf, G. 1998. *Becoming Roman: The Origins of Provincial Civilization in Gaul*. Cambridge.

Wooten, C. 1976. Petronius, the Mime, and Rhetorical Education. *Helios* 3: 67–74.

Wooten, C. 1984. Petronius and 'Camp'. *Helios* 11: 133–9.

Wrede, H. 1981. *Consecratio in formam deorum: Vergöttlichte Privatpersonen in der römischen Kaiserzeit*. Mainz.

Wyke, M. 1997. *Projecting the Past: Ancient Rome, Cinema and History*. New York and London.

Zanelli, D. (ed.) 1970a. *Fellini's Satyricon*. New York.

Zanelli, D. 1970b. From the Planet Rome. In Zanelli 1970a: 3–20.

Zanker, P. 1975. Grabreliefs römischer Freigelassener. *Jahrbuch des Deutschen Archäologischen Instituts* 90: 267–315.

Zapponi, B. 1970. The Strange Journey. In Zanelli 1970a: 33–9.

Zeitlin, F. 1971. Petronius as Paradox: Anarchy and Artistic Integrity. *Transactions of the American Philological Association* 102: 631–84. (Reprinted in Harrison 1999: 1–49.)

Index *locorum*

General Index

Note: In reference works Roman citizens are normally listed alphabetically by their *nomen* (e.g. Tullius Cicero, Marcus), and some appear in this way in the index; however, to aid the reader, in many cases we have listed Romans under their most commonly known name (e.g. Cicero), since this is also how they appear in the text. Uniformity has been rejected in favor of accessibility. At the same time, for clarity, and to assist further research, the full name is generally indicated within the index entry.

on tombs, 148
on wills, 143
Plocamus, 76
Plutarch, 6–7, 46, 130, 144, 163, 165
Polidoro, Gian Luigi, 202
Polyphemus, 36, 95, 110
Pompeii
   and *Fellini-Satyricon*, 210–11
   Herculaneum Gate necropolis, *156*
   House of the Ancient Hunt, 173
   House of the Ceii, 173
   House of the Labyrinth, 174, 175–6,
     175, 177–8
   House of the Tragic Poet, *166*, 167,
     183
   House of the Vettii, 162–3, *162*,
     167–9, *168*, 170, 172, 178
   Nocera Gate necropolis, *152*
   novels about, 183–4, 190–1
Pompeii (Harris), 190–1
Portus: Isola Sacra necropolis, *154*
Poseidon *see* Neptune
Potter, Martin, *216*
Powell, Antony, 197
Priapus, *162*
   Roman worship of, 83–4
   Trimalchio's pastry version, 92, 163
   wrath of, 25–6, 34–5, 42, 47, 92
Primigenius, 119, 130
Proselenus, 13, 145
Publilius (Publilius Syrus), 39, 60–1

Quartilla, 13, 72–3, 84, 88, 92, 93
Quintilian, 75
Quo Vadis? (Sienkiewicz and film),
   191–2

Ravenna: tombstones, *155*
reading
   reader's repertoire, 19–20
   Roman habits and methods, 16
Reden, S. von, 139
Rehm, R., 176
religion, 170

Remmius Palaemon, Quintus, 131, 137
Repath, Ian, 47
rhetoric, 19–20, 29, 48, 57, 59–60, 62,
   65, 66–81, 93
Richlin, Amy, 99–100
Rickman, G., 139
Rimell, Victoria, 61–2, 110
Rome
   compared to Croton, Tarentum, 109–10
   Fellini's vision of, 198, 199, 208, 210,
     215, 216
   houses in, 165
   Ianus Medius, 136
   Neronian, 105–9, 174, 193
   Porta Maggiore, *158*
   Titus's arch, 106
   tombs in, 129, 157
   triumphs in, 105, 107, 171
Rose, Kenneth, 101
Rostovtzeff, Michael, 115–16

Saller, R., 139
Satyrica
   absence of author, 123
   audience, 10
   characters' names, 96
   as comedy, 209
   date of composition, 8–9, 101
   early criticism, 71
   ending, 28–30
   as epic, 26, 32–8, 47, 52–5, 56–8, 72,
     95–6, 110, 179
   episodic outline, 10–11
   as fragment of larger work, 16,
     17–20, 33–4
   genre, 20–4, 25–6, 60, 66, 95–6
   glossary of characters, 11–13
   modern attempts to complete, 197
   moralizing in, 208
   narrator, 22–4
   as novel, 40–6, 47, 56, 58, 59, 94
   as Platonic dialogue, 38–40, 47
   prose/poetry mix, 19, 21–3, 41, 73,
     74, 81

Trimalchio (*cont'd*)
  jokes, 19–20, 121
  landed estates, 136–7, 137–8
  language, 69
  life as slave, 90, 118, 129–30, 138, 169–70
  as moneylender, 135
  as Nero, 102–9
  procession from baths to dinner, 102–8, 165
  and reading, 16
  relationship with other freedmen at dinner, 120
  relationship with slaves, 121, 122
  sexual preferences, 91
  tomb, 39, 141, 145, 147–59
  wealth, 135
  will, 77, 143, 148
  on zodiac dish, 49
  see also Cena Trimalchionis
triumphs, 105–8, 171
Troiae Halosis, 72, 73, 110, 112
Tryphaena
  breast-tearing, 78
  and Encolpius, 84, 88–9
  in *Fellini-Satyricon*, 205
  glossary entry, 13
  name, 37
  poem in epic style, 95–6
  reaction to "The Widow of Ephesus", 27
  role in plot, 26, 58

The Uncertain Hour (Browner), 194–6
urbanization, 128

Valerius Maximus, 95
Varro, 173
Velleius Paterculus, 165
Vernacchio, *216*

Veyne, Paul, 116, 128–9, 138
vibrare, 75–6
Virgil *see Aeneid; Eclogues*
Vitruvius, 165, 167, 174, 177
voyeurism, 93, 99

Wall Street (film), 188
Wallace-Hadrill, Andrew, 113, 179
Walsh, P. G., 30, 31, 47, 208, 209
Ward-Perkins, Bryan, 128
The Waste Land (Eliot), 195, 208
Whitehead, J., 160
Whittaker, Dick, 134
"The Widow of Ephesus"
  allusions to *Aeneid*, 53–4, 77, 95
  bawdy nature, 96
  breast-tearing, 78
  on death and sex, 145
  in *Fellini-Satyricon*, 209
  on inhumation, 144
  as Milesian tale, 46
  plot, 26–7
  sexual norms in, 89
  widow's devotion to husband, 145–6
Wilde, Oscar, 97, 98
wills, 29, 77, 143, 148
Wiseman, T. P., 179
Wodehouse, P. G., 197
Wolfe, Tom, 188–90
women, 89, 100, 145–6
Wonders beyond Thule (Antonius Diogenes), 40
Woolf, Greg, 127–8
Wyke, M., 217

Xenophon, 41, 42, 45

Zapponi, Bernardino, 201, 206
Zeitlin, F., 31, 208, 209
Zeuxis, 172